Bruce Wolpe is a Senior Fellow (non-resident) at the United States Studies Centre at the University of Sydney. He worked with the Democrats in the US Congress during President Barack Obama's first term, was a senior advisor to Prime Minister Julia Gillard and chief of staff to the former Prime Minister, and a senior executive at Fairfax Media from 1998 to 2009. Bruce is a regular contributor on US politics across media platforms in Australia. He is the author of *The Committee: A Study of Policy, Power, Politics and Obama's Historic Legislative Agenda on Capitol Hill* (with Bryan Marshall) and *Lobbying Congress: How the System Works*.

Praise for *Trump's Australia*

'I didn't think I wanted to read more about Donald Trump—but it turned out I did. This is a forceful reminder that Trump is not merely amusing, or old news: he is dangerous, and whatever he does next will affect Australia. True, timely and terrifying.'
Sean Kelly, columnist and author of *The Game*

'A forensic analysis of how President Donald Trump invaded Australia's politics and prospects, and a sobering look at what a second Trump term would mean for Australia in everything from foreign policy to media culture.'
Laura Tingle, Chief Political Correspondent, ABC TV's *7.30*

'Donald Trump was unfit to serve as president, idiotic, unhinged, racist, and dumb as shit—those are just some of the reported character assessments from the people who served in his chaotic administration. *Trump's Australia* is both a timely warning and a potential survival guide.'
John Barron, journalist and co-host of ABC TV's *Planet America*

'I applaud Bruce Wolpe's informed and salutary warning of the power of populism and of underestimating its consequences. In this AUKUS era it is a must read for anyone who cares about Australian democracy, our sovereignty and the threats they face.'
Zoe Daniel, Independent MP for Goldstein, author of *Greetings from Trumpland*

'Masterful'
Norman Ornstein, author of *One Nation after Trump*

'If you ever wondered about the Trump Presidency's long-term impact on the American way of life and its impact on Australia and our friendship with the US, this is a book you should read.'
Natalie Barr, co-host, Network Seven's *Sunrise*

What Trump's Second Term Means for Australia

The shocking consequences for us and the world

Bruce Wolpe

ALLEN&UNWIN
SYDNEY • MELBOURNE • AUCKLAND • LONDON

This edition published in 2025

First published in 2023 as *Trump's Australia*

Copyright © Bruce Wolpe 2023, 2025

Copyright in individual chapters remains with the authors

All rights reserved. No part of this book may be reproduced or transmitted in any form or by any means, electronic or mechanical, including photocopying, recording or by any information storage and retrieval system, without prior permission in writing from the publisher. The Australian *Copyright Act 1968* (the Act) allows a maximum of one chapter or 10 per cent of this book, whichever is the greater, to be photocopied by any educational institution for its educational purposes provided that the educational institution (or body that administers it) has given a remuneration notice to the Copyright Agency (Australia) under the Act.

Allen & Unwin
Cammeraygal Country
83 Alexander Street
Crows Nest NSW 2065
Australia
Phone: (61 2) 8425 0100
Email: info@allenandunwin.com
Web: www.allenandunwin.com

Allen & Unwin acknowledges the Traditional Owners of the Country on which we live and work. We pay our respects to all Aboriginal and Torres Strait Islander Elders, past and present.

A catalogue record for this book is available from the National Library of Australia

ISBN 978 1 76147 284 8

Author photo by Stefanie Zingsheim © United States Studies Centre
Set in Sabon LT Pro by Midland Typesetters, Australia
Printed and bound in Australia by the Opus Group

10 9 8 7 6 5 4 3 2

The paper in this book is FSC® certified. FSC® promotes environmentally responsible, socially beneficial and economically viable management of the world's forests.

*To Lesley, who came to America for our life there,
and brought me to Australia for our life here.*

Contents

Foreword: The Second Trump Administration		ix
Prologue: Growing Up with Kennedy, Surviving Trump		1
I.	**Trump and Australia's Foreign Policy**	
1.	Trump: America First Abroad	31
2.	China: Transactional and Unpredictable	43
3.	AUKUS: A Survivor of Trump II	57
4.	North Korea: Spectacle Diplomacy is Back	62
5.	Trump Redux: What Does Australia Need to Do?	66
6.	Chemistry: 'You Don't Look Like a Prime Minister'	71
II.	**Trump and Australia's Domestic Policy**	
7.	Economy: America First in America	77
8.	Trade: A World War of Tariffs	82
9.	Climate: Drill, Mine, Burn, Repeat	86

10.	Trump 2025: What Can Australia Do?	92
11.	Healthcare and the Coronavirus Pandemic, Lesley Russell	101

III. Trump and the Future of Democracy in America and Australia

12.	Trump Political Culture: Earthquakes in America, and the Aftershocks in Australia	129
13.	Endangered: American Democracy	138
14.	Culture Wars: Buttons Are Being Pushed	143
15.	The Big Lie: Blunting the Aftershocks in Australia	146
16.	Race: Trump's Voice versus the Voice	163
17.	Media: Will 'The Enemy of the People' Prevail?	179
18.	Is Trump an '-ism'?	201
19.	Trump 2024: We Know What We're Getting This Time	207

IV. The Democracy Guardrails in Australia

20.	The Safeguards of Australia's Democracy	219
21.	Futureproofing Australia's Democracy	233

V. Trump's Return

22.	The Existential Question for Australia	241

Epilogue: A Letter to Australia from an American Friend, Norman J. Ornstein	252
Acknowledgements	258
Notes	261

Foreword
The Second Trump Administration

On 5 November 2024, the American people voted to elect Donald J. Trump, the 45th president of the United States, running in his third consecutive election as the Republican nominee, to a second term, as the 47th president of the United States. Trump won a decisive victory in the electoral college and obtained a plurality just shy of 50 per cent of the national popular vote—a record turnout for him compared to 2016 and 2020. Trump will be inaugurated and take office on 20 January 2025. J.D. Vance, a senator from Ohio, will be sworn in as vice president.

In the first edition of this book, called *Trump's Australia*, I anticipated that Trump would again seek election as president and that there was a good likelihood he would be elected. I examined what Trump stood for and what his beliefs and outlook portended for Australia. I believed it was important, after everything we all endured as a country and as citizens of Australia during Trump's first term, to trigger some hard thinking in this country on what could come Australia's way in a renewed Trump presidency, and some strategic planning and wargaming of Trump policies against Australia's national interests. Trump has had a profound effect on America's democracy, institutions, and political culture, and it has affected us here. Trump changed how Australians view the United States and its democracy. I discussed Australia's becoming an echo chamber of issues—and noise—that Trump generated in the United States and, at times, the stress placed on Australia's democracy from Trump's attacks on America's democracy.

This new edition is a tune-up of the issues and themes discussed in *Trump's Australia*. The year 2025 will have an enormous impact on Australia's politics, strategic posture and outlook. It has every promise of being a savage year. There will be immense surprises—there always are with Trump—but we can anticipate much of what is coming our way, and how we might further harden Australia's posture in facing them.

At the end of 2022, in looking ahead to the 2024 US elections, I wrote:

> If Trump does defeat President Biden, or whoever is the Democratic nominee, he will come to office to wreak vengeance on his enemies, especially in Congress. His administration will be filled with Trump First loyalists; he will have no need to deal with well-intentioned establishment Republicans who want to curb his excesses. There will be no effective guardrails on a second Trump presidency. After being in office for four years, he will know exactly how to execute what he wants to accomplish—without interference from anyone.

It is crucial to appreciate what Trump has accomplished in returning to the presidency. His election—his political redemption—makes him, at least for now, the most consequential American political figure of the 21st century. As Peter Baker of the *New York Times* wrote the day after the election, 'As a result, for the first time in history, Americans have elected a convicted criminal as president. They handed power back to a leader who tried to overturn a previous election, called for the termination of the Constitution to reclaim his office, aspired to be a dictator on Day 1 and vowed to exact retribution against his adversaries.'[1] Shocking and breathtaking are understatements.

At his campaign rallies throughout 2024, Trump was emphatically clear: he intends to destroy the so-called Deep State—the elites who he claims have thwarted the aspirations and economic security of his loyal followers. 'In the end, they're not coming after me. They're coming after you . . . Either we have a Deep State or we have a Democracy . . . Either the Deep State destroys America, or WE destroy the Deep State. This is the final battle.'[2]

Trump railed against those enemies who wanted to take him down. 'Every time they indict me, I consider it a great badge of honour. I'm being indicted for you, and never forget, our enemies want to take away my freedom because I will never let them take away your freedom. They want to silence me because I will never let them silence you. And in the end, they're not after me. They're after you and I just happen to be standing in the way.'[3]

In the days immediately following the election, Trump began to assemble his cabinet and senior staff. In contrast with the chaotic scramble for positions in 2016, Trump engaged in a very clinical process with all deliberate speed. The fate of his nominees will be decided in the weeks following the inauguration, with Trump enjoying Republican control of both the House and Senate. But his most prominent nominees for the most crucial positions who will lead the attack on the Deep State all expressed their profuse loyalty to the Trump agenda. Matt Gaetz, an extremist Trump supporter in the House of Representatives, was selected by Trump to be attorney-general. Through the Justice Department, Trump can direct indictments and prosecutions of his enemies. Gaetz qualified himself for his appointment with these words: 'We either get this government back on our side or we defund and get rid of, abolish the FBI, CDC [Centers for Disease Control], ATF [Alcohol Tobacco and Firearms], DOJ [Department of Justice], every last one of them, if they do not come to heel.'[4]

Trump loathes the Department of Justice because of his belief that President Joe Biden and the Democrats weaponised the DOJ via all the investigations launched against him, all the ensuing indictments, and all the pending trials—which will never be concluded as Trump will ensure his attorney-general will win dismissal of the charges by the courts. According to a Trump advisor, Gaetz sealed his appointment this way: 'None of the attorneys had what Trump wants, and they didn't talk like Gaetz. Everyone else looked at AG as if they were applying for a judicial appointment. They talked about their vaunted legal theories and constitutional bullshit. Gaetz was the only one who said, "Yeah, I'll go over there and start cuttin' fuckin' heads."'[5]

Gaetz was ultimately forced to withdraw from consideration as attorney-general. But there is no doubt that Trump will ultimately have an attorney-general confirmed by the Senate who will carry out Trump's insistence that the 'disloyal' elements rife in the department are removed and punished.

Trump's appointment of Robert F. Kennedy Jr to head the Department of Health and Human Services is a baseball bat designed to bludgeon every vestige of medical science and public health as practised by former Chief Medical Advisor Dr Anthony Fauci, one of the world's most respected physician-scientists and immunologists, who Trump came to despise during the Covid pandemic.

Trump's selection of Tulsi Gabbard, a former member of Congress who has expressed sympathies to Putin and Russia,[6] as the Director of National Intelligence is designed to shut down the intelligence community's hostility to Russia and other international actors.[7] Trump's choice of Pete Hegseth, a veteran and Fox News star, is intended to start a purge of senior 'woke' military commanders for their disloyalty to Trump and resistance to his desire that they follow his orders in every instance, especially regarding the deployment of military forces to put down demonstrations on the streets of America's cities or enforce deportation orders against immigrants.[8]

As is the case with Gaetz, regardless of whether these other nominees are ultimately confirmed or rejected by the Senate, Trumpist policies will be enforced by whoever holds those cabinet positions.

Trump enters office at the zenith of his power. His first year will be marked by the most extensive use of executive power under the Constitution in United States history. A political reality that normally applies to incoming presidents is not in play for Trump. Trump is now term-limited and does not have to face the voters again.[9] Trump can exercise power to do what he wants and what he believes is right. At least until the midterm elections in 2026, there is nothing the voters can do to curb his exercise of his power. With Republican control of the House and Senate, there is virtually no likelihood Trump will be impeached or removed from office. Most importantly, the Supreme Court ruled in July 2024 that the president is immune from prosecution for 'official acts' he undertakes.[10] If Trump ignores laws passed by Congress or refuses to abide by court decisions that would block his policies, Trump will be immune from accountability under those laws and court orders.

Trump's power in this presidential term, in other words, is the closest to absolute.

Trump and Australia's foreign policy settings

There are four pillars to Trump's policies. Nativism and the protection of America's borders, and stopping illegal immigration. Protectionism through the use of tariffs to prevent imports from flooding American markets and to rebuild America's industries and factories. Isolationism, to keep America out of foreign wars and international institutions that constrain American policy and programs. And nationalism, to 'make America great again' by ensuring that all engagement with the world benefits America first and foremost. The ledger should always be tipped towards the benefit of the United States.

These pillars define Trumpism.

Trump's agenda with the rest of the world will be confrontational.

None of this will come as a surprise to Australia's leaders and policy makers.

There was a strong consensus among Australian and American officials I spoke with for this book about Trump's character and temperament. Their view was that Trump will never change; he is erratic, unhinged and foments chaos; he is arrogant, has no sense of history, and is completely transactional.

With respect to those he sees as enemies, he never apologises, recants or retreats. He never expresses regret for his actions. When under attack for scandalous behaviour or abuse of power, Trump has one playbook: deny, denounce, discredit, defame.

Trump will challenge, again, the structures erected after World War II to promote security, peace and prosperity across the globe. This is the world order that Trump wants to raze.

As discussed later in this book, Australia must maintain its membership in all the international organisations Trump wants to pull the United States out of: several agencies of the United Nations (including the World Health Organization and the World Trade Organization), the Paris Agreement and the International Criminal Court.

Australia should continue to stand with the world and the integrity of these institutions.

With respect to Australia's relationships across the Indo-Pacific, Trump will focus on several pressure points.

How much of the regional architecture will Trump want to continue supporting? Australia and the United States are in the ASEAN Regional Forum, the Asia-Pacific Economic Cooperation (APEC), and the Pacific Islands Forum. Australia is joined, together with Japan and India, in the Quad. The US, Australia and Japan have a trilateral cooperation agreement with respect to stability in the Taiwan Strait. The US, Japan and South Korea have a working group on regional issues, especially North Korea. Australia, Japan, the Philippines and the United States are engaged in maritime security agreements. Will Trump support or seek to dismantle or downplay these arrangements? China opposes the Quad. Will Trump seek openings with China by neglecting attention to or demoting the role of the Quad?

Trade and the economy

On trade, Trump will unleash the most comprehensive suite of tariffs since the protectionist policies of the 1930s. Trump has threatened tariffs of up to 20 per cent on all goods imported into the United States, and tariffs of 60 per cent on all imports from China. Tariffs imposed on Australian exports would go against the grain of the tariff-slashing United States–Australia Free Trade Agreement, concluded twenty years ago.

This will be an early test of Australia's relationship with Trump and his administration. Australia has had a structural trade deficit with the United States for over seventy-five years.[11] Australia is not, and should not be, a target of Trump's wrath on trade. Whether Australia is exempted from the Trump tariffs will be crucial in framing the relationship in the next several years.

Trump's tariffs will start a trade war with China. When Trump did this in his first term, Australia was swept up in the hostilities, with China's retaliation encompassing Australia's trade relationship with China. Why should Australia support Trump's trade war with Beijing and invite a reprise of the complete disruption of Australia's trade with China? It took four years to get this back on track. There is no need for Australia to go through it again.

Trump may also revive consideration of punishing China by 'decoupling' the US economy from China's. Again, Australia should resist any positioning that parallels such a stance with respect to China.

But if Australia opposes Trump's trade war with China, will Trump challenge Australia?

Trump's policy settings will have a profound effect on the US economy, which will in turn affect Australia's economic future. Many of the Trump tax cuts enacted in 2017 expire at the end of 2025.[12] Extending the law will add $4.6 trillion to the US deficit over the next ten years.[13] Trump's tariffs could cost each consumer US$2600 per year in higher prices for goods.[14] Mass deportations are expected to trigger extensive labour shortages, again leading to higher prices for goods and services.[15] The result could be both higher inflation and lower growth.[16]

These developments could harm prospects for any lessening of the cost-of-living pressures on households in Australia, leaving in place a regime of high interest rates.

AUKUS, Australia and Asia

As the Trump presidency begins, there is optimism among those most closely associated with AUKUS that it will not only survive but continue apace. As AUKUS was an initiative conceived and executed by President Biden, Trump may have some misgivings over its patrimony. More likely, Trump will interrogate the deal like the business CEO he is: what is the flow of money, jobs and technology, and who benefits the most, the United States or Australia? Trump may prompt a re-negotiation to get more favourable terms and returns to the US. AUKUS should survive this process.

Later in this book, I argue that Australia must step up across the Asia-Pacific as never before to protect its foreign policy objectives and secure its interests. This is the shared view of all the 'AusMin Chorus'—a group of Australian and American former officials with deep involvement in Australia's foreign policy. They counsel for deeper strategic engagement, building firmer relationships with Asian partners and landing high-quality trade deals. In short, strengthening Australia's independent relations across Asia—separate and apart from its alliance with the United States—all in order for Australia to continue to be fully engaged with the Asia-Pacific, notwithstanding whether the United States is retreating from the region. Foreign Minister Penny Wong has amply fulfilled this mission, and it will redound to Australia's benefit in the coming Trump years.[17]

Climate and global warming

Aside from withdrawing from international global warming agreements and targets, Trump will, with his 'drill baby drill' policies for full encouragement of oil, gas, fracking and other fossil fuels, set the United States apart from the policies and programs of Australia to meet the targets for renewable energy supplies under the Paris Accord. A retreat by an Australia under pressure from Trump on these issues will harm the bridges built by Australia with the nations across the Asia-Pacific, where the issue of global warming is exceptionally strong. Indeed, at the APEC meeting in Lima, Peru, in November 2024, Albanese saw a tactical advantage and signalled that Australia welcomes clean energy investments that are no longer welcome in the United States under Trump.[18]

Health and healthcare

The health and healthcare focuses from the first edition of this book are: how the Covid-19 pandemic and the way it was managed highlighted the frailties of the public health and healthcare systems in Australia and the United States, and the need to be better prepared for the next global health crisis; the threats to reproductive health and abortion rights; how Trump and his allies had politicised public health and demonised scientific and medical experts; how disinformation and misinformation around public health issues is a growing international problem; and the impacts of the Trump administration's policies on global health initiatives.

Those concerns and threats have only grown since this book was first published and, as the make-up of the new Trump administration emerges, health experts around the globe are rightly alarmed about what its policies will mean for health and healthcare.

The Covid-19 pandemic is far from over, despite political pronouncements to that effect. It is a major contributor to excess mortality rates and will continue to be unless vaccination rates—with updated vaccines to account for the continual emergence of new variants—improve. In the United States, an average of 1500 Covid-19 deaths a week were reported last year—this is comparable to fentanyl or firearms deaths.[19] Long-Covid has affected millions of Americans[20] and Australians[21] and is generating steep economic and social costs.

Meanwhile in North America the first human-to-human transmissions of H5N1 bird flu have been recorded. The virus has new mutations facilitating this transmission, and there are fears that, without appropriate actions, this could lead to widespread infections.[22] The United States also faces threats from mpox,[23] increasing numbers of measles outbreaks[24] and growing reports of tickborne diseases thought to be due to climate change.[25] The consequences of climate change and the impact on health and the delivery of healthcare services have been strikingly demonstrated in 2024: severe storms, cyclones, wildfires and winter storms have resulted in the deaths of 418 people.[26] Australia is not immune to any of these threats.

There is clear and growing evidence that the Dobbs decision from the US Supreme Court, which revoked the constitutional right to abortion, is not just harming reproductive health, but also means worsening health outcomes for American women as abortion bans force doctors to provide substandard care.[27] And the 2024 data show that the United States continues to be in a class by itself in the under-performance of its healthcare sector.[28]

Trump returns to the White House and assumes responsibility for these wicked problems having spent the election campaign flip-flopping on abortion rights, access to IVF, and repealing Obamacare. He has tried to rewrite history with respect to his handling of the pandemic,[29] denied any knowledge of the Heritage Foundation's Project 2025[30] and played word games about whether he would cut Medicare entitlements.[31] The Trump campaign demeaned transgender people, promised to undermine trans rights, and promulgated dreadful lies about schools secretly sending children for gender-affirming surgeries.[32]

Trump's capacity to manipulate the truth and to switch positions is now magnified by his cabinet appointments. The choice of Robert F. Kennedy Jr to be Secretary of Health and Human Services is described as 'an indication of the contempt with which Trump holds the federal health establishment, including the National Institutes of Health and the Food and Drug Administration'.[33]

'I'm going to let him go wild on health. I'm going to let him go wild on the food. I'm going to let him go wild on the medicines,' Trump has said,[34] at the same time saying Kennedy could 'do what he wants' with women's healthcare. Trump has refused to rule out Kennedy's plans to ban vaccines and has endorsed the removal of fluoride from water supplies.[35]

Much of this, including Kennedy's Make America Healthy Again agenda[36] (but barring Kennedy's status quo stance on abortion which Trump has—to date—supported), is in line with the health proposals from Project 2025.[37] Add to this mix the 'efficiency' operations of the Department of Government Efficiency and it's easy to see how much damage could be done with huge budget cuts, onerous restrictions on access to programs like Medicaid, Veterans' Health and food stamps, and a dangerous loosening of regulations designed to protect human and animal health. A Republican-dominated Congress is almost certain to try to dismantle key aspects of Obamacare, regardless of Trump's stance, and it is highly likely that the Republicans in Congress and the politicised Justice Department will engage in witch hunts of high-profile climate scientists and medical experts like Dr Anthony Fauci.

There will be significant consequences for Australia. These come at a time when the federal government is confronted with addressing the recommendations from the Covid-19 Response Inquiry report[38]—a key finding of which is that the government must rebuild trust in public health. A significant aspect of this is transparency about data and improved communications to ensure people understand the benefits of public health protections such as vaccines. Yet both federal and state levels of government have dramatically reduced reporting requirements for Covid-19 (data from the Australian Bureau of Statistics show that as of 1 October 2024, there were 4056 deaths from Covid-19 in that year[39]), vaccination rates for Covid-19 are depressingly low,[40] childhood vaccination rates are falling,[41] sexually transmissible infections are on the rise,[42] and cases of whooping cough (a vaccine-preventable disease) have passed 40,000 this year for the first time since recording began more than thirty years ago.[43]

The promised Australian Centre for Disease Control has never been more needed, but the Albanese Government has been slow to deliver: its formal establishment, which will require enacting legislation, is not due until 1 January 2026.[44] Between now and then there is a federal election (and there are no guarantees of Coalition support for this new agency) and we can expect the Trump administration to aggressively downgrade the US Centers for Disease Control and Prevention, which has been the gold standard for such agencies. Trump administration attacks on the Food and Drug Administration will potentially affect approvals of some medicines and medical devices in Australia, where the Therapeutic Goods Administration refers to FDA reviews to expedite approvals.[45]

The pandemic highlighted a range of challenges for the management of Australia's international relationships and revealed a serious vulnerability in medical supply chains, especially for protective equipment and vaccines.[46] Trump's insistence on 'America first' was a factor in determining which countries got early access to Covid-19 vaccines[47] and as president he signed an Executive Order requiring federal agencies to purchase American-made essential drugs and medical supplies.[48] This time around that approach will surely be hardened. This will impact Australia's vaccine manufacturers and supply chains.

The expectation is that Trump will also take a harder approach to the involvement of the United States in global health issues— this at a time when Pacific Island nations are threatened by climate change, there is a Marburg virus outbreak in Rwanda (which appears to have been successfully controlled due to support from the World Health Organization and a vaccine from the United States[49]), there are endemic polio outbreaks in Afghanistan and disease threats in Gaza, and there is a global outbreak of measles.[50]

The real impact of the return of Trump and Trumpism on Australia will emerge in the context of the next federal election. We should expect to see issues such as abortion, fluoride in drinking water, vaccine mandates and access to treatment for gender dysphoria enter the debate; ideological positioning about universal access to key social services such as Medicare; and increased levels of misinformation, disinformation and vilification of scientific and medical expertise from those on the extremes of politics and on social media.

The Trump stress tests on democracy

On many mornings over the next couple of years, our news bulletins will contain headlines out of Washington. In Trump's first term, many of us woke up in the morning to ask, 'What [expletive deleted] did he do overnight?' We are condemned to a renewal of that experience.

Australia is an echo chamber for what Trump initiates in America. We hear his policy decisions which in turn affect our thinking on those same issues here. When Trump ramps up on immigration, woke culture and racial issues, those events play into our media coverage and political discourse.

In the first few weeks of Trump's presidency, we will likely see a sweeping program of the rounding up and forced deportation of thousands—and perhaps hundreds and hundreds of thousands—of immigrants who are deemed by Trump to be in the country illegally. This will make the scenes of chaos and disruption under Trump's 'Muslim travel ban' of 2017[51] look like a stop-and-search operation. Immigration agents and military forces will be widely deployed. Families will likely be separated. Treatment will be harsh, likely with detention camps erected to house those ordered to leave. Where these immigrants are sent and how they will be received is likely to be disorderly and wrenching.

Trump was elected in significant part by the political potency of the immigration issue and the urgency of the government controlling America's borders. We in Australia have felt the power of this issue over many years and many elections since then-Prime Minister John Howard famously declared, in the wake of the Tampa affair in 2001, 'We will decide who comes to this country and the circumstances in which they come.'[52] This is now Trump's most powerful and emotive policy issue. Trump's language on immigration has been super-charged with hate. In his re-election campaign, Trump regularly resorted to Nazi talk that immigrants 'were poisoning the blood of our country' and were 'vermin' to be expunged.[53] Half the country will cheer; the other half of the country will be deeply distressed.

The world will witness it. This will further colour perceptions about Trump, his policies and the nature and character of the United States.

It is in this context that several other issues will erupt and be assessed. This will be especially true on cultural issues: the treatment and rights of gay and transgender people, the future of diversity, equity and inclusion programs, issues that play on identity politics, book banning in schools. Paramount in this class of issues is the ability of the states to restrict abortion rights, and opposition to gun control. Trumpists play the race card on voting rights issues with their support of voter ID requirements for elections.[54] Whatever Trump pushes in the US along these lines can easily emerge here by being taken up by political leaders who see an opportunity to exploit these issues for political advantage. Abortion rights, for example, was a major issue in last year's US presidential campaign. It is no coincidence that abortion rights came up late in the Queensland state election in October 2024, just as the issue was peaking in the US.[55]

At the same time as the immigration deportations are underway, Trump will pardon perhaps hundreds of extremists who have been convicted of crimes for attacking the US Capitol on January 6, 2021, in an insurrection to overturn the 2020 election. Trump has described them as 'hostages' who must be set free.[56] Trump's tolerance for extremists and white nationalists will continue to leach into the political culture here in Australia. Neo-Nazis marched in Charlottesville, Virginia, in 2017. In recent years, they have marched in Melbourne and Ballarat.[57] This is also no mere coincidence.

Trump has complained bitterly about the media, and especially mainstream media, which he consistently calls 'fake news' as he points them out with his index finger at his rallies. This also leaches into our political culture. When a politician does not want to answer a question with an ugly insinuation, the issue is dismissed as 'fake news'.[58] In the course of the 2024 campaign, Trump took on a more threatening posture against major mainstream media platforms, especially television and cable networks. Trump has attacked Comcast, owner of NBC, for its 'one-side and vicious' coverage that must be 'thoroughly scrutinized for their knowingly dishonest and corrupt coverage'.[59] Trump threatened to revoke CBS's license because of editing by *60 Minutes* of their campaign interview of Kamala Harris. He has sued CBS for US$10 billion in damages.[60] Trump has also threatened to jail reporters for their coverage.[61]

Trump was back in full force with Fox News throughout 2024, and Fox is all-in with Trump as his presidency takes shape. But new media stars in the political firmament have emerged: right wing, male-oriented streaming platforms that predominantly reach young men. As Axios has reported, 'Gone are the days of Fox dominance.

Instead, Musk's X and personality-dominated podcasts, led by Joe Rogan, will be the new power centers. All of this is unfolding on X, where the stars of the right-wing constellation congregate.' X, with Elon Musk's ownership, is in the process of transcending Fox News.[62] Tucker Carlson, ousted from Fox and now with his own streaming platform, has successfully re-established his close and powerful association with Trump.

Parallel developments in the media landscape have not yet emerged in Australia. For now, News Corp and Sky News are less strongly positioned in Australia.

Peter Dutton, currently leader of the Opposition, routinely criticises the ABC and its coverage of the issues of the day[63] and the culture of its journalists.[64] As Trump continues to normalise hostility to the media in America, his example will make it easier for political leaders here to more aggressively attack media they view as hostile to their politics.

The guardrails of Australia's democracy

Australia's democracy can more than withstand the stress tests Trump inflicts in America. First and always, we have compulsory voting, reinforced with preferential voting. In our elections, we always land on centre-left or centre-right—and not extreme left or extreme right.

With our Westminster system, a blow-in like Trump is impossible here. The prime minister is always the leader of the party with a majority in the House of Representatives. Clive Palmer, Gina Rinehart and Twiggy Forrest, for example, will never be prime minister.

Elections are administered by the Australian Electoral Commission, which ensures the machinery of elections is maintained and repaired on a completely nonpartisan basis to keep it in excellent working order. Getting on the electoral rolls is uniform across the country, from the most remote booths in the Northern Territory to the wealthiest suburbs in Melbourne. Race does not infect voting rights or the counting of votes. The votes are counted with scrutineers from the political parties present. Outcomes in seats where the margin is within some dozens of votes are very rarely taken to court. In Australia there is no Big Lie about who won the election.

As discussed later in this book, the appointment of judges is non-political. Unlike the confirmation process under the US Constitution, Parliament has no role in approving the appointment of judges. There are norms governing the vetting of judicial vacancies. As opposed to the practices of many states in the US, state and local judges are not elected in Australia. Similarly, the Reserve Bank of Australia is insulated from political pressure. Trump has made clear that he wants to have more direct say in the setting of interest rates.[65] Trump may also decide to take an unprecedented step and fire Jerome Powell, chair of the Fed.[66]

Australia's reckoning with Trump redux

It is clear that, over the past year, the Australian Government has done much to prepare for Trump's return to power. Extraordinary efforts at outreach to Trump and Trump's circle of contacts have been undertaken, from Ambassador Kevin Rudd's liaisons with Trump allies and advisers to former Prime Minister Scott Morrison's meeting with Trump to discuss AUKUS.[67]

That was all necessary and smartly executed. But in itself it is not sufficient to face the challenges at hand.

The main game will be the relationship between Prime Minister Anthony Albanese and President Trump. It is the prime minister who will need to make—and win—directly with Trump the argument that Australia should be exempt from Trump's new tariffs. It is the prime minister who will need to stand up to Trump's imposition of tariffs against China and declare Australia's opposition to Trump's trade war policies.

It is the prime minister who will need, if required, to dissuade Trump from blowing up the AUKUS deal by new terms which render the arrangement prohibitively injurious to Australia's interests.

Those will be the critical initial tests between the prime minister and the president, and will determine where Australia stands in Trump's firmament.

The results of those tests will serve as a reckoning on Australia's place in the Indo-Pacific and how it can protect its interests.

Trump and Australia: The existential threat

There might also be a reckoning on the US–Australia alliance itself. We are allies, and we are allied, because we share the same values: democracy, liberty, freedom, universal suffrage, the rule of law, freedom of religion, freedom of the press, freedom of assembly.

But Trump threatens to cripple America's democracy. Trump will command the biggest deportation of immigrants in American history and bring in the military to execute it. Trump will use the National Guard and perhaps US troops under the Pentagon to control protestors.

Trump wants to impose his will and loyalty across the bureaucracy. Under the terms of Project 2025, Trump will require civil servants to sign loyalty oaths. As Carlos Lozada of the *New York Times* concluded:

> It calls for a relentless politicizing of the federal government, with presidential appointees overpowering career officials at every turn and agencies and offices abolished on overtly ideological grounds. Though it assures readers that the president and his or her subordinates 'must be committed to the

Constitution and the rule of law,' it portrays the president as the personal embodiment of popular will and treats the law as an impediment to conservative governance. It elevates the role of religious beliefs in government affairs and regards the powers of Congress and the judiciary with dismissiveness.[68]

What if the struggle for democracy and the soul of America fails in 2025, 2026 or 2027? What happens if President Trump declares martial law, if troops are deployed to cities across the country to put down protests and restore law and order, if Trump disobeys court orders, including from the Supreme Court, to cease and desist acting under the authority of his executive actions, if Trump ignores laws and spending decisions enacted by Congress, if Trump orders the detention and imprisonment of his political enemies, if Trump has journalists arrested and jailed and shuts down media outlets that report truthfully on him? If Trump directs the regulatory agencies to put certain companies he perceives as enemies out of business?

If Trump dismantles American democracy, the American continent will no longer be populated by united states. They will be bitterly divided. There will be immense unrest. The country will no longer be the United States.

Trump redux therefore poses an existential question: How could Australia remain allied with a country that has discarded the fundamental values of democracy which have bound these two nations together? How can Australia be allied with a country that is drifting towards autocracy and authoritarianism?

The 2020s and the 1930s: Is this déjà vu all over again?

As we absorb Trump's re-ascension to the presidency, what decade does this feel like? With this election, the post-war world is now over. The architecture established after World War II—the

United Nations, the World Trade Organization, the World Health Organization, international accords on climate change and the environment, human rights bodies—are a shadow of their former stature. NATO will be under immense stress from Trump. We have authoritarian dictators invading other countries to extend their raw power. Isolationism has gripped the superpower that has been the engine of democracy, the United States, and trade wars will be unleashed.

With isolationism and a retreat from the world, protectionism and tariffs and trade wars in vogue, with nationalism coloured by nativism on the rise, it is beginning to look and feel like the 1930s. Few are alive from those times. As Santayana and Churchill observed, those who do not remember history are doomed to repeat it. We should remember how that decade ended.

Some final words of guidance for Australia from Norman Ornstein, Emeritus Scholar at the American Enterprise Institute:

> The American experience shows that any society, no matter longstanding norms, can slide towards authoritarianism and deep and irreconcilable internal divisions. The combination of ruthless demagogues, a pliant or complicit mainstream press, pernicious tribal media and manipulated social media can create conditions that lead to a slow movement in a bad direction. No society, including Australia, should be complacent.

Which is precisely why I am so thankful to you for reading these pages.

Bruce Wolpe
Sydney, Thanksgiving Day, November 2024

Prologue
Growing Up with Kennedy, Surviving Trump

On 22 January 2021, two days after Joe Biden's inauguration as president, my wife Lesley and I went for a morning swim at Balmoral just north of Sydney. It was a beautiful day. Blue water, great light, calm. I tweeted, 'Friday morning in Sydney. Joe Biden is President of the United States. @POTUS.' We were getting back to normal after nearly 1500 days of Donald Trump as president, waking up every morning and asking, 'What the hell did he do last night?' and absorbing what he had tweeted, what he had said on television, whom he had attacked and insulted, whom he had fired, which ally he had dissed, what norm of governance he had violated, what investigation he had monstered. The tension was gone. The collective blood pressure in Australia was declining, just as it was in the United States. The vice in the chest and tightness in the stomach were easing. The incidence of yelling really ugly epithets at the television was becoming more rare. Frowns receded. Smiling came easier.

I never really understood—I still don't—how the United States could go from Barack Obama to Donald Trump. How the country could unite and conquer the legacy issue of race and send the first Black American into the White House with an overwhelming margin and yet eight years later elect a man who embodied the urge to divide America to its very core. A man who was so unsuited to be president. A man who did not understand what the presidency meant and what it was. A man who had contempt for democracy's most basic values.

Lesley and I had listened to Obama's acceptance speech in 2008 while on the phone with our closest friends, and we were all crying and shrieking. We could not believe how wonderful that moment was and that it had come in our lifetimes. On election day 2016, it was impossible to absorb that three reliably Democratic states—Wisconsin, Michigan and Pennsylvania—had flipped to Trump, giving him victory in the Electoral College, and sending the country and the world into shock. The kick in the gut began there and did not go away for four years. After Trump's overwhelming win in November 2024, it's back again.

After Trump's first victory, I was heartened that Vice President-elect Mike Pence and his wife went to New York to see Lin-Manuel Miranda's *Hamilton* on Broadway. The musical is the story of the American Revolution and the democracy and Republic that Alexander Hamilton and the Founding Fathers wanted to establish. At the end of the performance, Miranda, with all the actors on stage, addressed Pence. 'We, sir—we—are the diverse America who are alarmed and anxious that your new administration will not protect us, our planet, our children, our parents, or defend us and uphold our inalienable rights. We truly hope that this show has inspired you to uphold our American values and to work on behalf of all of us.'[1] The crowd erupted in cheers. Pence did not react. Trump tweeted that Miranda had been very rude and had harassed the vice president to be, and demanded Miranda apologise—which he did not. Hamilton would have been proud.

In 2016, I had prominently predicted a Hillary Clinton victory. Four years later, on the eve of the 2020 election, at the National Press Club in Canberra, I was asked who was going to win, Biden or Trump, and I said, 'I am still atoning for predicting Hillary in 2016. Every day for me is Yom Kippur.'

I grew up in Washington, DC. My grandparents had made their way there in the 1910s from Lithuania and Eastern Europe. We lived in the north-west area of the city, off Connecticut Avenue, a major boulevard that runs north from the White House. The city was much smaller then, and it was, to us, two cities: a largely Black-majority city, with ghettoes and neighbourhoods with a Black middle class; and a white city, with government workers, and also white local communities.

The federal government was much smaller then too, and the armies of lobbyists and consultants that now pervade the city did not exist. For us, 'the government' was far away; we only knew a few people who worked for it. J. Edgar Hoover, the all-powerful and feared director of the FBI, lived nearby—his house was forbidding and we never played near it.

Our world was like a small town, with regular people building their lives. But living in Washington meant that you were closer to the government, and its power. You could feel the pulse of the city when something important was happening.

I went to President Kennedy's inauguration. Those who have read of that day know it was bitterly cold; it had snowed close to two feet the day before. But the sun was so bright at noon that January day that we sat in the stands along Pennsylvania Avenue, near the White House, and watched the parade that heralded the president's car, with Kennedy and Jackie smiling and waving. At forty-three, Kennedy was the youngest-ever president and had an air of vigour and informality.

We knew people who knew people. Our family barber, in a shop on Connecticut Avenue, was a very dapper fellow, who also cut President Kennedy's hair. He arranged a Secret Service tour of the White House for us. I remember we were in the West Wing, and suddenly there was a crush of journalists and photographers headed to the Oval Office. We followed them and Dad hoisted me up to see Kennedy at his desk, answering questions. Pretty exciting.

In school we had 'current events' classes in which Kennedy's press conferences were discussed, and his style made a huge impression on us.

Later, I was a staffer for Henry Waxman, a congressman from California who would become one of the most effective lawmakers of the post World War II years. I made the cut to be on the California float in Jimmy Carter's inaugural parade when he became president in 1977. In 1980, Ronald Reagan ousted Carter—hyperinflation and Americans held hostage by the Iranians were politically fatal—and in January 1981 I attended a Reagan inauguration party on Pennsylvania Avenue. With Reagan's victory, the Democrats lost the Senate and thirty-three House seats, and it hurt terribly. Reagan came in to slash social spending, beef up defence and champion conservative moral values, from abortion to guns to prayer. That 20th of January was a dramatic day; the hostages were released in Tehran moments after Carter ceased being president.

In 1993, we flew into Washington from Sydney to attend Bill Clinton's inauguration. We loved Maya Angelou's poem, 'On the Pulse of Morning', with all its promise for the future with our brothers and sisters.

When I grew up in DC, the city was segregated, and the schools were too. The only students of colour in my elementary and junior high school were the children of diplomats who lived in Northwest DC. During my senior year at Woodrow Wilson High School, Black students were bused in. The white and Black communities were separate and profoundly unequal. Race was always in the air—it impacted where you could walk or drive, whether you were safe at night. In the summers, I went to camp in West Virginia with other teens like me. All white. In the summer of 1963 the counsellors were listening to the radio one night and talk of plans for a major civil rights march on Washington. 'The niggers are coming,' one said. More than 200,000 people, Blacks and whites, headed to the Lincoln Memorial that day. It was where Martin Luther King, Jr delivered his most famous speech:

> I have a dream that one day on the red hills of Georgia, the sons of former slaves and the sons of former slave owners will be able to sit down together at the table of brotherhood.
>
> I have a dream that one day even the state of Mississippi, a state sweltering with the heat of injustice, sweltering with the heat of oppression will be transformed into an oasis of freedom and justice.
>
> I have a dream that my four little children will one day live in a nation where they will not be judged by the color of their skin but by the content of their character. I have a dream today.[2]

No one I knew went. We were told to stay home that day. And it was the same on the night of 4 April 1968 when King was murdered. Riots seized the city; Washington burned just blocks from the White House. The National Guard was deployed, and troops were on Connecticut Avenue, close to our house. The 4th of April is my birthday, shared ever since for memory, renewal and commitment to the man lost that day, but whose values and ideals ultimately were not.

More tragedy was to come just two months later. I watched Bobby Kennedy's victory speech after he won the California primary for his presidential run, and I went to sleep after he gave his famous 'V' for victory. I woke up to the horror of his assassination. Frank Mankiewicz, Kennedy's press secretary, announced the death the next day from the hospital. Frank later became head of National Public Radio, and I worked with him in the first Reagan term.

It was a summer of urban riots across the county and riots in the streets of Chicago at the Democratic Convention. Nixon beat Hubert Humphrey in the November general election, and Nixon and Kissinger prosecuted the Vietnam War for the duration of his presidency.

Those experiences and events of being close to politics in my teens had their effect. I loved political novels—*The Man* (about the first Black president), *Seven Days in May*, *Fail-Safe*, *The 480*, *Advise and Consent*, *All the Kings Men*, *1984*, *Soul on Ice*, *To Kill a Mockingbird*—and political films, especially *Dr Strangelove*, *The Best Man*, *The Manchurian Candidate*, *Citizen Kane* and *All the President's Men*. When I was in high school, the *New York Times* company gave students a huge discount on a subscription and I started reading the *Times* every day. Their editorials against the Vietnam War were immensely compelling to me. I've read the *Times* every day since, and the *Washington Post*. We got the afternoon paper at home too, *The Evening Star*. On Saturday mornings, driving to my dad's store, we would listen to the CBS World News Roundup at 8 am—fifteen minutes of what you needed to know. David Brinkley would come into the bar where I worked summers after his news broadcasts on NBC. An interest in politics and issues and the media was spawned in me and has been part of what I've done all my life.

I followed presidents—not so much the Congress; that would come later—and what they did, and when they were heroes, as Kennedy was in the Cuban Missile Crisis in 1962, and villains, as Lyndon B. Johnson was in the Vietnam War. And as Nixon was in Watergate of course, a tale of such an astonishing plot against the constitutional order—effectively a conspiracy to discredit the Democrats and take down Nixon's enemies in order to win re-election in 1972—that it became a test of the rule of law, and whether it would prevail. It was a civics course on the grandest scale for everyone who followed it. What was so thrilling about Watergate to me was that the institutions worked as they were supposed to. The scandal of Nixon's misdeeds provoked investigations by special counsel Archibald Cox, a highly regarded legal scholar; when he was fired, the attorney-general and several officials in the line of succession at the Department of Justice who refused to carry out Nixon's orders were fired or resigned. The White House was shaken. The country was shaken. Congress started a special investigation. When it was disclosed that Nixon had taped his White House meetings—a shocking revelation that sent everyone into a frenzy, because the tapes would reveal what the president said and knew throughout the scandal—the congressional committees sought the tapes. They won that battle in court—including a landmark decision by the Supreme Court. Nixon did not assert 'executive privilege' over his aides, who were compelled to give testimony. The country stopped every day to watch the Watergate hearings on television. There was wall-to-wall coverage on the three commercial networks. There was no Fox News and no internet to push out alternative narratives of what everyone was seeing. There was a crescendo of disclosures of what was in the tapes that led Nixon, facing impeachment and under pressure from Republican senators, to resign.

What was at stake? There's a wonderful scene in the movie *All the President's Men*, based on the Bob Woodward and Carl Bernstein book. Late at night, Ben Bradlee, editor of the *Washington Post*, meets with Woodward and Bernstein and outlines the scandal's inflection point for the country, and the imperative that the press—his reporters—do their job, and do it right. Bradlee says, 'Because we're under a lot of pressure too, and you put us there—not that I want it to worry you—nothing's riding on you except the First Amendment of the Constitution plus the freedom of the press plus the reputation of a hundred-year-old paper . . .'[3]

It was true. The First Amendment to the Constitution, which enshrines freedom of the press, and the *Washington Post* both survived. Nixon did not. Nor did all the president's men. President Gerald Ford's first words to the nation, on being sworn in to succeed Nixon, were, 'My fellow Americans, our long national nightmare is over. Our Constitution works; our great Republic is a government of laws and not of men.'

From Vietnam to Watergate and beyond, what I took with me was a belief that American democracy did work, could work, and that there were standards and values that were both enduring and essential. There were rules to the game, and the system was inherently just; corruption would be discovered and punished, and accountability exacted; and, just like William Hurt, as the network anchor in *Broadcast News*, said at the end of a crisis playing out on TV: 'In other words, I think we're okay.'[4]

While I was aware of Donald Trump through his TV show, *The Apprentice*, he first hit my radar as a political animal in 2010, when he began flirting with a run for presidency and became a champion of the 'birther' conspiracy movement that asserted Barack Obama was not a US citizen, was not born in Hawaii and was an illegitimate president. It was simply infuriating to see these falsities gain traction and media attention. Trump's movements into politically hot states such as New Hampshire, where presidential campaigns are born, crossed into the mainstream media. And so it was in 2011 when Trump, toying with a presidential candidacy for 2012 (he ultimately would not run), landed his branded chopper in New Hampshire as Obama released his birth certificate. The split-screen coverage sealed Trump's clout with cable news eyeballs.

Obama had his revenge a few days later at the White House Correspondents' Association dinner—the gala constellation of political and media power in Washington where a cutting speech by the president is expected. Trump had a table in the middle of the ballroom. Obama, the grandmaster of locution, did not hold back: 'Now, I know that he's taken some flak lately, but no one is happier, no one is prouder to put this birth certificate matter to rest than The Donald,' Obama said. 'And that's because he can finally get back to focusing on the issues that matter—like, did we fake the moon landing? What really happened in Roswell? And where are Biggie and Tupac?

'But all kidding aside, obviously, we all know about your credentials and breadth of experience. For example—no, seriously, just recently, in an episode of *Celebrity Apprentice*—at the steakhouse, the men's cooking team did not impress the judges from Omaha Steaks. And there was a lot of blame to go around. But you, Mr Trump, recognised that the real problem was a lack of leadership. And so ultimately, you didn't blame Lil Jon or Meatloaf. You fired Gary Busey. And these are the kind of decisions that would keep me up at night. Well handled, sir. Well handled.'[5]

Trump, humiliated, took it. Did he vow that night to take revenge? Hours before that dinner, Obama had approved the mission executed by the Navy Seals to kill Osama bin Laden. So by the end of that weekend, Trump and bin Laden had been terminated with extreme prejudice in the eyes of the Washington establishment.

Trump's entrance into the presidential race in 2016 reflected his ability to ensure the media were fixated on him. It did not matter that there were over a half-dozen Republican heavyweights—including Jeb Bush, Ted Cruz, Marco Rubio, Chris Christie and John Kasich—who were determined to ensure Trump would be beaten. Wherever Trump went, the cameras followed. Whenever he was on stage, he owned it. He beat the field into submission. His views were even more outrageous than accusing Obama of being born in Kenya.

After Trump called immigrants from Mexico 'criminals and rapists' and demanded a border wall with Mexico, the Pope said, 'A person who thinks only about building walls, wherever they may be, and not building bridges, is not Christian.'[6]

Trump has only one gear: attack. Even if the target is the Pope. 'For a religious leader to question a person's faith is disgraceful,' Trump said.[7] And it paid off. Trump won the Catholic vote in 2016. Trump proved, with his base, hardcore supporters who came to comprise overwhelming strength among Republican voters, he could do that again and again.

Trump has up-ended Republican orthodoxy going back five decades to Ronald Reagan. Reagan was for American world leadership, alliances, championing democracy, free trade and immigration as essential to nation building. Trump is for America First, isolationism, protectionism and nativism. His brutal personality and his shameless and shocking statements placed him outside what was thought to be mainstream national sentiment. But in 2016 he kept dominating the candidate debates and winning primaries, essential to securing the party's nomination for the presidential campaign. In the hall and on TV, Trump took all the oxygen out of the room. Viewers were fascinated—many repelled—by what they were seeing, because no serious candidate for president had ever acted or spoken like Trump did, and they kept watching to see what astonishing, outrageous things he would say next. In a field of seventeen candidates, Trump, with a base of 30 per cent and growing, enjoyed seeing his opponents splitting the field into popgun armies that he could overwhelm.

John Sununu, former Republican governor of New Hampshire and chief of staff to President George H.W. Bush, said early in 2016 that he did not understand what he was seeing—it did not compute that Trump could win the allegiance of the Republican Party. Before the New Hampshire primary, Sununu urged New Hampshire voters: do 'not drink the Trump Kool-Aid,' and said, 'You can't be commander-in-chief with such a thin skin. He may be rich, but he's not bright. The two don't necessarily go together.'

Why was Trump succeeding? 'I have no idea.'[8]

After Trump romped in New Hampshire, South Carolina and Nevada, and swept most of the Super Tuesday states on 1 March 2016 (so-called because so many states vote on the same day), it was beginning to become clear that he would be the Republican nominee. In mid-March, I was with Julia Gillard in Washington for working sessions at the Brookings Institution. The prospect of Trump as president was too shocking to take seriously. 'But if he becomes president,' I said, 'he will be impeached.' That stopped the conversation for a full minute. (I was wrong. Trump was impeached twice.)

The Trump atrocities continued throughout the campaign. He kept getting up at 3 am to attack a former Miss Universe on Twitter. To impugn a Vietnam War hero and prisoner-of-war. To stomp on the grief of an American Muslim family whose son sacrificed his life to save fellow American soldiers in Iraq. To disparage the integrity of a judge because his parents were from Mexico. To raise the implicit spectre of unleashed vigilante gun violence against his opponent, Hillary Clinton.[9]

How could a Trump follow an Obama, whose approval rating was close to 60 per cent at the end of his presidency?

We have to go back to 2008.

I was in Denver, Colorado, attending the Democratic Convention that had just made history in nominating Barack Obama for president—the first time a Black American had won that prize. The party and its supporters were ecstatic, with the concluding words of Obama's acceptance speech still in their ears: 'America, we cannot turn back. Not with so much work to be done. Not with so many children to educate, and so many veterans to care for. Not with an economy to fix and cities to rebuild and farms to save. Not with so many families to protect and so many lives to mend. America, we cannot turn back. We cannot walk alone. At this moment, in this election, we must pledge once more to march into the future. Let us keep that promise—that American promise—and in the words of Scripture hold firmly, without wavering, to the hope that we confess.'[10]

In order to take some air out of the Obama balloon, Republican presidential nominee Senator John McCain's campaign leaked that Sarah Palin would be his running mate.

The first reaction among the throng was, 'What? Sarah who?' The governor of Alaska was not well known at all. Then there was her life story: basketballer, beauty queen, journalism student, mayor of the Alaska hamlet of Wasilla, and a rebel against the party establishment with enough gumption to beat the sitting governor in 2006. A dear female friend and colleague who worked with Ronald Reagan told me, 'She will have appeal to suburban moms who think the Democrats are too extreme.' Palin could maybe help McCain flip the election.

But the second reaction followed immediately: Sarah Palin was not qualified to be president. The vice president has to be able to assume the office in a heartbeat if necessary. Palin proved her lack of competence and gravitas in the weeks that followed. In foreign policy, she said she could keep an eye on Russia from her house in Alaska. Tina Fey's send-up of Palin on *Saturday Night Live* reached millions. Obama and Biden romped home by over 9.5 million votes, and 365 Electoral College votes (way in excess of the 270 required to win).

But Palin had scratched an itch among white voters who felt let down and driven out by establishment politics. In his memoirs, Obama wrote: 'Palin's nomination was troubling on a deeper level. I noticed from the start that her incoherence didn't matter to the vast majority of Republicans. In fact, anytime she crumbled under questioning by a journalist, they seemed to view it as proof of a liberal conspiracy . . .

'Through Palin, it seemed as if the dark spirits that had long been lurking on the edges of the modern Republican Party—xenophobia, anti-intellectualism, paranoid conspiracy theories, an antipathy toward Black and brown folks—were finding their way to center stage.'[11]

Palin lost in 2008 but she helped pave the way for Trump in 2016 and again in 2024. Obama wrote in 2016: 'I see a straight line from the announcement of Sarah Palin as the vice-presidential nominee to what we see today in Donald Trump, the emergence of the Freedom Caucus, the tea party, and the shift in the center of gravity for the Republican Party.'[12]

Writing for *Quarterly Essay*, Don Watson, Australian author and former political adviser and prime ministerial speechwriter, went to Wisconsin, a key swing state that Trump had to win, to see the Trump effect on the electorate up close.

'Trump says, Hand your fear over to me. Hand your loathing over too. I will deal with your enemies as I have dealt with mine. I will give you back your freedom, and your country. Your old lives will be yours to live again. I will halt the terminal decline. American exceptionalism, in which you all hold shares, will be underwritten by an exceptional American.'[13]

Watson's reporting brought home why America was ripe for Trump's message. In particular, it showed the anger and frustration of non-college-educated white men, whose lives had been harmed by economic forces they did not understand and that were beyond their control, who saw the country becoming strange to their eyes as its demographic face changed in their lifetimes. Men who raged against an Imperial City that was dysfunctional, obsessed with itself and its power, and was greedy and unresponsive to their needs.

In 2016, people were stunned, reeling that Donald Trump could win the Electoral College, and the presidency, thanks to Wisconsin and two other traditionally Democratic states, Pennsylvania and Michigan. It was just 78,000 votes in those states, out of 128.8 million votes cast nationally, that secured his victory. That 78,000-vote difference in those three states gave Trump the presidency even though, in the total popular vote across the country, Hillary Clinton beat Trump by nearly 3 million votes.

When Trump first became president, I kept a list, added to every day, on his character traits. The exercise lasted a month, but it was telling: 'He can say anything. Can change his mind completely. He lies. Has to be the centre of attention. Distracts focus by attacking multiple subjects at the same time. Utterly conflicting views on the same person. Loves authority figures. Denies he has said what he said. Believes he is beyond conflicts of interest. Does not care he acts in ways that are beneath a president. Humiliates potential appointees. So smart he does not need intelligence briefings.

Lies about the size of his election victory. Trump only hears what he wants to hear.'

Within three years, it would be abundantly clear that Trump's presidency was the most disruptive and divisive in modern history.

The United States was more divided than at any time since the Vietnam War. Partisanship had never been stronger; it was as if the Westminster culture of government and opposition had descended not only on the Capitol, the seat of the US Congress, but across the country as well. Ninety per cent of supporters of the two major parties became locked in their view of Trump: Republicans approved of him, Democrats rejected him.

Trump vigorously prosecuted his agenda: America First; a strong military; a strong economy; taking on the post World War II global order: trade, NATO, the European Union, the World Trade Organization, the International Monetary Fund; getting the United States out of the Paris climate agreement; ensuring hard conservatives were placed on the courts; impeding any sensible gun control measures even in the face of horrific massacres in schools, churches and synagogues; relentless measures to seal the border and limit all immigration—legal and illegal; massive programs of deregulation for business; fidelity to religious views to roll back the access of women to abortions.

On trade, Trump was the first president to directly challenge China's structural advantages and barriers to foreign investment. He deployed tariffs against friends and enemies on a scale unseen since the protectionism (that preceded the Great Depression) of the 1930s. Seeing Iran as an unremittingly hostile terrorist state committed to harming the United States and Israel, and which had snookered President Obama and his Secretary of State John Kerry into an agreement that Iran would surely evade, Trump terminated the nuclear deal with Iran and established a strategic fault line between Iran and its proxies and the Sunni Muslim states together with Israel.

Trump consistently showed a clear preference for authoritarian leaders over democratic allies. Russia's Putin, China's Xi, North Korea's Kim, Saudi Arabia's Mohammed bin Salman, Brazil's Bolsonaro, Hungary's Orbán, the Philippines' Duterte and Turkey's Erdoğan were all favoured over Germany's Merkel, France's Macron and Canada's Trudeau. Japan's Abe and Australia's Morrison fared better, as did Boris Johnson, who championed and executed a Trumpian agenda with Brexit in the United Kingdom. (But before Boris, Trump rubbished Theresa May.)

Clearly, Trump had wilfully abdicated the role of leader of the West—a special mantle worn by every US president since Franklin Roosevelt.

Trump was incredibly chaotic in governance, with unprecedented turnover in his office and cabinet. Three chiefs of staff, four national security advisers, and more than a dozen changes to cabinet, including State and Defense: all power and policy flowed directly from the Oval Office.

Before Covid hit, with the benefit of a trillion-dollar tax cut and a trillion-dollar deficit, the economy indeed boomed, with unemployment at fifty-year lows, and markets hitting all-time highs.

I have been criticised for saying what follows. But taking all this into account—notwithstanding that Trump lied or made misleading claims more than 30,000 times during the course of his presidency[14]—*Trump has been the most ruthlessly honest president in modern times.*

He does what he says he will do. There is nothing hidden. He commits his atrocities in broad daylight. Shamelessly.

Which is why his base loves him and continues to love him.

When Joe Biden entered the presidential race in 2019, he was absolutely clear why he was determined to run:

> Charlottesville, Virginia, is home to the author of one of the great documents in human history. We know it by heart: 'We hold these truths to be self-evident, that all men are created equal, endowed by their Creator with certain unalienable Rights.'
>
> We've heard it so often, it's almost a cliché. But it's who we are. We haven't always lived up to these ideals; Jefferson himself didn't. But we have never before walked away from them.
>
> Charlottesville is also home to a defining moment for this nation in the last few years. It was there on August of 2017 we saw Klansmen and white supremacists and neo-Nazis come out in the open, their crazed faces illuminated by torches, veins bulging, and bearing the fangs of racism. Chanting the same anti-Semitic bile heard across Europe in the '30s. And they were met by a courageous group of Americans, and a violent clash ensued and a brave young woman lost her life.
>
> That's when we heard the words from the president of the United States that stunned the world and shocked the conscience of this nation. He said there were 'some very fine people on both sides.' Very fine people on both sides?
>
> With those words, the president of the United States assigned a moral equivalence between those spreading hate and those with the courage to stand against it. And in that moment, I knew the threat to this nation was unlike any I had ever seen in my lifetime.
>
> I wrote at the time that we're in the battle for the soul of this nation. Well, that's even more true today. We are in the battle for the soul of this nation.

I believe history will look back on four years of this president and all he embraces as an aberrant moment in time. But if we give Donald Trump eight years in the White House, he will forever and fundamentally alter the character of this nation—who we are—and I cannot stand by and watch that happen.

The core values of this nation, our standing in the world, our very democracy, everything that has made America, America, is at stake.

That's why today I'm announcing my candidacy for President of the United States.

Under Trump, three events that I thought simply could not occur in America occurred.

Jews have been murdered by other Americans in their synagogues. In years past, on the High Holy Days at synagogue in Washington, I feared that it was the perfect opportunity for a terrorist act by the PLO. That never happened. But there was an attack by my fellow Americans. In 2021, a gunman killed eleven people at the Tree of Life Synagogue in Pittsburgh. There have been other attacks on Jewish places of worship.

The Capitol was violently attacked by Americans. Trump has never tried to be the Uniter-in-Chief, or the Healer-in-Chief. His dog whistles to white supremacists have created an environment where the unthinkable occurs. From the day of his inauguration, Trump invoked 'American Carnage' as a theme—'This American carnage stops right here and stops right now.'[15] Almost four years to the day after Trump uttered those words, his American carnage visited the very Capitol where he took office, with his mob attacking Congress as it met to certify the election and seal the peaceful transfer of power to Joe Biden.

I worked in that building for over ten years, and never thought for a moment that armed Americans would attack it.

The loser of a presidential election refused to concede. In 1960, Nixon had good reason to believe that there were suspect votes for Kennedy in Chicago, and if Illinois flipped to his column, Nixon could win the election.

Peggy Noonan retells the tale: 'Nixon believed the election was stolen. President Dwight D. Eisenhower and Senate Minority Leader Everett Dirksen wanted him to challenge the results. Nixon thought it could take months and might not succeed, but his thoughts went deeper than that. In the Cold War, the nuclear age, unity at home and abroad was needed. Young democracies looked up to us. If they thought our elections could be stolen it would hurt the world's morale. The *New York Herald Tribune* had launched an investigative series, but Nixon talked the reporter into stopping it: "Our country cannot afford the agony of a constitutional crisis."'[16]

In Evan Thomas's brisk *Being Nixon: A Man Divided*, he reports that the GOP wise man Bryce Harlow urged Nixon to challenge, but Nixon said no: 'It'd tear the country to pieces. You can't do that.'

So he didn't.

The 2000 presidential election, between Vice President Al Gore and Texas Governor George W. Bush, came down to whichever candidate carried Florida. The recount was farcical, with election officials holding up computer ballot cards with 'hanging chads'—the shards of the punched ballot papers that had been put through the counting machines, fluttering on them. The recount was also very tense, with passions running high. In what became known as the 'Brooks Brothers Riot', well-dressed pro-Bush Floridians massed at the recount headquarters, confronted election officials, pounded on desks and demanded the recount be halted.

Some commentators draw a line between that putative push at election interference and the ultimate morphing of those anti-establishment passions into the January 6 attack on the Capitol. When the recount reached a legal impasse—both candidates contested the recount and how long it would go on in several courts, with Bush ultimately leading in Florida by 537 votes out of nearly 6 million cast—the Supreme Court ruled by a 5–4 vote that the election was over and Bush had won the state, and the presidency. Al Gore conceded to George W. Bush:

'I say to President-elect Bush that what remains of partisan rancor must now be put aside, and may God bless his stewardship of this country. Neither he nor I anticipated this long and difficult road. Certainly neither of us wanted it to happen. Yet it came, and now it has ended, resolved, as it must be resolved, through the honored institutions of our democracy . . . Now the U.S. Supreme Court has spoken. Let there be no doubt, while I strongly disagree with the court's decision, I accept it. I accept the finality of this outcome, which will be ratified next Monday in the Electoral College. And tonight, for the sake of our unity as a people and the strength of our democracy, I offer my concession.'

Bret Stephens, a staunchly conservative columnist for the *New York Times*, captured Trump's presidency this way: 'He is the only president in American history who has refused to concede an election, who has schemed with conspiracy theorists to remain in power, who has sought to bully state officials into finding him votes, who has egged on a mob, who has cheered an assault on Congress, who has put the life of his vice president in jeopardy, who has flouted the demands of the Justice Department to return classified documents, who has violated every norm of American politics and every form of democratic decency.'[17]

America's democracy is not undone. Yet.

But the second Trump term may do much more damage.

In June 2022, as the fiftieth anniversary of Watergate approached, Bob Woodward and Carl Bernstein joined by-lines for an essay in the *Washington Post*. They addressed Trump in the context of Nixon: 'A dominating personal trait binds Nixon and Trump together: Each viewed the world through the prism of hate.'

Woodward and Bernstein then recalled what Nixon, in the moments before he resigned in disgrace, acknowledged in farewell remarks to his staff, televised live to the nation.

'The day Nixon resigned the presidency, August 9, 1974, he gave his farewell address in the East Room of the White House. He had no script. His wife, Pat, his two daughters and their husbands stood behind him. Nixon spoke of how his mother and father were misunderstood and proceeded to unleash more grievances.

'Then suddenly, as if he had found a larger message, he smiled gently and offered his final counsel to all. "Always remember, others may hate you—but those who hate you don't win unless you hate them, and then you destroy yourself."

'It seemed a blinding moment of self-understanding. Hate had been the trademark of his presidency. But in the end he had come to realize that hate was the poison, the engine that had destroyed him.'[18]

Trump doesn't recognise the poison. It hasn't destroyed him yet.

Trump 2020

In an interview for ABC's flagship current affairs program *Four Corners* a month before the 2020 presidential election, I said that I felt the election was the most important in my lifetime, and that there was a real possibility, if Donald Trump were re-elected, that American democracy would not survive his second term:

'America faces a decisive choice. If he's re-elected and has another four years, incalculable and perhaps irreversible damage will be done to American democracy and how America operates and what it stands for in this world. So really, everything is at stake for the future of the country.'

Trump was defeated in 2020, but he did not concede the election. Trump's fervent belief that the election was stolen is accepted by upwards of 60 per cent of Republicans.[19]

After the 2020 election, what was exposed was not simply Trump's plot to overturn the election result, but a comprehensive campaign, focused on the state and local levels in key swing states, to alter the election mechanisms to change who counts the votes in these states, and who has the power to certify the votes in those states. In addition, nineteen states have passed laws to make it harder—not easier—to vote, disadvantaging voters who are poorer and voters of colour from enjoying equitable access to the polls.

During the Biden term, Trump continued to dominate the Republican Party and its legislative agenda in Congress, and the passage of legislation supported by President Biden and Democrats to strengthen voting rights was systematically blocked.

Trump's success in shifting the balance of the Supreme Court through the appointment of three staunch conservatives during his term has sharply constricted the rights of women to access abortion and greatly expanded the rights of Americans to obtain guns.

Trump announced his candidacy for the 2024 election on 15 November 2022. He spoke of a return to glory in America:

> But just as I promised in 2016, I am your voice. I am your voice. The Washington establishment wants to silence us, but we will not let them do that. What we have built together over the past six years is the greatest movement in history because it

is not about politics. It's about our love for this great country, America. And we're not going to let it fail. I am running because I believe the world has not yet seen the true glory of what this nation can be.

Trump made it very clear during the 2024 election campaign that on his return to office he will wreak vengeance on his enemies, especially in Congress. His administration will be filled with Trump First loyalists; he will have no need to deal with well-intentioned establishment Republicans who want to curb his excesses. There will be no effective guardrails on a second Trump presidency. This time he knows exactly how to execute what he wants to accomplish—without interference from anyone.

As part of a larger projection of what Trump back in power would look like, assembled by Thomas Edsall of the *New York Times*, Stanford professor Cécile Alduy wrote that the Republican agenda under Trump redux 'would be fueled by increased moral panic about white America's decline, a professed sense of having been spoliated and "stolen the election" and a renewed sentiment of impunity for his most extreme backers from the Jan. 6 insurrection. My bet is that there is an active plan to reshape the political system so that elections are not winnable by Democrats, and the state be run without the foundation of a democracy.'[20]

In other words, American democracy as we have known it will come to an end.

Trump's second term will call into question Australia's alliance with the United States, as reflected in the historic ANZUS treaty, now over seventy years old, and what Australia does with it. Australia loves America, but can we love a divided America under Trump?

The consequences for Australia, given the bedrock alliance between the two countries, and two democracies, are as incalculable as they are immense.

Trump and the future of Australia

If Trump destroys America's democracy, does that pose an existential threat to Australia's alliance with the United States? What should Australia do to protect its future?

Part I turns to Trump's foreign policy and Australia, including discussions of China, the Australia–US–UK alliance to counterbalance China in the Indo–Pacific, North Korea, and related issues.

Part II turns to Australia's domestic policy settings on the economy, trade, and climate, and how Trump policies affect the debate on those issues here.

Part III explores the future of democracy in Australia and the United States in the context of Trump's shaping of the political culture in both countries. I focus on how elections in both countries are conducted, racial issues, the media, and the emergence of Trumpism.

Part IV turns to the key safeguards of democracy in Australia, including mandatory voting, the Westminster system, and how some critical institutions here are insulated to a degree from political pressure.

Trump's Australia explores what Australia needs to do to maintain and strengthen its democracy and political culture in the face of its most important ally's retreat from democracy. What trends in the United States will affect us here in Trump's second term? What Trumpist themes are seeding foreign and domestic policy issues and Australia's political culture? And what guardrails in policy and politics need to be erected or reinforced to withstand and protect Australia's society and way of life from a second Trump presidency?

Waleed Aly and Scott Stephens explored some of these issues in their masterful *Quarterly Essay*, 'Uncivil Wars', in September 2022. Although their analysis focused on political debate in Australia, and how toxic it became especially over recent years, they looked to events in the United States as a window on the political culture in Australia. 'We inevitably draw heavily on American examples. This may seem strange in an Australian essay intended largely for an Australian audience, but we do so for two reasons. The first is that since social media drives so much contemptuous public exchange, America has an oversized influence on public conversation in Australia. English-speaking social media is dominated by American ideas and trends.'[21] This book has a similar lens.

A note on sources for this book. I have worked on the staff of the US Congress, in a prime minister's office in Australia, and in the private sector. I have brought my experience to bear on researching issues and questions that are important to the future of two countries I love and am a citizen of: Australia and the United States. I engaged in several dozen conversations with Australians and Americans for this book. In the foreign policy section, I spoke with nearly two dozen senior officials who served in both the Australian and United States governments, under Liberal and Labor prime ministers, foreign ministers and defence ministers, and under Republican and Democratic US presidents, secretaries of state and secretaries of defense. What struck me about those interviews was the overriding consensus in the views of this wide-ranging group of individuals who have been deeply engaged in the Australia–US alliance and who have reflected on what Trump could do in a second term, and what that could mean for Australia. They all had extraordinarily clear views on Trump, how he acts and what his policies are and portend. I was astonished at how highly consistent they are in their views on a Trump return to power and Australia's national interests. I could call them the 'AusMin Chorus' because they were singing in harmony—and that is what they project in these pages. I have chosen not to name them when their quotes are used so I can publish their most candid assessments. Similar treatment was afforded to other officials in discussions of economic and trade issues and the Reserve Bank.

This book includes a chapter on Covid-19 and larger health policy issues, written by Dr Lesley Russell. Lesley's analysis of the pandemic helps us understand the public health and healthcare issues presented for Australia and how the actions (and inaction) of the Trump administration have had far-reaching ramifications nationally and internationally.

Lesley is an expert in health policy issues and has worked at the interface of politics and policy in both the United States and Australia. I'm proud to be married to her. She is an Adjunct Associate Professor at the Menzies Centre for Health Policy and Economics at the University of Sydney. Lesley has served as a senior health policy adviser to both the federal Australian Labor Party and the Democrats on the Energy and Commerce Committee in the United States House of Representatives. She was also a senior policy adviser to the United States surgeon-general during the Obama administration.

Norman Ornstein, one of America's foremost political scientists, is a senior fellow emeritus at the American Enterprise Institute (AEI), where he has been studying politics, elections and the US Congress for more than four decades. His books include the *New York Times* and *Washington Post* bestseller *One Nation After Trump: A Guide for the Perplexed, the Disillusioned, the Desperate, and the Not-Yet Deported* (St Martin's Press, 2017) with E.J. Dionne Jr and Thomas E. Mann. Norm has visited Australia several times and is an avid follower of politics in Australia. It is a special honour to include his observations on what is discussed in these pages in an epilogue.

Trump's Australia was conceived and written independently of my position as a non-resident senior fellow at the United States Studies Centre (USSC) at the University of Sydney. This book is not a USSC publication and its views should not be attributed to USSC.

TRUMP AND AUSTRALIA'S FOREIGN POLICY

1
Trump
America First Abroad

When Donald Trump was inaugurated as the forty-fifth President of the United States on 20 January 2017, the world would quickly see that he would do exactly what he had said he would. At the Capitol that day, he said:

> The oath of office, I take today, is an oath of allegiance to all Americans. For many decades, we've enriched foreign industry at the expense of American industry, subsidized the armies of other countries, while allowing for the very sad depletion of our military. We've defended other nations' borders while refusing to defend our own. And spent trillions and trillions of dollars overseas, while America's infrastructure has fallen into disrepair and decay. We've made other countries rich while the wealth, strength and confidence of our country has dissipated over the horizon. One by one, the factories shuddered and left our shores, with not even a thought about the millions and millions of American workers that were left behind. The wealth

of our middle class has been ripped from their homes and then redistributed all across the world.

But that is the past, and now we are looking only to the future. We assembled here today are issuing a new decree to be heard in every city, in every foreign capital, and in every hall of power, from this day forward: a new vision will govern our land, from this day forward, it's going to be only America first. America first.

Every decision on trade, on taxes, on immigration, on foreign affairs will be made to benefit American workers and American families. We must protect our borders from the ravages of other countries making our products, stealing our companies and destroying our jobs. Protection will lead to great prosperity and strength. I will fight for you with every breath in my body, and I will never, ever let you down. America will start winning again, winning like never before. We will bring back our jobs. We will bring back our borders. We will bring back our wealth, and we will bring back our dreams. We will build new roads and highways and bridges and airports and tunnels, and railways, all across our wonderful nation. We will get our people off of welfare and back to work, rebuilding our country with American hands and American labor.

We will follow two simple rules: buy American, and hire American. We will seek friendship and goodwill with the nations of the world, but we do so with the understanding that it is the right of all nations to put their own interests first. We do not seek to impose our way of life on anyone, but rather to let it shine as an example. We will shine for everyone to follow. We will reinforce old alliances and form new ones, and unite the civilized world against radical Islamic terrorism, which we will eradicate completely from the face of the Earth.[1]

Trump was unleashed, in head-snapping fashion. On any given day, his thrusts were stunning.

A few days after promising to 'unite the civilized world against radical Islamic terrorism', Trump announced a ban on travellers from six Muslim-majority countries, throwing travellers and airports into confusion. It would take months for Trump to get the legal basis for his decrees in sufficient shape to withstand the courts striking down his actions.

This tumultuous decision was a signal that Trump would lurch from issue to issue, often in dramatic fashion, to project his policies and beliefs. This meant that Trump's overall approach to foreign policy was confusing and chaotic. He played real estate tycoon with other countries. He advised North Korea's Kim Jong-Un on hotel and resort developments. At one stage he wanted to buy Greenland and he had the National Security staff work up options for a deal. 'It's just something we've talked about,' he said. 'Denmark essentially owns it. We're very good allies with Denmark. We've protected Denmark like we protect large portions of the world, so the concept came up. Strategically, it's interesting. And, we'd be interested. We'll talk to them a little bit.' Denmark's prime minister was clear: 'Greenland is not for sale.'[2]

Trump was known for his aggressive and bizarre stagecraft, such as the intense, weaponised handshakes with France's Emmanuel Macron. He literally shoved aside the President of Montenegro before the official photo for a 2017 NATO summit. He broke protocol and steamed ahead of Queen Elizabeth II at Windsor Castle.

He was hostile to America's best friends and allies, notably British Prime Minister Theresa May and Germany's Chancellor Angela Merkel. Yet, he professed 'love' for dictators such as North Korea's Kim Jong-Un only months after calling him 'short and fat' and 'Little Rocket Man', and threatening to meet him with 'fire and fury' and 'totally destroy' his country.

Trump was enamoured with leaders with absolute power. China's Xi Jinping got Trump's highest praise for his 'great' efforts to abolish China's presidential term limits in 2018. 'He's now president for life, president for life. And he's great. And look, he was able to do that. I think it's great. Maybe we'll have to give that a shot someday,' Trump said.[3] Philippines' President Rodrigo Duterte was lauded for his 'unbelievable job on the drug problem'[4] despite his extrajudicial killings of drug suspects.

Trump was eager to cross 'red lines' on national security issues. His top economic adviser stole a memo from Trump's desk to prevent him from signing an order that would have withdrawn the United States from a trade agreement with South Korea. Trump argued he did not understand why US troops were in South Korea. 'It's to prevent World War III,' his secretary of defense replied.[5] Leaving NATO was not a heavy lift to Trump because 'he didn't think NATO was good for America'.[6]

Trump's engagements with Russia were in a special category. He maintained a close and secretive relationship with Russia's president, Vladimir Putin, including an off-the-record hour-long conversation with Putin during the 2018 G20 summit. Trump seized the translator's notes so that there was no record of what transpired. Trump's relationship with Putin spawned intense speculation as to what Putin has on him.

Trump was erratic in carrying through his threats to use force. In 2019, Trump called off an attack against Iran in response to the downing of a US drone. He dithered at the last minute, when planes were already in the air, stunning the Pentagon and leading to the departure of John Bolton as national security adviser. A year later, Trump would decisively order the attack that killed

Qassim Soleimani, Iran's top security and intelligence commander, an act that threatened a counterstrike by Iran directly on US forces in the region.

Trump loved taking dramatic action that would have worldwide impact. He decreed moving the US embassy in Israel from Tel Aviv to Jerusalem in the context of the Abraham Accords. He unilaterally reached agreement to withdraw US forces from Afghanistan. He wanted to bring the Taliban leaders to Camp David to celebrate the accord. 'Unbeknownst to almost everyone, the major Taliban leaders and, separately, the President of Afghanistan, were going to secretly meet with me at Camp David on Sunday. They were coming to the United States tonight,' Trump tweeted. The thought of the Taliban at Camp David sent Washington's political class into apoplexy.

Trump consistently played power politics over prosecuting human rights issues. It is all but certain that Crown Prince Mohammed bin Salman of Saudi Arabia ordered the assassination of *Washington Post* journalist and Saudi dissident Jamal Khashoggi. But throughout his presidency, Trump had only praise for Saudi Arabia and the prince as a friend of the United States. Trump never held the prince accountable for murder.

Trump also never expressed sympathy for the assault on press freedom. Indeed, in 2018, Trump took his hostility to what he called the 'mainstream media' or 'lamestream media' to new levels, labelling the media 'the true Enemy of the People'[7]—just as Joseph Stalin would do in Russia throughout his dictatorship.[8]

But on policy issues, Trump was clear and consistent in unleashing his America First strategy—protectionism, isolationism and nativism—across the board.

On day three of the Trump presidency, the United States withdrew from the Transpacific Partnership—a deal designed, as the

United States Trade Representative said at the time, to 'open markets, set high-standard trade rules, and address 21st-century issues in the global economy. By doing so, TPP will promote jobs and growth in the United States and across the Asia-Pacific region.'[9]

The US signature on the 2015 Paris climate agreement was also erased within six months of Trump's inauguration.

He withdrew the United States from the Iran Nuclear Deal and the Intermediate-Range Nuclear Forces (INF) Treaty, and the Treaty on Open Skies. Trump also withdrew the United States from the UN Human Rights Council and the UN Education, Science and Cultural Organization.

The United States also withdrew from The Global Compact on Refugees in December 2018, which was not surprising after President Trump reportedly refused to take immigrants from 'shithole countries' and complained that Nigerian immigrants would never 'go back to their huts' and Haitians 'all have AIDS'. He doubled down in an Oval Office meeting. 'Why do we need more Haitians?' Trump asked. 'Take them out.'[10]

In July 2020, during the most major global pandemic in over one hundred years, the United States withdrew from the World Health Organization and refused to join the Covid-19 Vaccine Global Access Facility to provide vaccinations throughout the world.

Trump's vendetta against international engagement also included the International Criminal Court (ICC) and World Trade Organization (WTO).

It is no wonder then that Trump's September 2018 speech at the UN General Assembly was met with laughter when he said, 'In less than two years, my administration has accomplished more than almost any administration in the history of our country. So true!' Later on, he said, 'Didn't expect that reaction, but okay.'

Trump sought to distance the United States from commitments that were considered to sap it of energy and resources. He was driven by the idea of preserving 'American sovereignty' and shielding it from the type of restrictive international accountability that might curb America's freedom to choose what it wants for itself.

Trump's dominion over foreign policy was administered by a White House chronically infested with chaos. During his presidency, there were five national security advisers, two secretaries of state and five secretaries of defense, several of them serving in 'acting' roles. 'I like acting,' Trump said in 2019. 'It gives me more flexibility. Do you understand that? I like acting. So we have a few that are acting. We have a great, great cabinet.'[11] He did it to keep a short leash on everyone. It also meant that Trump could place these men in power without seeking Senate confirmation in their role.

Australia opposed virtually all of Trump's major foreign policy decisions that aimed to decouple the United States from the framework of international organisations and institutions designed to promote the world's security, prosperity and growth. But none of those differences reached a make-or-break point in terms of the overall US–Australia alliance.

There was a very rocky beginning to the relationship between Trump and Prime Minister Malcolm Turnbull, which threatened to put Australia into Trump purgatory. Days after Trump's inauguration there was an infamous call between Trump and Turnbull on an immigration deal under which the United States would accept 1200 refugees under Australian control in Nauru. Trump was trapped by an official agreement made before he took office but he excoriated Turnbull over the deal. The call was ugly. But the shocker was that someone in the White House leaked a transcript of that call (and one with the president of Mexico) to the *Washington Post*.

As Joe Hockey, Australia's Ambassador to the United States at the time, recounts in his memoirs, *Diplomatic*, everyone's reaction was that it was outrageous for Trump to rubbish the leader of the country that is America's strongest ally. Members of Congress, led by Senator John McCain, fell over themselves to stand with Australia. The media could not get enough of the atrocity Trump had committed against his strongest mate. The bipartisan, bicameral Friends of Australia Caucus in Congress was rejuvenated. Hockey initiated a campaign in Washington to celebrate '100 Years of Mateship'.

Turnbull writes in his memoirs that he was able to successfully deal with Trump because he stood up to him. Reflecting on that first term with Trump, and the incendiary call over the refugees, in which Turnbull prevailed, he writes: 'In my experience the successful narcissistic bully is able to manipulate others effectively because he has a keen sense of others' vulnerabilities. Like any predator, he can sense fear and weakness from miles away.

'So the best way to deal with someone like Trump is to be frank and forthright. Be yourself, always be courteous—there's nothing to be gained from rudeness or scratchiness. But stand your ground. That suited me.

'If you suck up to Trump, he just wants more sucking up.'[12]

The refugees deal stuck. Fifteen months later the two leaders met at a gala event in New York under the penumbra of Rupert Murdoch and all major Australian luminaries in the United States, from golfer Greg Norman to cardboard box billionaire Anthony Pratt.

The relationship was repaired, and when Scott Morrison, more conservative than Turnbull, won the May 2019 election after abruptly taking over the prime ministership, Trump provided a state dinner for him in September 2019. There was only one other state dinner during Trump's presidency, for France's Macron.

That evening cemented Australia's prime position in the Trump firmament.

Morrison was a truer conservative in Trump's eyes and there was no refugee issue for Trump to face on Morrison's watch. Morrison's hardline policies on refugees fit perfectly with Trump's fear of immigrants overrunning the United States. As Hockey relates in his book, Trump initially did not want to meet Morrison because he thought Morrison was a loser. But when Morrison won, Trump gave exceptional praise. 'Congratulations to Scott on a GREAT WIN!'[13] Trump tweeted. Trump loves winners. And Morrison was a winner with no issues to offend Trump's sensibilities, such as a trade partner who runs surpluses against the United States, or a defence ally who doesn't carry their weight in the Pacific.

Trump's first term was a clear win for Australia. Of all the countries doing business with Donald Trump, Australia emerged with a better relationship than any other country, including Israel.

What will Trump do on his return to the Resolute Desk in the Oval Office, and how will that affect Australia and its future?

Australians involved deeply in the relationship between Australia and the United States have remarkably consistent views on Trump's character, nature, how he thinks, his operating instincts, mindset and attitudes. There is no mystery or riddle to solve or unpack with Trump. He is known all too well. At his age, if anything, his internal gyroscope is locked even harder in its settings. Trump knows what he wants: vindication, redemption and most especially revenge against those who took his presidency away.

Trump also knows, from four years in the job, how the White House functions, and what he can do—or try to do—with the power of his office. Trump does not want to be hampered in acting on some of his most basic instincts; he knows he cannot afford to have around him any staff, or cabinet officials, or military chiefs, who will resist his demands. Trump fired FBI Director James Comey and his attorney-general, Jeff Sessions, because he believed they did not protect him from investigations probing his ties with Russia. Early in his presidency, Trump screamed at his generals, who were baulking at his desire to withdraw American military forces from the wars in the Middle East and bases around the world, 'I wouldn't go to war with you people. You're a bunch of dopes and babies.'[14] This time Trump has a vice president in J.D. Vance who would be unlikely to refuse to obey his orders to overturn the presidential election.

In Trump's second term, with respect to his power and how he wishes to wield it, there will be no checks, only greater imbalances. Australians will not die wondering what Trump is capable of in his second term.

Australia faces not a changed Trump but a harder Trump.

Trump's leadership, character and style

The senior Australian and American officials I interviewed for this book were in complete agreement that Trump would never change from the president we experienced in his four years in office. One official related, 'I thought Trump had changed when he got elected. But Trump never stopped being Trump ... He will never stop being Trump going forward unless he has a compelling reason to change.' Another added, 'He will be the same person as he was the first time around. He has learned that he needs people completely beholden to him—in his cabinet and throughout his staff. Ditto with the military. He will not want independently thinking people. He wants people who can help him manipulate the law and the Constitution.'

Trump will continue to be erratic. 'Trump is not anchored to a philosophical foundation; he can change dramatically. He has a fixation on authoritarian leaders. He admires them and that they can make tough decisions and can do so without being slowed down by democratic norms or the bureaucracy.'

Trump's ability to act on his whims at any given moment is also apparent. A former diplomat and senior public servant says, 'As president he can be just as inconsistent as he was in the first term. He can call Putin a genius one day, and call Ukraine brave the next.' Or as another said, 'Trump is confident in the extreme but inconsistent in the extreme. Inconsistency can lead to miscalculation, such as the need for General Mark Milley, Chairman of the Joint Chiefs of Staff, to call his Chinese counterpart to assure him that the US would not invade China as the US was preparing the transfer of power from Trump to Biden.'

Trump has no shortage of confidence: 'He firmly believes in his own powers of persuasion and his capacity to deal with others, such as with Putin and Kim Jong-Un.'

Trump is self-centred and determined. 'Trump does not listen. He is totally in a world of his own. He is impossible to talk to. He does not engage with what you are saying—only with what he is saying.' 'Trump's cabinet and staff will have less guardrails, and fewer adults. Trump will be able to move more quickly on whatever he wants to do.'

Trump does not operate with a coherent, consistent plan: 'Trump conflates the notion of revenge with having a strategy, such as with Covid and trade policy.'

Trump does not have the benefit of understanding history. 'We want America to be engaged in the Indo-Pacific. The starting point for Trump is that he does not know history or care about the geostrategic interests at stake.'

Democracy and freedom are not primary considerations or drivers of Trump's policies: 'Trump does not believe America should be defending freedom and democracy', and 'Trump will represent an autocratic approach to decision-making based on uninformed authority and force of personality—and as a result, Democracy will lose its edge in winning over other countries.'

Trump does not change his spots. The Trump who returns to power will act in exactly the same ways as he did in the first term, but with his resolve even deeper to conduct foreign policy and wield his authority without restraint from those who seek to oppose or impede him.

2
China
Transactional and Unpredictable

Under Prime Minister Malcom Turnbull, concerns about Chinese Communist Party interference and influence in Australian government and universities became a growing issue of public currency. In August 2018, the Turnbull Government banned Chinese technology company Huawei from providing 5G infrastructure in Australia, and advocated for other countries to also blacklist Huawei.

Under Prime Minister Morrison, the relationship with China was initially collegial. Morrison was keen to keep relations free from tensions, saying that his government would not make relations with China 'any more complex than they need to be'.[1] Morrison's first major foreign policy speech in 2018 talked of a 'peaceful evolution of our region'. His speech to Asialink in 2019 was positive: 'It is in no one's interest in the Indo-Pacific to see an inevitably more competitive US–China relationship become adversarial.'[2] This was buttressed by Secretary of State Mike Pompeo in May 2020, when he declared that the United States 'stands with Australia' against China's bullying on Covid and trade issues.

Morrison's meetings in Washington and the state dinner in his honour in September 2019 provided him with an opportunity to see Trump's prosecution of his trade war with China directly, and to appreciate the advantages and rewards of being all in with Trump as a political ally. Political journalist Andrew Probyn of the ABC saw this dynamic emerge: 'There's no pretending anymore. It's out in the open. Scott Morrison and Donald Trump are on a joint ticket when it comes to China.'[3]

Trump will miss Morrison. He was among Trump's strongest supporters in the trade wars with China, and for Trump's strategic posture against China's assertive strategy and tactics across the Asia-Pacific.

After the state dinner, Morrison joined Trump for a campaign-style rally at a Pratt Industries factory in Ohio. 'We believe in jobs. We believe in the way that jobs transform lives, how jobs give people choices. We're making jobs great again.'[4] No, those words weren't Trump's—they were Morrison's. The president then said in reply that Morrison was 'one of America's greatest friends', and continued:

> Australia is one of our most important allies and trading partners with more than $65 billion in trade between our nations last year and I believe we're the largest investor in Australia by quite a bit. We invest a lot of money in Australia, it's an incredible, incredible people to deal with. Unlike so many other nations, Australia upholds the principles of fair and reciprocal trade. For this reason, America is committed to further growing, expanding and strengthening our trade and commerce relationships between the United States and Australia.

This closeness would deepen in very substantive terms over the next several months. In late April 2020, with Covid beginning to rage across the United States, and with the United States going into lockdowns and suffering an immense loss in employment with the economy reeling, Trump demanded 'substantial'[5] compensation from China for the costs of the Covid pandemic. In May 2020, Trump claimed there was a strong basis that the Covid virus originated in a laboratory in Wuhan, and not in the wet markets, making the virus's eruption much more suspicious. Days before, Morrison also called for an investigation into the origins of the virus in China.

China would start its trade war with Australia in May 2020, with an 80.5 per cent tariff on barley—just days after Morrison's tag team with Trump on an international investigation into China's role in the Covid pandemic.

China's war on trade with Australia was extremely wide-ranging and damaging. In August China launched an anti-dumping investigation into Australian wine exports. The wine trade was valued at A$1.25 billion (more than a third of the whole wine export market). In October China imposed informal bans on Australian cotton and coal. The unofficial ban on coal remained through 2021 with significant costs for Chinese importers. In November 2020 Beijing unofficially told Chinese traders to stop importing Australian coal, sugar, barley, lobsters, wine, copper and log timber. In March 2021 China officially imposed anti-dumping tariffs on Australian wine. In May China announced that it was suspending its participation in the China–Australia Strategic Economic Dialogue. That same month China informally banned Australian liquefied natural gas (LNG) exports.

In addition to the tag team on the origins of Covid, in July 2020, the Morrison Government formally declared to the United Nations that China's claims to the South China Sea were illegal—a direct alignment of views with the United States.

This timeline suggests that the intensity of alignment between Trump and Morrison was a significant factor in the scope and severity of the trade retaliation China took against Australia. President Xi may not have been able to exact the same degree of hurt on Trump, but he could certainly vent China's anger and exact some real pain on America's closest ally.

By November 2020, the Australian Government's language and rhetoric around China and Chinese trade was more adversarial and overt, and the list of open criticisms of China grew. In response, China stepped up its rhetoric on Australia and, in a very provocative move, issued a list of fourteen 'grievances' about Australia, its policies and its governance, from blocking China's investment to 'wanton interference' in Hong Kong, Taiwan and Xinjiang province, and 'outrageous condemnation' of China by members of Australia's parliament. China put the relationship into deep freeze. Calls from ministers in the Morrison Government were not returned during the last two years of his second term. The Chinese foreign ministry tweeted a doctored image of an Australian soldier committing war crimes.

The atmosphere remained quite hostile. Throughout the deep freeze with China, Australian public attitudes towards China plummeted. Substantial majorities of Australians came to see China as a security threat, and far fewer saw China as an economic partner.

In contrast, Australia's relationship with the United States deepened throughout Trump's first term in office, largely over the shared China threat. Morrison was loyal to Trump to the end. Morrison did not, for instance, condemn Trump for the January 6 insurrection of the Capitol, even though Labor leader Anthony

Albanese said, 'The fact that we saw last week an attempted insurrection against democracy which was encouraged, of course, by Donald Trump is, quite frankly, shocking.'[6] An astute leader had to weigh what any words of criticism about Trump would mean for their relationship, personally and diplomatically. Morrison did not test it, even after the January 6 attack on the Capitol—even knowing that Trump would be leaving office days later.

In the first year of the Biden presidency, Morrison brought the list of China's grievances to the G7. He received very strong support from Western leaders. The top Asia policy chief in the National Security Council, Kurt Campbell, famously said, 'We are not going to leave Australia alone on the field,'[7] a statement that has since been backed repeatedly by US officials.

By contrast, the Albanese Government made it a priority after its election in May 2022 to hose down the tensions in Australia's relationship with China, and it succeeded in restoring much of the trade which had been cut off by China in response to Morrison's attacks.

Trump and China

It all started so well. It was to end in anger, bitterness and rancour.

In 2017, President Xi of China paid the highest respect to the new president by coming to Trump's Mar-a-Lago resort in Florida for their first summit meeting. Trump was very clear about his agenda. 'We have been treated unfairly and have made terrible trade deals with China for many, many years. That's one of the things we are going to be talking about.'[8] Trump also said he would press Xi to put more pressure on Pyongyang to curb North Korea's nuclear program.

There was drama. At their concluding dinner, Trump informed Xi that he had just launched a strike on Syria in response to Syrian

President Bashar al-Assad's use of chemical weapons. It was an exquisite moment for Trump—that he could project such military power, so ably executed by the generals, as he sat in communal repast with the president of the second-most powerful country in the world:

> I was sitting at the table. We had finished dinner. We are now having dessert. And we had the most beautiful piece of chocolate cake that you have ever seen. And President Xi was enjoying it.
>
> And I was given the message from the generals that the ships are locked and loaded. What do you do? And we made a determination to do it. So the missiles were on the way.
>
> And I said: 'Mr President, let me explain something to you . . . we've just launched fifty-nine missiles, heading to Iraq [sic] . . . heading toward Syria and I want you to know that.'
>
> And he said to me, anybody that uses gases—you could almost say, or anything else—but anybody that was so brutal and uses gases to do that to young children and babies, it's OK. He was OK with it. He was OK.[9]

The Chinese left Mar-a-Lago very pleased. 'President Trump made excellent preparations for our country's representatives and gave us a warm reception,' Xi said. 'We recently have had in-depth and lengthy communications to this end and arrived at many common understandings, the most important being deepening our friendship and building a kind of trust in keeping with the Sino–US working relationship and friendship.'[10]

In November 2017, Xi reciprocated by inviting Trump to Beijing, where the visit and choreography of events, including dinner in the Forbidden City, reflected the warmth of the Florida summit and contributed to a mood of cooperation and goodwill between the leaders. 'My feeling toward you is an incredibly warm one,' Trump told Xi, adding later, 'As we said, there's great chemistry, and I think we're going to do tremendous things, both for China and the United States.'[11]

The core of Trump's posture to China in these visits was that America had only itself to blame for being so weak and at a competitive disadvantage in trade with China. 'After all,' Trump said in Beijing, 'who can blame a country for being able to take advantage of another country to the benefit of its citizens?' Trump added, just to show how poor a hand he had been left by his predecessors from both parties, 'But in actuality, I do blame past [US] administrations for allowing this out-of-control trade deficit to take place and to grow. We have to fix this because it just doesn't work for our great American companies and it doesn't work for our great American workers. It is just not sustainable.'[12]

Following these summits in 2017, analysts predicted that Trump would take a harder US line on China, on both trade and seeking China's pressure on North Korea's nuclear program. That indeed came to pass. There would ultimately be an open debate in the White House on whether the United States should decouple its economy from China.

By the end of Trump's presidency though, Trump had taken a far darker view of China. Trump came to believe that China deliberately inflicted the coronavirus on the world—and especially on the United States.

Trump told US journalist Bob Woodward, in his book *Rage*, that he wanted to send a medical team to China when the outbreak became public knowledge. 'I wanted people to go into China. He [Xi] didn't want to do it. I was OK with it. You know why? Because I figured they knew what they were doing. Okay?'[13]

On 15 January 2020, as the virus was spreading in China, but before it was first detected in the United States, Trump and China's Vice Premier Liu He signed the Phase One trade agreement between the two countries. It was, Trump said, 'A momentous step.'[14]

But later in 2020, weeks before the presidential election, Trump vented his new judgement, which reflected the toll the 'China virus' was taking on his presidency and the country. Trump shared his thoughts with Bob Woodward. 'I think what could have happened, Bob, is it got away from them and he [Xi] didn't want to contain it from the rest of the world because it would have put him in a big disadvantage. And we were already beating them very badly. You know, on trade.' Woodward wrote that Trump thought, 'President Xi had intentionally let the virus spread.'[15]

The January 2020 trade agreement collapsed under the pressure of the economic hit from the pandemic to both economies. Trump's calls for China to account for how the pandemic started, and how the country handled the outbreak, also increased tensions. A year later, authoritative data[16] would show that the trade agreement failed to deliver a lift in US exports to China.

Covid inflicted a huge political hit on Trump. Given the relatively close vote in the 2020 presidential election—a change of just 43,000 votes in Georgia, Wisconsin and Arizona would have delivered Trump another victory—many observers believe, given the roaring US economy in 2019 and the growing support Trump was receiving from Black and Hispanic voters as a result, that without the Covid pandemic Trump would have won re-election. As opinion poll analysis website FiveThirtyEight concluded in January 2021: 'Had there been no pandemic, he may have still lost the popular vote, but considering how close the election was, he may have had a decent chance of winning the Electoral College.'[17]

To Trump, China infected the world and welshed on what he believed was one of the greatest ever trade deals.

In the words of a former diplomat, 'China reneged on its trade deals. Trump will want to rectify that.'

Protecting Australia's interests

A former Australian senior intelligence official framed the issues of what a 2025 President Trump will do and what Australia needs to do to protect its interests this way: 'The issues presented by Trump are not just Trump—it is the Republican Party. That may not be well understood by the political class here. We tend to fall back on our paradigms that America can course-correct and redeem itself. But maybe not with the party under Trump as it is now. So the context is: what is confronting America, how divided is the country, how significant are the risks of a party that is working to dismantle important parts of America's democracy. Trump is a proto-autocrat. He is just a symptom of an underlying malaise in the American political system and culture.'

What are the implications for Australia's posture and its alliances in Asia? The official continued: 'The Australian political class should be alarmed and watchful, and be ready for a different kind of relationship with the US. We will need to stand our ground. We will need to say "no" more often. We will have to hedge more against American policy in the region. Indonesia, Japan, South Korea become more important to us. We may no longer have much in terms of shared values with the United States under Trump. And if that is the case, what happens to the constellation of democracies that are poised against Russia and China if you have Viktor Orbán running America? America's reputation in Asia will be hit hard again. Asia wants America in the region, but now they are openly doubtful about America, its future, its staying power. They look at America and ask, "How can we rely on you?"'

Hugh White, a scholar and former senior defence official, says, 'The ties with Australia are strong and enduring and not dependent on Trump. China's rise plus the evolution of the world mean that the traditional notion of the US global role and the global order in Europe and the Mideast is unsustainable. America will struggle to keep faith with the leadership of its past. Trump amplifies this trend—he's an accelerant for this trend.'

These are important themes, with big questions. How tightly tied will, and should, Australia be to the United States under Trump? How much should Australia hedge its interests and objectives? How much independence from Trump policy will Australia want to stake out?

There is a growing sense that the United States and Australia are behind the eight ball with China—that the actions to implement strategy have lagged badly, with so much ground to make up. This, in turn, feeds uncertainty over whether both nations have the will and ability to execute their policies and strategies with respect to China.

The answers to these questions will lie in Australia's ability to understand the range of possibilities under Trump's policies with China and across Asia.

The experts I consulted had very firm views. They see Trump's China policy as guided by the following factors.

Trump is transactional

Trump loves the deal, and the art of the deal. He knows a tough deal from an easy deal—and considers himself a grandmaster of deal-making.

On the one hand, as he assumed the presidency in 2017, Trump was daunted by the prospects for Middle East peace.

> I want to see peace with Israel and the Palestinians. There is no reason there's not peace between Israel and the Palestinians—none whatsoever. It's something, frankly, maybe not as difficult as people have thought over the years. If you can't produce peace in the Middle East, nobody can. OK. All my life I've been hearing that's the toughest deal in the world to make. And I've seen it, but I have a feeling that Jared [Kushner] is going to do a great job.[18]

Trump was proved right. The Abraham Accords between Israel and several Gulf states were a realignment of strategic interests in the Middle East and constitute a diplomatic breakthrough of historic proportions.

Trump loved the diplomacy he opened up with Kim Jong-Un—not just for the substance of what was discussed but for the shock factor of agreeing to meet with North Korean emissaries in the White House to open the dialogue, and then to stage summits with Kim that commanded global media attention. Aside from meeting with Kim and, in a first for a US president, stepping into North Korean territory with Kim at his side, nothing was accomplished in their meetings. North Korea has a larger nuclear arsenal today than it had before Trump became president, and Kim is testing missiles that are close to violating limits defined by the United Nations. North Korea startled NATO in late 2024 when it supplied thousands of troops to assist Russia in its invasion of Ukraine.

Trump also loved making trade deals with China—and breaking trade deals with Europe, Canada, Mexico and others.

On China, two American scholars said Trump 'will want to find a deal that he can claim as a total winner', and 'Trump will stick with his China trade deal objectives, and get deals done.'

Trump wants to deal, but there is also nothing to prevent him from venturing into any no-go area. Trump will put any proposition on the table to see what can be carved up.

Trump is unpredictable

The core issue in security and stability in the Indo-Pacific is China and its militarisation, reach and influence across the region. The flashpoint of this geostrategic threat is Taiwan. Will China take it by force, just as Russia attempted to take Ukraine by force in 2022?

Trump has no default position on Taiwan.

As two senior Australian officials observe, in his first term, 'Trump's very unpredictability worked in the United States' favour. His unpredictability held back China on Taiwan—and it held back North Korea too. Whoever is the object of his attention cannot be certain about what Trump will do or not do, and it puts them off balance.'

But this has other consequences. In approaching China, 'There is a range of possibilities. He could establish, as Trump consistently said he wanted to, an "incredible relationship" with Xi and reach accords with him. This would be bad for Australia and the region. He could also try to tap into a different view: the Chinese are taking our jobs, attacking US primacy. Trump needs to assert America First and protect America's interests.'[19]

Australian and American officials and scholars alike were clear that Trump is not unequivocally wedded to Taiwan. A former Australian diplomat says, 'If Trump were re-elected, China would attack Taiwan. Trump would not lift a finger to defend Taiwan. He wants one thing from China: a trade deal.' A former senior

Australian official says, 'Trump's instinct is to let them have Taiwan.' Hugh White agrees. 'Trump lets China take Taiwan. It's theirs.'

How this could play out depends on what China does with respect to Taiwan. 'Trump may not react to increasing China pressure on Taiwan short of an invasion.' Why? A scholar and former foreign policy official says that for all of his bombast, Trump is not anxious to initiate a war. 'Trump does not like war. He does not want one over Taiwan. Trump may be able to cut a deal: favourable US trade in exchange for Taiwan?'

The other powerful political factor that will limit what Trump can do with respect to China and Taiwan is the hardening attitudes in Congress—across both political parties—against China. This has been building for years from Chinese excesses on trade, currency manipulation, restrictions on Big Tech companies—Apple, Facebook, X (formerly Twitter)—and whether their platforms can operate in China, and China's human rights violations in Hong Kong and Xinjiang province and their very aggressive military build-up.

This political reality increases the complexity of the China–Taiwan issue. Former Australian and American diplomats, assessing the increasingly headline anti-China attitudes within the Republican Party, and the strong bipartisan consensus that Taiwan should not be abandoned, assess that Trump will not have significant manoeuvrability in dealing with Xi on Taiwan and a resort to military force by China to occupy it. As several former US and Australian officials relate: 'Trump cannot simply let China have Taiwan. There is much too much pro-Taiwan sentiment in Congress. Trump's views are less powerful on that issue and he may need to change and be more confrontational with China over Taiwan.'

In balder terms: 'If China invades there will be overwhelming pressure to respond militarily. Trump could be trapped into doing that.'

Taiwan is extremely active in courting high-level US delegations to visit. This was especially evident when House Speaker Nancy Pelosi headed a congressional delegation to Taiwan in August 2022. As she said after her visit, 'Our congressional delegation's visit should be seen as a strong statement that America stands with Taiwan. We came to Taiwan to listen to, learn from and show our support for the people of Taiwan, who have built a thriving democracy that stands as one of the freest and most open in the world . . . America's solidarity with the people of Taiwan is more important today than ever, as we continue to support the defense of democracy against autocracy in the region and in the world.'[20]

This was the last thing Beijing wanted to hear.

3
AUKUS
A Survivor of Trump II

The strategic agreement between Australia, the United Kingdom and the United States—AUKUS—is directly related to China and the threat it poses.

There were ringing words from the leaders on 15 September 2021, the day AUKUS was announced. Prime Minister Morrison spoke first:

> Today, we join our nations in a next-generation partnership built on a strong foundation of proven trust.
>
> We have always seen the world through a similar lens. We have always believed in a world that favours freedom; that respects human dignity, the rule of law, the independence of sovereign states, and the peaceful fellowship of nations.
>
> And while we've always looked to each other to do what we believe is right . . . Always together. Never alone.
>
> Our world is becoming more complex, especially here in our region, the Indo-Pacific. This affects us all. The future of the Indo-Pacific will impact all our futures.

> To meet these challenges, to help deliver the security and stability our region needs, we must now take our partnership to a new level—a partnership that seeks to engage, not to exclude; to contribute, not take; and to enable and empower, not to control or coerce.

President Biden reinforced the message:

> Our nations and our brave fighting forces have stood shoulder-to-shoulder for literally more than 100 years: through the trench fighting in World War I, the island hopping of World War II, during the frigid winters in Korea, and the scorching heat of the Persian Gulf. The United States, Australia, and the United Kingdom have long been faithful and capable partners, and we're even closer today.
>
> Today, we're taking another historic step to deepen and formalize cooperation among all three of our nations because we all recognize the imperative of ensuring peace and stability in the Indo-Pacific over the long term.
>
> We need to be able to address both the current strategic environment in the region and how it may evolve. Because the future of each of our nations—and indeed the world—depends on a free and open Indo-Pacific enduring and flourishing in the decades ahead.
>
> This is about investing in our greatest source of strength—our alliances—and updating them to better meet the threats of today and tomorrow.
>
> It's about connecting America's existing allies and partners in new ways and amplifying our ability to collaborate, recognizing that there is no regional divide separating the interests of our Atlantic and Pacific partners.

Core to AUKUS is the development and deployment of nuclear-powered—not nuclear-armed—submarines to Australia. The AUKUS agreement disrupted and ended a contract for France to supply Australia with submarines. The French, not consulted and deeply offended, went ballistic in both Canberra and Washington. France recalled its Ambassador to the United States—an unprecedented act of anger from a country that has been allied with America since the Revolutionary War. President Macron was crystal clear about how Prime Minister Morrison handled the shredding of France's submarine agreement. When asked if he thought Morrison had lied to him, Macron responded, 'I don't think, I know.'[1] Two months after this rift in ties, France's Ambassador chose the most prominent media platform in Canberra, the National Press Club, to continue to drip the acidic Gallic anger: 'The deceit was intentional. The way it was handled was plainly a stab in the back.'

AUKUS was not conceived on Trump's watch so what would he do with the alliance as president in 2025?

Trump would keep AUKUS, but he would massage it to suit his interests and priorities.

There is strong consensus among former officials on this point: 'AUKUS will even survive Trump II'; 'AUKUS will remain strong under Trump. The UK and Australia mean a lot to Trump. But he will look at it as: what are you doing for me now?'; 'Australia is a very good ally. Australia has seen a need to increase defence and responded, and Australia will be rewarded by Trump for this.'

This is because of how Trump sees China. 'Trump hates China. China hates AUKUS. Trump likes the UK. Trump likes Australia. So AUKUS is OK under Trump.'

But Trump will keep tension in the deal in order to ensure returns to the United States. AUKUS is not a blank cheque—nothing with Trump ever is. Trump will be looking for commercial advantage for the United States as the agreement is implemented—especially with respect to the contracts and delivery associated with the submarines. The transaction costs could be significant.

'AUKUS will survive with Trump as long as it is a good commercial deal for the US—and the Aussies do a lot in the region to make it less of a burden on the US.' There are consequences that flow from this. 'Making Australia more powerful is attractive—it lets Trump pull back a bit and allows Australia to be a bigger player in the region.' 'The US presence in northern Australia will pick up.' 'It is possible we will soon see a visible increase in US troops in Australia.' This has in fact occurred. In late 2024, the US presence in the Northern Territory has been expanded, reflecting a greater Australian integration into the US military force structures.

Other experts expanded on this.

'Trump will support AUKUS. He will focus less on the strategic aspects and will focus more on the transactional benefits.' 'Trump's instinct: we will sell the subs and make money, and will want to ensure the subs are made in America.' 'Trump may exact a price for AUKUS: no net costs to the US for AUKUS. All the key defence assets for AUKUS built in the US.' 'AUKUS under Trump: he will go forward with it if Australia is prepared to pay in full.'

In the view of several Australian experts, however, there could be a significant reassessment of support in Australia for AUKUS depending on how events unfold under Trump. For Australia, it is critical that AUKUS fully serve Australia's interests. 'AUKUS is a partnership. Can Trump treat it as such?' 'The heart of the AUKUS issue is: Australian resilience and independence. How much more autonomy will Australia have under AUKUS?' 'AUKUS could be weakened significantly here if Trump goes very extremist and there is a backlash here—with pressure to dial down Australia's ties with the US.' 'If Trump is really bad for Australia, that could calibrate the degree of American presence that is welcome by Australia.'

There could be further trade-offs affecting the balancing roles of the military ties with South Korea and Japan. 'Of all the allies of the US, Australia would appear to be the last bastion. Trump will give up on South Korea and Japan.' 'If the price of AUKUS and US troops is a Trump-ordered US drawdown in Japan and South Korea—that is a problem' in terms of the balance of power with China.

Australia will not be the main focus in Trump's desire to realign US interests in the Indo-Pacific. A retreat of US forces and the overall strategic posture with Japan and South Korea will have huge collateral implications for Australia. It is these trade-offs that pose the highest risks for Australia, and Australia will need to manage them.

4
North Korea
Spectacle Diplomacy is Back

John Bolton was named national security adviser to Trump in March 2018, and his resignation and firing occurred simultaneously (as could only happen in the Trump White House) in September 2019. The day before Trump named Bolton, the two had met to discuss the appointment and his role. The next day, Trump accepted Kim Jong-Un's invitation to meet, news that rocked the world. In his memoirs, *The Room Where It Happened*, Bolton writes: 'I was beyond speechless, appalled at this foolish mistake. For a US president to grant Kim a summit with no sign whatsoever of a strategic decision to renounce nuclear weapons—in fact, giving it away for nothing[1]—was a propaganda gift beyond measure.'

In preparing for the summit, Bolton wrote, 'The more I learned, the more discouraged and pessimistic I became about a Trump–Kim summit . . . Here we were, at it again, having learned nothing. Worse, we were legitimising Kim Jong-Un, commandant of the North Korean prison camp, by giving him a free meeting with Trump . . . I was sick at heart over Trump's zeal to meet with Kim Jong-Un.'[2]

The Trump–Kim meetings were spectacle diplomacy. Trump was all about the show. Before Trump and Kim shook hands at their first summit, in Singapore, Trump said to Bolton, 'This is an exercise in publicity.'[3] Bolton's assessment of the decisive first meeting was that Kim 'had Trump hooked'. Trump was all in on dealing with the world's most reclusive and highly dangerous nuclear-armed leader. As Trump has often said, they fell in love.[4]

In the preparation for the first summit, there was work on three issues: North Korea's nuclear program; the massive sanctions that had been applied by the United States and much of the world against North Korea, deeply hurting their economy; and reaching a peace agreement with North Korea, South Korea and the United States to finally proclaim an end to the Korean War, and ensure that North Korea would not be invaded.

None of these objectives were met. The spectacle simply continued as Trump and Kim met in Hanoi in February 2019 and again at the Demilitarised Zone between the two Koreas in July 2019. What should have occurred—what would have tested the prospects for a truly historic outcome—would have been to formally set up three parallel streams on the key strategic issues, with nothing agreed until everything was agreed. Whether Trump, Bolton and Secretary of State Pompeo were up for it, or whether Kim had no intentions of any serious discussion of his nuclear weapons, even if other major concessions on sanctions and the integrity of his country could be met, we do not know.

All that is left are the love letters between Trump and Kim that Bob Woodward obtained for his book, *Rage*. Woodward wrote that 'The CIA never figured out conclusively who wrote and crafted Kim's letters to Trump. They were masterpieces. The analysts marveled at the skill someone brought to finding the exact mixture of flattery while appealing to Trump's sense of grandiosity and being centre stage in history.'[5]

For Trump's second period in the Oval Office, there is no clear path forward on North Korea. Foreign policy experts in Australia and the United States do not have a clear read on this, and the outlook is clouded.

'Who knows? Kim will never give up those nukes.' 'There are two scenarios: rekindle the special relationship with Kim. Or lose interest in it.' 'North Korea? Likely a replay by Trump of his relationship with Kim.' 'What's crucial is not what Trump does—it's what Kim does. They never offer concessions. But just watch: Trump will do all the things he did with Kim again.' 'Trump has nothing to show for it. Trump will probably reach out and see what happens.' 'Trump probably feels burnt by Kim. He will not try again to be Kim's special friend. And with South Korea, and the new government there—which is more hardline and supportive of a stronger military force—Trump could be much stronger and friendlier. It is not clear we will have Kim in power. The real crisis in North Korea is the economy. That could become a leadership crisis.'

It is clear Kim is amassing new weapons, making threats and pushing the limits on testing his missiles. To what end? There is increasing speculation that the lesson Kim Jong-Un is absorbing from the war in Ukraine is that he too has a nuclear shield he can wield to protect against a US military strike on his nuclear assets.

In 2018, after Trump abandoned his 'fire and fury' posture against Kim in the North, he ordered the Pentagon to develop options to take US troops out from the South. In 2019, Trump stepped up pressure to withdraw US forces if South Korea did not provide more financial support for the US presence. In 2020, in conjunction with an order to take out 9500 US troops from Germany, Trump again raised the prospect for reducing US forces in South Korea.

In his memoir, John Bolton records Trump saying: 'Get out of there [South Korea] if we don't get the five billion-dollar deal [for South Korean support of US bases]. We lose $38 billion in trade in Korea. Let's get out.'[6]

Which Trump Korea policy will he embrace this time: spectacle diplomacy with the North—even as Kim has provided thousands of North Korean troops to augment Russia's forces in Ukraine—a move below critical mass in deterrence by cutting American forces in the South, or reinforcement of South Korea as part of a strategic arc to punish Kim for failing to reach a deal with Trump on the North's nuclear weapons?

5
Trump Redux
What Does Australia Need to Do?

What Australia needs to do in Donald Trump's second presidency is shaped by two compelling premises.

First, the alliance with the United States is enduring and it is not to be abandoned.

While there is sentiment among some policy elites, and in the community, for Australia to assert a more independent foreign policy, that impulse has been constrained for now. After the US withdrawal from Afghanistan, and the collapse of the government and the lightning success of the Taliban seizing control of the country, many asked: what were these twenty years of war for? Was it worth it? Underneath that question is deeper consideration of the value of Australia being tied so closely to American views and policies on China and the region. Former Prime Minister Paul Keating has made several powerful expressions of this concern, and about the entire trajectory of Australia–US relations.[1] Hugh White has also written extensively on these issues, concluding that the United States should abandon Taiwan to China.[2]

Trump is unpopular in Southeast Asia. Before Anthony Albanese became prime minister in May 2022, Australia had not hedged its interests in Asia. There was no Plan B, and Australia is sharply exposed to anti-Trump sentiment that spawns anti-US sentiment. What really hurts Trump in the region—and can blow back on Australia as a staunch ally of the United States—are Trump's anti-Muslim policies, his confrontational posture towards China, his complete disdain for tackling global warming, his withdrawing from the Trans-Pacific Partnership, and his spurning of the regional architecture. As a US ally, Australia is vulnerable to some of the backlash.

This debate will continue to evolve and deepen. But for at least the beginning of Trump's second term, the US–Australia alliance, as it stands today, is not to be diminished, much less abandoned. An American diplomat and an Australian scholar agree: 'Do not align with another power'; 'Australia can't realise its goals without the Americans.'

Second, Australia has to step up across the Asia-Pacific as never before to project its foreign policy objectives and secure its interests.

The imperative of what has to happen was clear from the crisis over the Solomon Islands and their agreement to provide access to China for a military base, along with many other programs that extended Chinese influence within the Solomons. The Morrison Government's failure to absorb and act on what it apparently knew to be underway betrayed a failure of both its policies and the engagement required to protect Australia's geostrategic interests in the Asia-Pacific.

One of the legacies of the Morrison Government was the alarming gap in Australia's active ongoing involvement across the region, from diplomacy to economic aid to participation in dialogue with our Pacific neighbours, which left Australia at an enormous disadvantage. From the Albanese Government's election in 2022, Foreign Minister Penny Wong and Trade Minister Don Farrell made it a high priority to rebuild relationships with our Asian and Pacific neighbours, with considerable success. However, China remains heavily engaged across the region, and Australia will continue to have to compete for influence. Australia's ongoing investment in new coal and gas compromises its credibility with the Pacific Island nations on the frontline of rising sea levels driven by climate change.

The advice from senior officials and scholars across both countries is unanimous.

'We need to look after our own interests: more and better diplomacy, more investment in our capacity to engage in the region, and we need to be better. Stronger militarily so that Australia can protect its interests.'

'We have neglected key countries in the region. Much more is required—we have to deepen those relationships, especially with Indonesia and through the region, especially the Philippines and Vietnam. We need high-quality trade deals through the region— deals that are like and complementary to the Trans-Pacific Partnership.'

'We need to strengthen Australia's independent relations—independent of China and the US—with Asia. This will work for us in all possible scenarios. Double down on all those investments.'

'In Asia, it is very important for Australia to find partners in the neighbourhood—to walk the walk, not just talk the talk. We need to deepen cooperation with Japan especially, and also South Korea and India. If Trump is blowing up NATO, Australia needs deeper bilateral ties in Europe.'

'Double down with the US. Double down with other allies, especially Japan, the Quad (Japan, India, United States, Australia), and AUKUS. Increase the aid and development budget. Double down on regional diplomacy on trade and investment. More engagement with Indonesia and South Korea.'

Australia's presence in Washington also needs to be augmented and reinforced in order to further cement the advantages Australia secured both under Trump's first term and with President Biden.

'Continue to engage in an overt and covert influence campaign so that Australia can register its concerns in Washington—more think tanks, more efforts on the Hill, more in the media—more influence generally. Sell "Brand Australia".'

'Play the Washington political establishment all the way on the importance of the relationship and the emotional support it can command.'

There is concerted work to be done to enhance Australia's political and diplomatic assets now Trump is back in power.

'Do the basics now. Grow DFAT. Launch much more diplomacy and aid in the region. In Washington: even deeper ties with Congress and the private sector.' This is where success stories like Anthony Pratt and Visy are so important. 'Cultivate Trump's mates—get close to Trump's people.'

The objective of this step-up is to protect Australia's interests under Trump's presidency—so that by building much deeper and stronger ties across Asia, Australia can better withstand the blowback that Trump is destined to provoke.

Hugh White spoke for many others whom I consulted: 'Australia needs a more independent foreign policy and the assets to execute it. We need to enhance Australia's independent diplomacy in Asia. We need to do much more in Southeast Asia. We need to engage with all the Southeast Asian nations, so that Australia can better navigate and manage China. We need more money for diplomacy and defence hardware.'

Australia can also continue to lock in AUKUS benefits before Trump tries to take control over AUKUS hard assets in America's favour. Where will the nuclear submarines be built? Trump may take control of that decision, and may overrule Australia on any decision to proceed with UK model subs instead of US subs.

But these risks can be hedged. An Australian scholar and former official said, 'Also, lock in other trade agreements with the US (such as digital products, services and networks). Align policy on export controls. In development assistance, align USAID with AusAid.'

Australia's embassy in Washington and the Australian Ambassador to the United States in Washington, Kevin Rudd, had been laying the groundwork for a second Trump presidency, and they will need to draw on all Australia's personal and institutional relationships to keep the US relationship on an even keel.

6
Chemistry
'You Don't Look Like a Prime Minister'

For Trump, as former Ambassador Hockey told me, 'Chemistry is everything. Trump did not want to meet Morrison, but when Morrison won—Trump was all over him. Trump loves winners. Trump will have goodwill towards Australia. But with Albo, there is likely bad chemistry there.'

For Trump, appearances are everything. As Trump was assembling his cabinet in December 2016, a close Trump associate in the media industry, Chris Ruddy, told the *Washington Post*: 'He likes people who present themselves very well, and he's very impressed when somebody has a background of being good on television because he thinks it's a very important medium for public policy. Don't forget, he's a showbiz guy. He was at the pinnacle of showbiz, and he thinks about showbiz. He sees this as a business that relates to the public. The look might not necessarily be somebody who should be on the cover of *GQ* magazine or *Vanity Fair*. It's more about the look and the demeanor and the swagger.'[1]

Trump's former defense secretary, James Mattis, reminded him of General George S. Patton. His former UN Ambassador, Nikki Haley, had a rising-star quality. Rex Tillerson, as secretary of state, had silver-haired boardroom command. But his 2016 opponent, Hillary Clinton, didn't have the needed 'presidential look'.

Foreign leaders Trump really respects—Russia's Putin and China's Xi—have all the swagger and more. But a video of European leaders mocking Trump at a NATO summit in London went viral and captured the tensions between them.

Before the first meeting between Trump and Albanese, Trump would have been briefed on how Albanese has acted as prime minister, and the state of the alliance. Trump would have also been reminded of what Albanese said in the wake of the January 6 attack on the Capitol. On 8 January, Albanese re-tweeted a post from Joe Biden, and personally added: 'Democracy is precious and cannot be taken for granted—the violent insurrection in Washington is an assault on the rule of law and democracy. Donald Trump has encouraged this response and must now call on his supporters to stand down.'[2]

Trump would have been briefed on all the warm and engaging discussions Albanese has had with Biden. He would have been advised of what Albanese said in an interview, shortly before Trump declared his run for president for 2024, about how Morrison did not voice any concerns about the attack on the Capitol: 'Then-prime minister Scott Morrison was alone, really, among democratic leaders in not calling it out; in the UK, France, Germany, Canada, it was called out and it should have been. The circumstances in the US, with people almost in paramilitary gear, is a concern. That concern has been expressed, quite rightly, by President Biden.'[3]

Trump will not follow, or be tempted to follow, in Biden's footsteps as far as Albanese is concerned. Yes, Trump supports the ANZUS. Yes, he is moved by ardent Aussies such as Greg Norman and Anthony Pratt. Yes, he even came to respect Malcom Turnbull, after their very unpleasant first telephone call, when Trump came to understand that Turnbull had dealt with Kerry Packer. Trump had known Packer. As Turnbull recounts in his memoirs, 'He talked about Kerry Packer a lot; he knew I'd been Kerry's lawyer and "kept him out of jail", something Donald mentioned every time we met.'[4] If Turnbull was good enough for someone as rich and powerful and domineering as Packer, Turnbull was good enough for Trump.

To Trump, Albanese is no Turnbull, and Albanese defeated Morrison. Trump will look at Anthony Albanese and think: *You don't look like a prime minister. You come from poverty. You lived in public housing. You're Labor. You're unions. I hate unions. Just a party apparatchik. I hate labor parties. Your clothes aren't right. You're bad on TV. Your voice isn't right for the part. My hair is much better than yours. You're a lefty—even worse. You're a socialist. You're radical. You're even to the left of Biden. No way in hell will we play golf together. Why the hell should we 'be mates'? You will never get a state dinner in my White House.*

This relationship will have to be intensively managed, every day, at major levels directly below the two leaders, and for whoever succeeds Albanese as prime minister. Close working relationships between the US secretaries of state and defense and the Australian ministers for foreign affairs and defence, the president's trade advisers and the minister for trade, between the two ambassadors in their respective capitals, and between the prime minister's foreign policy team and the president's National Security Council, will be essential. There will not be any stress on the military and intelligence ties—they run too deep to be disturbed by the occupant of the Oval Office. But the relationship will be tested regularly by Trump's fixations and whims.

As a former senior leader said, 'Albo and Trump will not have a great relationship, but Albo will work hard to protect the relationship.'

Albo will have to.

II
TRUMP AND AUSTRALIA'S DOMESTIC POLICY

7
Economy
America First in America

On 5 February 2020, just a month before the Covid pandemic would ravage America and take its toll on the American economy, President Trump delivered what would be the last State of the Union address of that presidency before a joint session of Congress. His real audience was not the 535 lawmakers seated before him, but the American people. Over 37 million watched that night—the largest audience since Barack Obama's first address to Congress in 2009. Earlier in the day, the Senate was preparing to vote to acquit Trump of the impeachment charges of abuse of power and obstruction of Congress for his quid-pro-quo demand that President Zelensky of Ukraine help provide damning information on Hunter Biden, the son of Democratic presidential candidate Joe Biden, in exchange for receiving military and security assistance from the United States. Trump feared Biden the most going into the presidential election in November. The circus-like spectacle that evening was astonishing: a president stained by impeachment, unrepentant, unashamed, addressing the Congress. Trump was on the offensive as always, prosecuting his case to the American people that thanks to him the country was booming, the American people never had it so good, and its greatest days were still ahead.

> From the instant I took office, I moved rapidly to revive the US economy—slashing a record number of job-killing regulations, enacting historic and record-setting tax cuts, and fighting for fair and reciprocal trade agreements. Our agenda is relentlessly pro-worker, pro-family, pro-growth, and, most of all, pro-American. Thank you. We are advancing with unbridled optimism and lifting our citizens of every race, color, religion and creed very, very high.
>
> Since my election, we have created seven million new jobs—five million more than government experts projected during the previous administration.
>
> The unemployment rate is the lowest in over half a century. And very incredibly, the average unemployment rate under my administration is lower than any administration in the history of our country. True. If we hadn't reversed the failed economic policies of the previous administration, the world would not now be witnessing this great economic success.
>
> The unemployment rate for African-Americans, Hispanic Americans and Asian-Americans has reached the lowest levels in history. African-American youth unemployment has reached an all-time low. African-American poverty has declined to the lowest rate ever recorded.
>
> The unemployment rate for women reached the lowest level in almost 70 years. And, last year, women filled 72 per cent of all new jobs added.
>
> The veterans' unemployment rate dropped to a record low. The unemployment rate for disabled Americans has reached an all-time low.

Workers without a high school diploma have achieved the lowest unemployment rate recorded in US history. A record number of young Americans are now employed.

Under the last administration, more than 10 million people were added to the food stamp rolls. Under my administration, seven million Americans have come off food stamps, and 10 million people have been lifted off of welfare.

In eight years under the last administration, over 300,000 working-age people dropped out of the work force. In just three years of my administration, 3.5 million people—working-age people—have joined the work force.

Since my election, the net worth of the bottom half of wage earners has increased by 47 per cent—three times faster than the increase for the top 1 per cent. After decades of flat and falling incomes, wages are rising fast—and, wonderfully, they are rising fastest for low-income workers, who have seen a 16 per cent pay increase since my election. This is a blue-collar boom.

Real median household income is now at the highest level ever recorded.

Since my election, US stock markets have soared 70 per cent, adding more than $12 trillion to our nation's wealth, transcending anything anyone believed was possible. This is a record. It is something that every country in the world is looking up to. They admire. Consumer confidence has just reached amazing new highs.

All of those millions of people with 401[k]s and pensions are doing far better than they have ever done before with increases of 60, 70, 80, 90 and 100 per cent, and even more.

Likewise, we are restoring our nation's manufacturing might, even though predictions were, as you all know, that this could never, ever be done. After losing 60,000 factories under the previous two administrations, America has now gained 12,000 new factories under my administration, with thousands upon thousands of plants and factories being planned or being built. Companies are not leaving; they are coming back to the USA. The fact is that everybody wants to be where the action is, and the United States of America is indeed the place where the action is.[1]

It was a very politically potent presentation. While Trump's overall approval rating was below 50 per cent throughout his presidency, his approval score for the economy that January was 56 per cent.[2] Trump's pitch was premised on the crusades of populism and protectionism that were at the heart of his economic policies and programs. It became the cornerstone of the campaign he ran for re-election.

Trump, the billionaire businessman, projected himself as champion of the working class, flaunting his deal-cutting skills. 'I'll be the greatest jobs president that God ever created,' he said during the 2020 campaign.[3] Trump bragged he was delivering more for Blacks and Hispanics than any Democrat ever had. He would take their votes and win a second term.

Trump entered the 2020 presidential election campaign with plenty to boast about. Median annual household income rose from US$54,000 to US$65,000 from 2016 to 2020. Over those four years, the poverty rate dropped from 15.5 per cent to 12.8 per cent.[4]

In the three years prior to the pandemic, 6.4 million jobs were created. Wages, adjusted for inflation, grew throughout Trump's first three years in office. Trump's major legislative achievement in his presidency, enacted in December 2017, was the *Tax Cuts and Jobs Act*, a US$1.5 trillion package that cut individual taxes for eight years and lowered the corporate tax rate from 35 per cent to 21 per cent.

Trump's tax cuts came at a cost though. The deficit, driven by the cuts, was projected to rise by US$3.1 trillion through the 2020s. But Trump, deeply experienced in bankruptcies that had engulfed his businesses, was quite comfortable with debt.

Trump's America First theology started with the economy, supplemented by his tireless efforts to muscle the stock markets—especially when he highlighted optimism of good news with China on trade in order to boost the Dow—and the Federal Reserve, especially with regard to keeping interest rates low. As documented by Peter Baker and Susan Glasser in their authoritative book, *The Divider*, Trump regularly attacked and denigrated Jerome Powell, chairman of the Fed, for not keeping interest rates low—'the key, Trump believed, to his re-election'.[5] In 2018, Trump was so angry with Powell's leadership of the Fed and what monetary policy was doing to the stock market that he sought to fire him—but ultimately shied away from it.

These policy settings were joined at the hip to his embrace of protectionism on trade and his savaging of the existential issue of global warming.

8
Trade
A World War of Tariffs

Trump shook the status quo on neoliberal economics, which from the 1990s posited that globalisation in trade was ideal, with steady success in building the World Trade Organization and putting in place a series of trade agreements to lower tariffs and increase investment. Trump slammed shut the door of open trade. He attacked virtually every major international institution that was set up after World War II to help ensure peace, security, economic growth and prosperity. The United Nations, NATO, the G20 and G7, the European Union, the World Trade Organization, World Health Organization, the Asia-Pacific Economic Cooperation, the Association of Southeast Asian Nations: all were dissed, impugned, belittled, disregarded. It may have been inevitable that seventy years after the victory over Fascism in Germany and Japan, with faded memories and forgotten lessons of history, the consensus that drove the post-war era would collapse. Today, there is a deep reconsideration of where the world is headed. Trump, with his isolationism, nativism and protectionism, has certainly been an accelerant of these trends. Putin's invasion of

Ukraine in 2022, reflecting his desire to re-establish the lost Russian empire; the insistent march of China's Xi to domination in the Indo-Pacific, and absorption of Taiwan into the People's Republic; the breakdown of the authority of the United Nations and the powerlessness of whoever has the title of secretary-general; even the lesser role of the Pope in bridging tectonic differences (as Pope John Paul II did in breaking down the Cold War)—the issue is clearly posed: are we at the end of the era of globalisation?

A major Trump front in this epic devolution of global arrangements was on trade. In his first term, Trump's attacks were systematic and thorough, with his America First sword cutting across all geographies and alliances, and foreign imports seen as a national security threat.[1]

Nothing was overlooked in Trump's insistence that no country should enjoy a trade surplus with the United States, and that no overseas industry should threaten American jobs. The targets were everywhere: solar panels, cars, semiconductors, steel and aluminium, technology transfers, intellectual property, machinery, appliances and electrical equipment. Retaliation from trading partners against American products included agriculture, bourbon, motorboats, blue jeans, corn, peanut butter and soybeans.

China was the biggest trade target, hit by Trump with US$360 billion in US-imposed tariffs. Trump's trade war with China was a defining policy of his presidency. While the trade war appeared to take the United States and China to the brink of decoupling their economies, an interim agreement to freeze the trade hostilities was signed just before the Covid pandemic erupted. This 'Phase One' deal left most Trump tariffs in place and committed China to buying US$200 billion worth of US products over two years.

But the costs of the trade war were significant. A Brookings study highlighted that US companies had to pay tens of billions in tariffs for Chinese imported goods while US farmers lost most of their US$24 billion export market to China.[2] There were also perverse outcomes. The US trade deficit with China clocked in at US$345 billion in 2019, and as a consequence trade was diverted to Japan, South Korea, Taiwan and other countries, resulting in the US trade deficit actually increasing overall throughout Trump's presidency. When the Trump trade wars came fully into effect in 2018, the US goods and services trade deficit was US$627.7 billion, and grew to US$678.7 billion in 2020.[3]

Australia dodged Trump's bullets. The framers of the US–Australia Free Trade Agreement, signed in 2005, never imagined what their negotiating skills would deliver in terms of future-proofing against a Trump presidency: Australia has a significant—and structural—trade deficit with the United States. It was A$18.3 billion in 2020. Under the FTA's terms, the chances of Australia enjoying a trade surplus with the United States would be equal to the chances of snow in Sydney. Even though Australia was not on Trump's principal hit list of trading partners to retaliate against, Australia's steel and aluminium exports[4] were under direct threat from Trump and his trade czar, Peter Navarro. But Australia's Ambassador in Washington, Joe Hockey, played the alliance card to the hilt with the White House officials who truly cared about the alliance and was successful in avoiding the tariffs on those products that Trump imposed on Canada, Mexico and the EU.

There were, however, real setbacks for Australia. The United States rebuffed all entreaties to come into the Trans-Pacific Partnership (TPP). On his first full working day as president in the Oval Office, Trump abandoned the deal. 'We're going to stop the ridiculous trade deals that have taken everybody out of our country and taken companies out of our country, and it's going to be reversed. I think you're going to have a lot of companies come back to our country.'⁵ No amount of lobbying by Australia could convince him otherwise. Hockey would implore Trump's senior advisers to reconsider but he was blown off every time. In 2016, Hockey directly asked Stephen Miller, who would become one of Trump's fiercest acolytes in the White House—Miller designed and implemented Trump's vicious anti-immigration policies—whether Trump would support TPP. 'Well,' Miller told Hockey, 'that's not going to happen.'⁶ And it didn't. In 2019, Hockey tried again to make the case for the United States to come in from the cold on TPP in a speech at the college campus where Winston Churchill gave his famous 'Iron Curtain' speech. Press reports reached the White House. Trump's deputy national security adviser called Hockey. 'What are you doing? I thought you were on our side,' he said. 'Why are you attacking us?'⁷

Trump was wilfully blind to the fact that TPP was designed, and operates, as a counter to China's economic power in Asia, and in fact would have been much more effective in reducing China's power and trade imbalance with the United States. As Tom Friedman wrote in the *New York Times*, TPP 'included restrictions on foreign state-owned enterprises that dumped subsidized products into our markets. It detailed intellectual property protections for the newest and most advanced American-made tech products—like free access for all cloud computing services, which China restricts. It set out explicit anti-human-trafficking provisions that prohibited turning guest workers into slave labor. It banned trafficking in endangered wildlife parts, a practice still common in China that may have played a role in the pandemic. It required signatories to permit their workers to form independent trade unions to collectively bargain and to eliminate all child labor practices.'⁸

In the Trump White House, there were no second thoughts, and apparently no regrets. Tariffs on imported goods and a mega tariff on Chinese goods were central to his 2024 re-election campaign.

9
Climate
Drill, Mine, Burn, Repeat

Less than five months after taking office in 2017, President Trump announced that the United States would withdraw from the Paris climate agreement.

> I am fighting every day for the great people of this country. Therefore, in order to fulfill my solemn duty to protect America and its citizens, the United States will withdraw from the Paris Climate Accord—thank you, thank you—but begin negotiations to re-enter either the Paris Accord or a really entirely new transaction on terms that are fair to the United States, its businesses, its workers, its people, its taxpayers. So we're getting out.
>
> Not only does this deal subject our citizens to harsh economic restrictions, it fails to live up to our environmental ideals. As someone who cares deeply about the environment, which I do, I cannot in good conscience support a deal that punishes the United States—which is what it does—the world's

leader in environmental protection, while imposing no meaningful obligations on the world's leading polluters.

For example, under the agreement, China will be able to increase these emissions by a staggering number of years—13. They can do whatever they want for 13 years. Not us. India makes its participation contingent on receiving billions and billions and billions of dollars in foreign aid from developed countries . . .

China will be allowed to build hundreds of additional coal plants. So we can't build the plants, but they can, according to this agreement. India will be allowed to double its coal production by 2020 . . .

The rest of the world applauded when we signed the Paris Agreement—they went wild; they were so happy—for the simple reason that it put our country, the United States of America, which we all love, at a very, very big economic disadvantage.[1]

Trump made no secret of his deregulatory agenda: cripple Obama's green energy ambitions and transform the United States from a net energy importer to a global energy superpower.

The Trump administration did not hold back in implementing its new energy vision. It lifted 'burdensome' environmental and other restrictions on the domestic energy sector. This included the rollback of about seventy environmental regulations, including the Obama-era Clean Power Plan. Permissions were granted to construct new oil pipeline infrastructure (the Dakota Access Pipeline, the Keystone XL Pipeline and the New Burgos Pipeline). Trump promoted American energy exports in foreign markets, and tightened sanctions against large energy-producing countries such as Iran and Venezuela. Trump appointed cabinet members who shared his ambitions and vision, including Rex Tillerson, a former ExxonMobil chief executive, who was secretary of state; and Rick Perry, former Republican governor of oil- and gas-rich Texas, who served as secretary of energy.

Trump's war on climate policies was wide-ranging. Over one hundred rules were adopted to eliminate or neuter regulations on air and water pollution, drilling, toxic substances, wildlife and species protection, and wetlands. Trump officials conceded nothing about their scorched-earth approach to protecting the environment. Days before the end of his presidency, an Environmental Protection Agency spokeswoman said, 'We have fulfilled President Trump's promises to provide certainty for states, tribes, and local governments [while] delivering on President Trump's commitment to return the agency to its core mission: Providing cleaner air, water and land to the American people.'[2]

Climate denial was convenient. It enabled Trump to turn a blind eye to the environmental costs of his sought-after shale revolution—to open up as much fracking as possible to expand gas supplies—and his goal of reopening coalmines. Trump's regression of climate action enabled Australia to similarly take a back seat in terms of the urgency with which it looked to transition its own economy from heavy-emitting energy sources to greener alternatives.

To be certain, Australia had gone through the climate wars for several years before Trump won the 2016 election. In 2009, the Greens entered into an unholy alliance with the Liberal Party under Tony Abbott to defeat Prime Minister Kevin Rudd's landmark carbon pollution reduction scheme, which would have established a carbon trading system. In 2011, Prime Minister Julia Gillard enacted one of the most far-reaching programs to establish a price on carbon to drive reduction in carbon emissions. Tony Abbott's highest objective on winning government in 2013 was to repeal Gillard's law, and he succeeded. In the ensuing decade, the Liberal–National coalition was locked in an endless battle with Labor on carbon reduction targets and the means necessary to meet them.

The bitter debate in Australia over global warming, and energy and climate—which over a decade would come to destroy the prime ministerships of two Labor and three Liberal leaders—was fully entrenched by the time Trump became president. For years, the Murdoch media was deeply invested in the political debate on these issues, attacking[3] Prime Minister Kevin Rudd's election pledge to combat climate change as the 'moral challenge of our time'[4] and Julia Gillard's prime ministership, when she was lacerated for her 'carbon tax' policies. These media campaigns fed a hyper-political atmosphere on energy and climate issues, leaving in its wake a 'lost decade'[5] on addressing climate change.

Trump's utter hostility to climate change goals and programs had an echo-chamber effect in Australia. Objections to coal and fossil fuel emitting industries were seen as a 'war on coal' and a 'war on jobs'. The president's relentless prosecution of pro-carbon energy resources—oil, gas, shale, coal—encouraged Australia's debate on climate change to become ever less susceptible to compromise.

Throughout the Trump presidency, which coincided with the Turnbull and Morrison Governments, Australia refused to give up on coal. Scott Morrison, then Treasurer, brought a lump of coal into Parliament. 'This is coal. Don't be afraid. Don't be scared,' he said to all the MPs. Morrison's message: coal would keep the lights on.[6] Government policy provided support for new coalmines and billions in tax subsidies. Instead of phasing out coal, Australia was committed to digging for more. Coal remained the country's second biggest export.

WHAT TRUMP'S SECOND TERM MEANS FOR AUSTRALIA

During Morrison's visit to Washington in September 2019, Trump had high praise in the Oval Office for Australia and its commitment to coal: 'Australia has really been so focused on the economy. They do minerals. They have incredible wealth in minerals and coal and other things. And they are really at the leading edge of coal technology. It's clean coal. We call it "clean coal," but it's also great for the workers. And things that would happen to—because it was very dangerous years ago, and very bad for a lot of people. And you've rectified that 100 per cent. It's incredible. I looked at your statistics the other day and coalminers are very, very safe in Australia.'[7] A month before meeting Trump in Washington, Morrison refused to join a Pacific Islands Forum communiqué highlighting climate change and coal—even though climate change and rising seas are threatening several Pacific Island nations and their livelihood, and these nations view Australia's reliance on coal with intense alarm.

Leading into the 2020 presidential election there was a sense in the United States, and in countries committed to action on global warming, that a second Trump term would make any climate action or efforts to mitigate emissions an impossibility. Trump enabled climate deniers to have space in Australia's national debate on global warming, continuing the decade-long trend of slowing down and politicising strategies to reduce climate change. It changed the conversation from prioritising action to prioritising debate on the cost of action. For Australia, Trump provided a buffer for its lagging efforts to face up to carbon reduction targets. The Morrison Government was shielded to a degree from international accountability for Australia's relative lack of restrictions on coal emissions. The Pacific Island nations were despondent, but Morrison had a climate mate in the White House and there was no pressure on a heavy-polluting nation such as Australia to act.

It was only when Joe Biden took office in 2021 that the Morrison Government shifted its position in the runup to the United Nations Climate Change Conference (COP26) at Glasgow. Under intense pressure from the White House, Morrison finally committed to Australia adopting net-zero carbon emissions by 2050. But he did not outline any improvement on the interim 2030 targets of 26 to 28 per cent reduction, nor was any pledge made to phase out coal-fired power.

The bushfires and floods that ravaged Australia from 2019 through 2022 transformed public opinion on climate change. There was a new politico-climate syllogism: climate change = weather catastrophes = drought and fires or deluges and floods = economic hardship and destruction of our way of life.

Morrison paid the highest price for his equivocation on these issues in the 2022 election as blue-ribbon Liberal seats were lost to 'Teal' candidates who championed much stronger action on climate, cleaning up government corruption and securing real progress on women's equity in the workplace. The Australian people, and growing sectors of the business and investment communities, were way ahead of the Liberal–National Government on climate.

10
Trump 2025
What Can Australia Do?

As with foreign policy, with Trump's high tolerance for chaos and disruption re-creating more policy uncertainty across the globe, there will be collateral effects on international trade and investment.

As president in 2025, Trump will renew his nationalist, protectionist America First agenda that cuts across economic policy, trade and climate. Coming after the Biden presidency, and the strong ties and strategic alignment between Biden and the Albanese Government that reflected a degree of harmonisation in domestic policy settings in both countries, Trump's re-emergence will, in the words of Australian economist Stephen Kirchner, a financial market and academic economist in Sydney, 'hit the US–Australia relationship hard. It will be harder to have business as usual.'

Economy
There will certainly be more stress on the international economy in Trump's second term.

Trump does not—cannot—change his spots. He is isolationist and xenophobic. He believes in bilateral trade, not multilateral trade. And we are in a world, as Australian economist and former secretary of the New South Wales Treasury, Percy Allan, related, where 'China has become globalist and Trump is anti-globalist'.

Trade is in Trump's crosshairs, with trade wars—tariffs—again his weapon of choice.

As Stephen Bartholomeusz, a leading economic columnist for the *Age*, says, 'Trump is very transactional. He sees things in the simplest terms. He sees any trade deficit as the United States being weak. He always sees winners and losers, and he wants America to be winners.'

This has the potential for immense damage to Australia. Australian economist Stephen Koukoulas, former chief economist at Citibank and adviser to Prime Minister Gillard, warns, 'A re-escalated trade war with China will hurt Australian exports even further. Trump's belligerence will get us caught up in that—China will react, will see us aligned with Trump, and will punish us.'

A person who has served on the Reserve Bank board underscored this. 'The biggest threat from Trump to Australia was his protectionism. He can certainly launch more trade wars. Globally the world will be very anxious about Trump and what he will do on trade and economic policy.'

Craig Emerson, a minister in the Gillard Government and an economist, believes Trump will keep up the trade war with China. 'The world will go into a divided, two-part system: a China-aligned world, and a US-aligned world. This will be the worst of both worlds for Australia,' Emerson says. 'Aligned with the US, no relief from China, with Australia hostage to every statement Trump makes.'

In this game, Australia will find itself stuck. Economist Percy Allan says: 'There is no way for Australia to hedge against Trump policies while Australia is still the closest ally of America—even if America is under Trump.'

Trump will again up-end the United States' participation in the World Trade Organization, renewing friction with Australia's interests in a world with more orderly trading arrangements. The only significant good news is that the Free Trade Agreement with the United States will protect that bilateral market.

On overall economic policy, Trump will reprise his high stimulus, deficit spending, tax cut regime.

Stephen Koukoulas told me: 'If Trump comes back in, and has a cooperative Fed, easy money, tax cuts, and deregulation, the US economy will overheat again—and we will have to deal with the consequences here.'

We have already seen what this looks like. The Trump tax cuts will renew the debate here on the corporate tax rate. Last time, that prompted concern that Australia would become far less competitive in attracting investment capital, especially from the United States. The debate was very vocal and confronting. Australia's business community was rapt, eagerly seeking a me-too moment for their bottom lines: 'A powerful group of CEOs, including Mr Forrest, Wesfarmers chairman Michael Chaney and Rio Tinto chief executive Jean-Sebastien Jacques, said Australia was at risk of being left behind if its corporate tax stayed at 30 per cent,' *The Australian* reported. '"The competition is not between Rio or BHP, it is about Australia versus India, versus Brazil. We should not forget the big picture here," Mr Jacques said.'[1]

While the legislation was pending in Congress, then-Treasurer Morrison said, 'The Labor Party seem hell-bent on leaving Australian businesses stranded on a tax island, uncompetitive with the US, uncompetitive with the UK, uncompetitive with our biggest trading partner, China.'[2]

After Congress enacted the Trump tax cuts in December 2017, Morrison continued to warn, 'International companies will flee the country while Australia is at the beach this summer.'[3]

The sky did not fall in from the tax differential between the United States and Australia. But Trump back in power will renew the pressures. Percy Allan says, 'The Trump policies on corporate tax cuts make it hard for Australia not to match them. Also, the average corporate tax rate in OECD countries is now almost 20 per cent versus Australia's 30 per cent. Funding a corporate tax rate cut would make budget repair impossible . . . Trump is for tax cuts, not tax reform.'

The differences between President Trump and Prime Minister Albanese are impossible to bridge on this issue. This will become further complicated by where the fight against inflation sits by early 2025, with Trump wanting to stimulate the economy and the Albanese Government assessing the inflationary effects of further tax cuts. Further Trump tax cuts will spur further pressures on Australia to do the same, lest the country become more uncompetitive globally. The way to get ahead of what could be coming is for the prime minister and the treasurer to lock into law whatever they decide is optimal on tax policy for 2025–28 before Trump takes office in January 2025. Delay means vulnerability to Trump's policies.

Trump, the Fed and the Reserve Bank of Australia

As Trump regains the presidency in 2025, the roles of the Federal Reserve board in the United States, and the Reserve Bank of Australia, will become very important. The Fed and the Reserve Bank are the last resort in terms of wielding tools—most critically, interest rates—to deal with the consequences of excessive inflationary pressures in the economy. Both central banks also have a mandate to promote maximum employment as well as meeting inflation targets.

Stephen Koukoulas has framed it this way: 'There will be more stress on the international economy—so we will need a stronger, more robust, more transparent Reserve Bank board, with more accountability, to both promote and ensure the integrity of the decisions it makes on Australia's economic settings.

'Trump will want to pump tonnes of money into the economy, leading to excess liquidity and inflation. If Trump comes in with a cooperative Fed, easy money and more tax cuts, the US economy will overheat again—and we will also have to live with the consequences.'

The Fed and the Reserve Bank are both independent from direct political pressure, but in his first term, Trump 'blew up'[4] these norms. Trump repeatedly pressured the Fed to lower interest rates and criticised any Fed decision to raise them. He publicly toyed with the prospect of firing the chairman, Jerome Powell.

'If Trump stacks the Fed with stooges, you will get inappropriate policy settings such as intense pressure for lower interest rates—rates below what is justified,' Koukoulas added.

The recent politicisation of the process of appointing governors to the Federal Reserve board has made this prospect more real in a second Trump term, and it could well affect the governance of the Fed.

The chair and vice chair of the Fed are chosen by the president from among the serving governors. Fed governors are generally drawn from the ranks of economists and those who serve in the network of Federal Reserve subsidiary banks across the country.

In Trump's first term, three of his nominees failed to win Senate support. One was blocked because of her strong advocacy of returning the United States to the gold standard. Two other Trump nominees were withdrawn because of their economic views, among other issues. A Senate with more Trumpists in its ranks in 2025 may be more amenable to packing the Fed with governors who have radical populist views on what Fed policies, and the country's economic settings, should be.

The Reserve Bank of Australia operates differently. In contrast with the United States, it is fundamentally de-politicised. The prime minister and Parliament have no direct role in nominating or confirming governors of the Reserve Bank board. All the members of the board are appointed by the treasurer, including the appointment of three key members: the governor, the deputy governor, and secretary of the treasury.

On its face, the appointment of Reserve Bank board members by the Treasurer is highly political, but extra-legislative norms ensure that the treasurer embarks on a consultation process. This process has evolved over the years and ensures a focus by the treasurer on expertise and a wide perspective on economic issues. Insulating the appointment of Reserve Bank board members from an approval process in Parliament—which would be similar to what occurs in the United States—effectively lowers the temperature for the RBA and its work.

While three positions are appointed by the treasurer, the other six are drawn from business, labour, academia and related fields. This wider experience of Reserve Bank board members in Australia provides a different perspective and culture for their decision-making than the Fed has in the United States. But, given the inflation crisis that erupted in Australia in 2022, and the RBA's aggressive interest rate rises, there is pressure to ensure the board has members with even wider social and policy experience.

One who has served on the Reserve Bank board underscored this default setting towards diversity and independence: 'The Reserve

Bank is certainly able to maintain its independence. We have very thoughtful and socially aware governance at the RBA. When there is an appointment to be made to the RBA board, the Governor recommends a list of potential directors to Treasury.' This is often drawn from suggestions made by the RBA board members.[5]

The RBA's monetary policies are premised on its independence. 'The Reserve Bank Board makes decisions about monetary policy independently of the political process—that is, it does not accept instruction from the government of the day on monetary policy. This principle of central bank independence in the operation of monetary policy, in pursuit of accepted goals, is the international norm. It prevents manipulation of monetary policy for political ends, and keeps monetary policy focused on its long-term goals.'[6]

Trump consistently jawboned, with tweets and running commentary in the media, the stock markets and the Fed in his first term. The norms that Trump violated remain in place in Australia, even under intensive political circumstances. Just days before the 2022 general election, the RBA raised interest rates for the first time since 2010. This decision, taken in the wake of rising inflation, undoubtedly hurt the Morrison campaign, and may well have contributed to his defeat. What was clear to many political observers at the time, however, was that a decision *not* to raise interest rates at such a pivotal political moment would have been seen as a political act. In the days before the election, the RBA made the decision it would have made, given the inflationary economic landscape it was surveying, on any other day. It did the right thing.

The Reserve Bank of Australia will play a major role in containing damage to Australia's economy inflicted by a returning President Trump. The RBA, through its control of monetary policy, is the last line of defence against Trump excesses, even if a government in power in Canberra ultimately succumbs to pressures unleashed by Trump on fiscal and tax policy.

Trade and climate wars

On trade, Australia can hedge against Trump's protectionist, unilateralist trade policies with expanded markets overseas. Redouble efforts to strike as many bilateral and regional trade deals as possible. Lock these buffers in now with countries throughout Asia, Europe, Africa and South America. They will not only limit the potency of Trump's punches for the United States to dominate key trading markets, but they will also provide a hedge against China and a return to trading restrictions with Australia.

Kirchner offers this example: 'Australia has really tried to support multilateralism. Australia could be a bridge to the WTO. Australia could help form an EU–Australia–Japan coalition within the WTO to take on China, rather than tackling China unilaterally.'

It is also possible that Trump could renege on his decision in 2019 not to impose tariffs on Australian steel and aluminium. He could also try to order Australia to stop selling China iron ore—perhaps Australia's most crucial export to China. When faced with these prospects, Australia will have to play the alliance card in Washington as effectively as it ever has.

On climate, President Trump's return to the White House will herald the end, once again, of any support from the United States for concerted action on climate change. Trump will want full development of all of America's energy resources—from the coalmines in West Virginia to the tar sands along the Canada–US border, to oil fields beneath the now-protected tundra of Alaska and off the coasts of California and Florida.

The pro-carbon president will collide with the carbon-neutral prime minister.

WHAT TRUMP'S SECOND TERM MEANS FOR AUSTRALIA

As prime minister, Anthony Albanese has enacted many of his climate change policies for Australia—and he has done so with strong support across Parliament, with the exception of hard-right factions among the opposition Liberals, Nationals and some independents in the Senate.

Specifically, Albanese has met with success in writing into law in 2022 emissions cuts of 43 per cent by 2039 and moving to net zero by 2050—the first climate legislation in a decade.

Trump will come into office with deep hostility to the policy settings of the Albanese Government on climate. There is only one choice for Australia: forward. Trump's pro-carbon energy and climate programs will start being enacted in the second half of 2025. If Australia wants to protect the progress it has made on carbon emissions, it needs to ensure that everything that can be put into law on climate is fully legislated by then.

This is the best insurance policy Australia can take out to protect its future in a world ever more deeply overwhelmed by global warming.

11
Healthcare and the Coronavirus Pandemic
Lesley Russell

Australia's recent Coalition Governments have not needed the Trump administration as an exemplar of how to undermine the existing healthcare system, ignore needed reforms, neglect preventive health and hand off crucial public health responsibilities to the states: they were well ahead of Trump on these issues and will clearly return to this agenda should they again hold the reins of power.

However, the political ideologies of conservative Australian governments are constrained by the concerns and needs of Australian voters, who consistently see (and vote for) a major role for government in the delivery of health and healthcare services.[1] Voters' concerns about the future of Medicare have played a major role in the outcomes of several federal elections, and polling also shows that trust in government rose during the pandemic.[2]

In Australia, the coronavirus pandemic highlighted national, community and individual resilience and a raft of issues around health and healthcare. These include: the value of the public healthcare system and also its failings; the importance of sustained investment in prevention and preparedness; the heavy reliance on overseas manufacturers of essential medical supplies, including vaccines; and the critical need for evidence-based policies and effective strategies for their communication and delivery. At a time of such crisis it is important that decisions are based on expert advice and that community leaders are consulted about their local needs, there are clear lines of responsibility and reporting, and policies are designed to prioritise those with the greatest risk and need.

In the United States, the long-recognised failures of the healthcare system and the leadership failures of President Donald Trump meant that the pandemic severely undermined national resilience and wreaked havoc and death on an increasingly divided society.

A report by *The Lancet* Commission on Public Policy and Health in the Trump Era issued in February 2021 assessed the repercussions of Trump's health-related policies. Trump failed in his efforts to repeal the *Affordable Care Act* (Obamacare), but he weakened its coverage, increased the number of uninsured people by 2.3 million, and accelerated the privatisation of government health programs. His disdain for science and cuts to public health agencies and global health programs impeded the country's response to the Covid-19 pandemic, resulting in tens of thousands of unnecessary deaths.[3]

Recent research highlights the extent to which the toxicity of American partisan politics is fuelling an increase in US mortality rates, both from Covid-19 and overall. Residents of counties that strongly supported Trump in 2020 are more than twice as likely to die from Covid-19 than those who live in areas that supported

Biden.[4] Deaths from alcohol, suicide and drug abuse (the so-called 'deaths of despair') are also higher in those counties where support for Trump is high.[5] The blame for these dreadful and growing disparities lies with policies of both the Trump administration and Republican-controlled state legislatures.

The world now looks on with disdain as the United States appears to be headed back to the early part of the last century with increasing restrictions on abortion rights and women's reproductive health services, growing rates of maternal mortality, and outbreaks of diseases such as polio and measles that are preventable by vaccination. To this we must add the uncontrolled gun violence and murders, gun suicides and the fact that gun violence has surpassed car accidents and infectious diseases as the leading cause of death for American children.[6] The result is a decline in life expectancy since 2019 that is the largest decrease in nearly one hundred years.[7]

Australians cannot blithely dismiss these problems as unlikely to arrive here. The rejection of mainstream science and medicine that, under Trump, became a feature of the American political right has gained ground in Australia and globally.

While life expectancy in Australia continues to climb,[8] emerging (and currently incomplete) data suggest that the Covid-19 pandemic is—either directly or indirectly—responsible for an increase in the number of deaths over that expected.[9] Some of these 'excess deaths' are due to an over-stretched and under-resourced healthcare system that is now desperately in need of reform.

Ironically, some aspects of healthcare in the United States would be beneficial in Australia, and many of the possible new models of care and financing (for example, bundled payments and a focus on high-value care) are based on those developed and implemented in the United States.

The politicisation of healthcare

It has long been the case that the worst threat that could be thrown against any proposed change (or failure to act to make change) to Australian healthcare is that this will lead to the Americanisation of the healthcare system. The dreadful irony is that is increasingly the case: Australia's healthcare system is becoming more and more like the expensive, privatised version in the United States.

In the United States, the effort to ensure all Americans have affordable access to care has come a long way, but the battle for an iteration of Medicare-for-all is hindered by the larger political dialogue. The roots of conservative opposition and public misunderstanding of national health insurance are rooted in the toxic residues of the McCarthy era and the subsequent demonisation of 'socialised medicine'.

Most Australians readily understand the principle on which Medicare is founded—that people pay in, via taxes, according to their means and then have a universal right to coverage and access to services according to their needs. In contrast, despite the popularity of the US version of Medicare and the significant numbers of Americans who rely on the encompassing healthcare services provided by the military and the Department of Veterans Affairs, the pervading fear in the United States has long been that socialised medicine will erode individual freedoms and choice.[10]

Trump used the prospect of socialised medicine as part of a fearmongering campaign against Obamacare, despite having previously lauded the virtues of universal healthcare in Canada and Scotland, and praised Australia's healthcare system.

It is no easy task to legislate, implement and then oversee a national healthcare system; the history of Medibank then Medicare in Australia and of Medicare, Medicaid, the Clinton efforts on healthcare reform and the *Affordable Care Act* in the United States are testament to this. As Trump (accurately for once) attested: 'Nobody knew health care could be so complicated.'[11]

The political battles to implement and then maintain these government-funded healthcare systems are driven by two key issues: divisive arguments between political parties over the role of government in the delivery of societal benefits, and the failure by most politicians to see improving health outcomes as a driver of productivity and the economy, rather than a budget impost.

Political attacks on these healthcare programs are constrained by voters' support for the benefits they derive from the investment of their tax dollars. In Australia, Labor has routinely invoked the fact that it built Medicare and will always protect it. The Coalition's history of hostility to Medicare and ambivalence towards universal coverage makes this an easy sell.[12]

In 2016, 73 per cent of Australians said they were 'very concerned' about the creeping Americanisation of the Australian healthcare system, and a further 18.6 per cent said they were 'somewhat concerned'.[13] Australians are strongly opposed to paying fees to see a doctor and (rightly) believe a Medicare co-payment simply means more people going to emergency departments.[14] They have consistently indicated their willingness to pay more taxes if it means better health and aged care services.[15]

The erosion of Australia's healthcare

In a 2021 international comparison of healthcare system performance among high-income countries of the Organisation for Economic Cooperation and Development (OECD), Australia takes third place and the United States is ranked last.[16]

Four features distinguish top-performing countries from the United States: universal coverage and the removal of cost barriers; investment in primary care systems to provide high-value services that are equitably available in all communities; reduction of the administrative burdens that divert healthcare providers' time and health improvement efforts; and investments in social services, especially for children and working-age adults.

Australia's high ranking for health status, as measured by life expectancy, is an average national measurement that hides the disparities seen when such factors are measured with more granularity, for example, by postcode.[17] These disparities are underpinned by failure to invest in population health and primary prevention measures and to address the factors such as poverty, housing and discrimination that are as important as doctors, hospitals and prescriptions in determining health outcomes.

The Australian claim of a universal healthcare system is now a cruel fallacy—perhaps it always was. The universality of Medicare has been allowed to erode[18] as reimbursements increasingly fail to match medical costs, leading to burgeoning out-of-pocket costs for patients. Access to general practitioners and specialists is limited by geography and affordability, and needed investments and reforms have been desultory and ad hoc. Out-of-pocket costs (16 per cent of total health expenditure in 2019) are now higher than those in the United States (11.3 per cent)[19] and are the largest non-government contribution to healthcare spending. The increasing privatisation of healthcare, especially specialist and surgical services, means that access is too often governed by ability to pay rather than medical need. For too many Australians, the healthcare system looks very American.

Social spending in areas such as family, old age benefits, disability supports and education is associated with population health outcomes.[20] Government spending on social services and education as a percentage of GDP for both Australia and the United States is less than the OECD average.[21] These issues matter because health is about more than access to healthcare. It is also about safe housing, education and employment, social justice and equity—the social and economic determinants of health.[22]

The Covid-19 pandemic served to highlight both the national dependence on the public healthcare system (and its extraordinary capacity to cope despite enormous pressures) and the vulnerability of many communities and population groups based on their socio-economic status, race and ethnicity, and rurality. We can expect these existing health disparities to be widened by the increasing impacts of climate change.

Health versus healthcare

The history of improvements in life expectancy and health outcomes highlights the importance of addressing community health and wellbeing through public health services that ensure clean drinking water, clean air, safe food supplies and infectious disease controls, preventive health services, and social services that address poverty, housing, literacy, social justice and social isolation.[23] There is growing recognition that the only way to contain burgeoning healthcare costs and the burden of preventable chronic illness and disability is to focus on health and wellbeing.[24] Despite lip service to this idea, the Australian healthcare system is relentlessly focused on treating sick people.

Secondary prevention efforts such as vaccinations and cancer screenings are done well, but population-level, primary prevention efforts were cast aside under a decade of Coalition Government. In 2021 a National Preventive Health Strategy was developed but there was no meaningful increase in funding for prevention. There has been a steadfast refusal to address obesity, its causes and consequences, despite the huge costs involved. Coalition Governments have seen advertising junk food to children, warning labels on alcohol, curtailing the sale of sugar-sweetened beverages, and more accurate food labelling as issues for families and have looked for voluntary compliance from the food and beverage and advertising industries rather than invoking government actions.

In many ways, Australia and the United States present a similar picture in terms of the failure to privilege prevention and early intervention over treatment. Just as the last Coalition Government defunded the National Partnership Agreement on Preventive Health and dismantled the Australian National Preventative Health Agency (done as part of the 2014–15 federal budget), the first Trump administration allowed funding for the Prevention and Public Health Fund, the National Prevention Strategy and the National Prevention Council established under the *Affordable Care Act* to expire.

In both Australia and the United States, significant public health responsibilities have been delegated to the states, and capabilities have been allowed to erode. There is a failure to address the impact of natural disasters and climate change on health. And there are widening disparities in the health status of population groups, based on race, ethnicity and socio-economic status.

The Trump effect

Trump came to his first presidency determined to undo the progress made on healthcare reforms under the Obama administration. This approach was purely pragmatic—a way to lock in his conservative base.

Initially he promised a better replacement, but he soon came to realise that delivering this was no easy task. Instead, he and his cabinet allowed the states to go their own ways, and adopted a 'just let Obamacare fail' approach.[25] The net result was a weakened program even as it was increasingly valued by the population.

It's easy to see this approach reflected in the neglect that characterised so much of the Morrison Government's approach to over-burdened hospitals, health workforce shortages, preventive health, and aged care. Likewise, there are echoes of the Trump efforts to constrain government spending on social safety net programs and longstanding entitlement programs for the poor in the Morrison Government's failures to invest in essential social security payments, disability and community services, and affordable access to healthcare.

As a result, Australia has been headed stealthily but inexorably towards a two-tiered healthcare system in which those with resources and access can purchase the services they want, and Medicare becomes a ragged safety net for the less well-off. This was underway well before Trump appeared on the political scene. It is inherent in the system as it was constructed, first under Whitlam and then under Hawke.[26]

The conservative view of government-funded healthcare as a last-ditch safety net for the less well-off (somehow also seen as the less deserving) will certainly be extended in the second Trump White House. Australians should worry that it could find resonance with the return of a Coalition Government in Australia. There are decades of evidence that the Coalition agenda favours private health insurance over Medicare. 'Private health insurance is an article of faith for us. Private health insurance is in our DNA,' proclaimed Tony Abbott, then Opposition Leader, in 2012.[27]

The past decade of Coalition Government saw a hollowing out of the capabilities and capacity of the Department of Health and associated agencies. Valuable public expertise was lost and advice was devalued. Trump also sidelined the expertise in his government agencies, often ignoring the advice of his political appointees and regularly undermining or outright denying the science that underpinned the expert advice he was given. This approach reached its apogee during the Covid-19 pandemic, with disastrous results.

The election of the Albanese Government meant an increased level of optimism that the universality of Medicare will be restored, and the issues around health and healthcare that languished under the Coalition Government will be addressed.[28] This will require significant reforms and investments from the Albanese Government that are yet to eventuate and, if and when they do, will take time to deliver the needed changes. But without major reforms, the so-called Americanisation of our healthcare system will continue.

Reproductive health and abortion rights

The June 2022 decision of the US Supreme Court that overturned the constitutional right to abortion has led to international concerns about the need to protect abortion rights and access to reproductive healthcare.[29] Australian women have marched in the streets in support of abortion rights, provoked by statements from anti-abortion groups and some Australian politicians that the US Supreme Court decision will energise efforts to roll back access to reproductive health in Australia.[30]

The Australian situation is much more akin to the US situation, and much more fragile, than most people realise. There is no nationally enshrined right to abortion in Australia; abortion laws are determined by the states and territories, which all have different rules about when and how women can access terminations.[31] The decriminalisation of abortion is relatively recent, and abortion still remains under the criminal code in Western Australia.

There are varying limits on surgical abortions, from sixteen weeks in the ACT to twenty-four weeks in Victoria, before further approvals are needed. Medical abortions are available across the nation until nine weeks' gestation and require a doctor's prescription. There are, however, some serious access barriers to abortions: these include out-of-pocket costs and geography.[32]

An anti-abortion stand has become a litmus test for conservatives in the United States. It represents a total inversion of the usual conservative position—that there is something inherently dangerous about the government's role in healthcare—even as Republican politicians increasingly meddle in women's reproductive health.

Trump (whose personal stance on the issue has varied over the years[33]) was first elected promising to appoint anti-abortion judges to the Supreme Court and he delivered threefold on that promise.[34] While abortion rights play out as a very black and white political issue, dividing primarily along party lines, positions in the community are much more nuanced: 60 per cent of Americans support the right to abortion, and less than half of Republican women (48 per cent) support banning the procedure.[35] Abortion rights in the United States are an inflammatory political issue, as shown by the critical role the 2022 US Supreme Court decision that overturned *Roe v Wade*—taking away the federal right to abortion—played in getting Americans out to vote in the 2022 midterm elections.

Abortion is not seen as a partisan political issue in Australia. The last time the Australian Parliament faced a vote on legislation dealing with abortion was in 2006 with a bill to lift a ten-year ban on RU486 (the combination of drugs used to deliver a medical abortion) by stripping the powers to limit its use from the minister for health. Then Prime Minister John Howard, and then Minister for Health Tony Abbott, opposed the bill, but it had been declared subject to a conscience vote and female politicians united across party lines to ensure its passage.[36]

Trump's attacks on abortion were not limited to his own country. Within days of first being sworn in as president, Trump signed an executive order reinstating the so-called 'global gag rule',[37] banning international non-government organisations (NGOs) from providing abortion services or offering information about abortions if they receive US family planning funding. Later that year, in an unprecedented move to weaponise aid funding, the rule was expanded to apply to all American global health assistance. It was estimated that in 2018 this affected about US$12 billion in NGO funds in seventy-two countries.[38]

Abortion rights will continue to be a frontline health issue in the United States, but it's hard to see it becoming such in Australia. Moves underway to further limit reproductive health rights and access in American states are likely to provide an impetus for Australian efforts to ensure a national guarantee for those rights (as outlined in the bipartisan National Women's Health Strategy 2020–2030).[39] The recent announcement of a National Women's Health Advisory Council, with the specific aim of addressing 'medical misogyny', highlights the very different focus on women's health in Australia.[40]

The Covid-19 pandemic

No country in the world has had a perfect response to the Covid-19 pandemic and no country is emerging unscathed. Australia and the United States have not been alone in their struggles to develop, communicate and deliver effective policies around the pandemic. The pandemic has been mismanaged everywhere, although some countries have dealt with the chaotic times better than others.

Australia was poorly prepared for this new pandemic, which turned out to be much more widespread and harmful than any other infectious outbreak in recent times. The nationally agreed *Australian health management plan for pandemic influenza* was developed in 2014, based on lessons learned from a review of

Australia's health sector response to the 2009 H1N1 pandemic. But there had been no large-scale national pandemic exercise since 2008 and the federal government had not considered the risks a pandemic would pose to the availability of personal protective equipment (PPE) in the National Medical Stockpile. The rapid global spread of the virus meant that Australia faced stiff international competition for PPE, tests, vaccines and drugs for treatment, leading to shortages and rationing.

An examination of the Morrison Government's approach to the Covid-19 pandemic is a seesawing tale of best practice, policy-making on the run, overreaction and delayed responses, responsibilities denied and dismissed, and conflicting and poor-quality communications. Expert advice was followed, ignored and misused.[41] Nevertheless, in the early months of the pandemic the rates of infections, hospitalisations and mortality were well controlled in the community (with the dreadful and glaring exception of aged care homes), and government supports for those who lost business and employment helped ease the financial implications of lockdowns and required isolation periods (again with some glaring exceptions).

Australians put up with the social and financial imposts of the harsh pandemic management measures because they trusted the authoritative advice, respected the government sources of that advice and were promised that vaccines would bring relief. But government failures meant that there were delays in getting vaccine supplies and further delays in getting vaccine shots into arms.[42] Very few Australians were protected by vaccination when the delta strain arrived in late 2021.[43]

Sadly, despite Morrison's acknowledgement in December 2021 that 'mistakes have been made',[44] he and his government went on to compound mistakes already made and to make new mistakes.

The most egregious of these was the push to open national and international borders, schools and businesses, and 'live with the virus', before the population was fully vaccinated.

There was no backtracking on this approach when the omicron variant arrived, even as it became obvious that maximal protection against this viral strain required three vaccine shots, and very few Australians had received the booster dose. The national vaccination program faltered when it was most needed. A review of Australia's vaccine and treatment readiness highlighted that this was due to a slow-moving bureaucracy, the lack of a central, regularly updated policy statement, and the failure to see that vaccine procurement from international suppliers was 'a race'.[45]

At the same time, Morrison showed an increasing tendency to keep decision-making under wraps, to dismiss the advice of scientific experts, and to engage in political argy-bargy with the states. By the end of 2021, his government had switched from a public health approach to pandemic management to one that promoted 'living with the virus' and personal responsibility for infection control.

It was no surprise that in 2022 the rates of infection and deaths climbed to numbers that would have been totally unacceptable in 2020. At the time of the federal election in May 2022, Australia's cumulative incidence of infections was 276,678 reported cases per million people,[46] higher than that of the United States (248,649 reported cases per million people). The mortality rate, highest among older people, rarely rated a public mention by politicians or the media.

Australians had been outraged at deaths in residential aged care in 2020, a situation that provoked a royal commission,[47] but during the first five months of 2022, 1418 people died with Covid-19 in aged care facilities, more than in the first two years of the pandemic.[48] Morrison dismissed this distressing figure: 'As the number of cases has risen, that's what was always going to happen. What you see when you have case numbers of that level is that people, when they pass away from many other causes, they will die with Covid, and their deaths are recorded as Covid deaths—but that doesn't necessarily mean ... that they passed away because of Covid. That's a very different proposition.'[49] The Australian approach was looking increasingly like the Trump approach.

Morrison and state and territory leaders themselves might not have sought consciously to emulate Trump (or British Prime Minister Boris Johnson), but they were urged to cast aside travel restrictions, social isolation requirements and vaccine and mask mandates and 'open up' by big business and conservative media commentators who downplayed the health risks. The latter, along with the small but vocal and visible groups of 'freedom' protesters and anti-vaxxers, were acting out Trumpist ideologies, and it was common to see Trump flags and merchandise at their rallies.

Morrison might have wanted to go further sooner in his efforts to dump pandemic management mechanisms but he was, fortunately, constrained by some inherent Australian traits. These included: respect for the research and knowledge that Australian scientists, clinicians and public health experts worked daily to communicate through the media; and relatively high levels of social cohesion that meant Australians valued the efforts and tough times they and their communities had put into protecting family and friends.

After his May 2022 election loss, and in the face of a growing scandal about his secret assumption of five cabinet portfolios (including Health) during the pandemic, Morrison was moved to offer an apology that was more like a set of justifications for his actions (or failures to act).[50] There were some very Trumpian overtones, most particularly in his exaggerated claim that he was responsible for saving 40,000 lives.[51] That Australia has done remarkably better than the United States in this regard is indisputable: one estimate, made in May 2022, is that if the United States had the same death rate as Australia, about 900,000 lives would have been saved.[52] But the fact remains that many Australian deaths and the emerging and growing burden of long-Covid could have been prevented.

The story of the end of the pandemic is yet to be told. It's not clear that the end is in sight or even achievable. Sadly, in Australia a change in federal government has brought no obvious changes to the management of the pandemic, and the death toll continues to rise.

By the beginning of December 2022, Australia's cumulative incidence was 407,217 reported cases per million people, dramatically higher than that of the United States (292,105 cases per million), despite the much more comprehensive vaccination coverage in Australia.[53] It should be noted that in both countries reported cases are a fraction of the true number of infections. It is estimated that some 80 per cent of Australians of all ages have had Covid-19, in some cases asymptomatically, in other cases multiple times.[54] Covid-19 became the third leading cause of death nationwide[55] and in the six months after the 2022 election, more than 1800 people in residential aged care died from Covid-19.

The Albanese Government's National Covid-19 Health Management Plan for 2023 stated: 'Australia will transition to managing Covid-19 in a similar way to other respiratory viruses, moving away from Covid exceptionalism and bespoke arrangements.'[56] The national economy, the healthcare system and the health of Australians remain at serious risk from the abandonment of Covid restrictions and the failure to renew Covid-specific hospital and healthcare funding.[57]

It is interesting to compare and contrast Australia's abandonment of 'Covid exceptionalism' with the Biden administration's National Covid-19 Preparedness Plan, released in March 2022, which stated: 'We are not going to just live with Covid.'[58]

Preparations for the next pandemic

In both Australia and the United States, comprehensive reports assessing the national response to the pandemic are beginning to emerge.

In the United States, the House of Representatives Select Subcommittee on the Coronavirus Crisis released its final report, which was particularly critical of the Trump administration's failure to recognise and prepare for the threats posed by the coronavirus pandemic.[59] A report from Democrats on the House Intelligence Committee outlines how Trump's distrust of the intelligence community and his consistent failure to read briefing papers and even attend daily briefing sessions meant that he failed to see the pandemic as a threat to global health and security.[60]

In Australia, the Senate Select Committee on Covid-19 published a report in April 2022 that assessed the Australian Government response to that date as a series of failures: failure to plan, to take responsibility, to get it right.[61] Its key recommendation, for the establishment of an Australian Centre for Disease Control, was instantly dismissed by the Morrison Government.

An independent review, 'Fault Lines: an independent review into Australia's response to Covid-19', led by former senior public servant Peter Shergold, was released in October 2022. It found that low socio-economic families, aged care residents, people with disabilities, temporary migrants, multicultural communities, and others already experiencing disadvantage bore the brunt of the pandemic.[62]

While many of the lessons learned from such reviews will be about failures of planning, policies and initiatives, there are also examples of great success, most obviously in the rapid development of an array of new vaccines. The Trump administration's Operation Warp Speed,[63] a multibillion-dollar joint venture of the Pentagon, the Department of Health and Human Services, and private pharmaceutical companies, led to approval of four new vaccines in record time, accomplishing in under a year what might normally have taken a decade.

Australia also benefited from its onshore capacity to research and manufacture vaccines, although the Morrison Government was slow to capitalise on this and it was not until December 2021 that the announcement was made that Australia would acquire new manufacturing capability for mRNA vaccines.[64] Local researchers have argued that Australia 'could and should' set itself up to supply not only itself but the region with all future vaccine and essential drug needs, and that failure to do so puts the nation at grave risk of remaining hostage to a market captured by a small number of manufacturers—a situation that enables profiteering.

Vaccination failures in both Australia and the United States demonstrate that acquiring enough vaccines is merely the first step in getting jabs into arms. That requires not just nationwide distribution mechanisms and availability of the appropriate healthcare workforce, but also ethical decisions about priorities, data on which to assess need, and trusted, culturally safe sources of communication to encourage the population to present for vaccination.

Both Morrison and Trump wanted to claim credit for the things that worked and to offload the blame for problems and failures to others. Their interventions were rarely helpful (for example, Morrison's rush to talk about serious side effects from the AstraZeneca vaccine[65]) and often harmful (for example, Trump's claims about the virus-killing properties of disinfectant and UV light[66]). Their predilections for overriding the advice from experts and public servants meant confused communications and unclear chains of responsibility. Both political leaders dumped the difficult issues to the states (but then interfered) and offloaded responsibility to others when problems arose. There is, however, no way that Morrison's behaviour reached the levels of mendacity, incompetence and outright stupidity delivered by Trump. Under Trump, the silencing of health officials was overt, and even the most senior officials struggled to contradict his foolish statements.[67]

The pandemic highlighted existing weaknesses in the Australian healthcare and aged care system. These pressures result not just from patients hospitalised with Covid-19 and its consequences, but workforce shortages and burnout and delays in the treatment of other medical conditions. Despite these problems, Australia's publicly funded system has coped well and has surely helped reduce levels of mortality and morbidity.

In contrast, the United States has seen a dramatic decrease in life expectancy since the advent of the pandemic.[68] Factors such as gun violence and the opioid epidemic have contributed to this, but researchers also believe that the lack of affordable access to healthcare services was an issue. A Yale study estimates that around 212,000 lives lost to Covid-19 in 2020 would have been saved if the United States had a single-payer, universal healthcare system, and that a Medicare-for-all system would have saved US$105.6 billion in hospital expenses.[69]

There is growing recognition that the pandemic must be a driver for healthcare and health workforce reforms.

Trump's pandemic legacy

The damage that Trump wrought to the status of US public health, and specifically the Centers for Disease Control and Prevention, will continue for some time. The politicisation of public health has led to the harassment of public health officials and has gone as far as death threats for high-profile officials such as Dr Anthony Fauci.[70]

Attempts by the Biden administration to restore public trust in America's public health agencies and apparatus have had little effect. Public distrust, uncertainty and scepticism are at an all-time high. This will affect the ability of the public health system to respond to future threats from infectious disease, natural disasters and climate change. There are also concerns that the second Trump term could see requirements for total fealty from political appointments including scientists and medical advisers.

Australian public health experts have also faced harassment, driven in large part by the pervasive influence of misinformation about the virus and the severity of infections, the safety of vaccines, and unproven and speculative treatments.[71] Much of this information has arrived in Australia from overseas, especially from the United States. A recent parliamentary inquiry into media diversity heard evidence that News Corp–owned media outlets have played a critical role in driving misinformation and conspiracy theories around Covid-19 and 'actively undermining public health through commentary marked by racism, ridiculing of science and ideological warfare'.[72] These efforts continue today and include an active campaign to undermine the science that points to the health and environmental impacts of climate change.

Shock events such as pandemics and natural disasters uncover the deficits in social cohesion and exacerbate existing social inequalities at every level.[73] One of the few constants of the pandemic is that countries with high levels of social cohesion and trust in leadership and government fare better than those without it.[74]

The Trump presidency was defined by its divisiveness.[75] He actively undermined trust in government, national security agencies, academia and mainstream media, encouraged irrationality and insecurities, and set different segments of society against each other. This played out in the pandemic when something as simple and as responsive to community needs as mask-wearing was highly politicised (and remains so). This divisiveness was fuelled by misinformation and was capitalised on by other political figures and some media commentators. It is now deeply entrenched in the United States, its tribalism evident in the Make America Great Again movement, which the majority of Americans now see as a threat to democracy.[76]

Elements of this behaviour are also seen in Australia. The Australian protests against lockdowns, mask-wearing and vaccination mandates were not deeply rooted in political ideologies—and to the extent that they were political, the divisions were not along party lines; they often reflected concerns about poverty and discrimination.

International health issues

The United States and Australia both have important roles to play in supporting international health issues.

Under President Obama, the United States was the largest single contributor to international development assistance for health. Every year of his first term, Trump pushed efforts to reduce overseas aid and to withdraw the United States from international agencies and collaborative efforts. Trump's America First policy vastly under-valued the importance of American aid to improving global health, especially in areas such as malaria, tuberculosis and HIV/AIDS, and he failed to see the importance of American efforts to help defeat the coronavirus pandemic abroad.[77]

The Obama administration's last fiscal appropriation, in 2016, provided nearly US$8.5 billion for global health in fiscal year 2017.[78] Trump's first budget called for a 24 per cent reduction in that funding in FY2018.[79] This was seen as diminishing the international capacity to prevent and coordinate interventions to tackle human health security issues,[80] and Congress did not enact these cuts. Regardless, every year Trump pushed similar efforts to reduce overseas aid. In the last week of his first term, in January 2021, he sent Congress a sweeping package of spending cuts totally US$27.4 billion, including funds for global health and food programs and research.[81]

Trump's efforts to withdraw the United States from international agencies and collaborative efforts began even before the pandemic arrived. He withdrew the United States from the United Nations Educational, Scientific and Cultural Organization (UNESCO) in October 2017 and from the United Nations Human Rights Council (UNHRC) in June 2018. In July 2020, Trump announced that the United States would withdraw from the World Health Organization, effective July 2021. This move was a threat to highlight Trump's annoyance at what he characterised as the WHO's 'China-centric' response to the pandemic.[82] Trump's unwillingness to work with the WHO had further ramifications when, in September 2020, it was announced that the Trump administration would not participate in the Covid-19 Vaccines Global Access (COVAX) Facility because the WHO was involved.[83]

Trump's vendetta against the American research establishment also had potential international ramifications. His budget proposals always included massive cuts to funding for research bodies such as the National Institutes of Health, the Centers for Disease Control and Prevention and the National Science Foundation—all bodies that fund international research, including the work of Australian scientists.[84] Fortunately, these proposals were routinely rejected by Congress.[85] Most of these first Trump-era actions were undone by the Biden administration. In stark contrast to the actions of his predecessor, President Biden called for a boost in funding for overseas aid,[86] including support for vulnerable nations dealing with climate change,[87] and for promotion of gender equality.[88] His administration put aid at the centre of its foreign policy. Biden rescinded Trump's WHO withdrawal letter and pledged US$4 billion to the Covid-19 Vaccines Global Access (COVAX) Facility, becoming the biggest contributor. His administration was confronted with contracts signed by the Trump administration that prohibited the United States from sharing surplus Covid-19 vaccines with the rest of the world,[89] but has since pledged to provide at least 1.1 billion doses by 2023.[90]

An examination of Australia's international aid efforts in the last decade highlights the reluctance of recent governments to spend money to assist less well-off nations. Australia's Official Development Assistance (ODA) budget was effectively frozen during the term of the last Coalition Government. Australia has signed on to the UN target of spending 0.7 per cent of gross national income on aid but has never come close to realising that level. The figure now is around 0.2 per cent of gross national income.[91] As a proportion of federal government expenditure, the ODA declined from 1.32 per cent in 2012–13 to 0.62 per cent in 2020–21. Australia is among the least generous OECD donors. The recent focus has been on Papua New Guinea and the Pacific, which means that funding for Africa and South and West Asia has declined considerably.[92]

The website of the Australian Department of Foreign Affairs and Trade lays out the development efforts in health and provides some limited information about funding levels for these.[93] The total Overseas Development Aid budget for 2021–22 was A$4.089 billion, of which A$625.2 million went to health initiatives, down from A$1067.5 million in 2020–21. In both 2020–21 and 2021–22, further sums (A$327.9 million and A$460 million) were provided for 'temporary and targeted' measures to assist countries in the Pacific and Southeast Asia with pandemic management and vaccinations. Australian National University academic Stephen Howes, who has consistently monitored Australian aid, suggested that the government reported these much-needed pandemic measures separately in order to be seen as 'tough on aid' and to ward off attacks from independent politicians on the right such as Pauline Hanson.[94] The Albanese Government has already acted to increase foreign aid by A$1.4 billion over the next four years, with most of this focused on the Pacific and Southeast Asia, although Australia remains one of the least generous OECD countries.[95]

Despite the rapid and generous response from the Biden administration, the first Trump era's disruptive approach to international aid led to international distrust and the interruption of aid programs.[96] Under the Morrison Government, Australia made no effort to address these deficits. Trump's return to the presidency will see a return to funding cuts for international aid and research efforts. The whole world will be impacted.

What will 2024 bring?

There are worries about how a resurgent Trump and persistent Trumpism might influence Australia's health and healthcare policies in the years ahead. The damage that Trump can inflict is already known, but future possible Republican presidential candidates might be no better, even worse. As just one example, Florida Governor Ron DeSantis said in September 2021 of Australia's approach to the pandemic: '[T]hat's not a free country. It's not a free country at all. In fact, I wonder why we would still have the same diplomatic relations when they're doing that. Is Australia freer than communist China right now? I don't know. The fact that that's even a question tells you something has gone dramatically off the rails with some of this stuff.'[97] In late 2022, in an apparent attempt to move to the right of Trump, DeSantis—once a proponent of Covid vaccines—demanded a grand jury investigate 'criminal or wrongful activity in Florida' involving the 'development, promotion, and distribution' of coronavirus vaccines.[98] This policy flip-flop came as vaccine hesitancy grew in the United States even as a new wave of Covid-19 infections arrived with the northern winter.

The future of American democracy was at stake again in 2024, as it was in January 2021, along with the future of Americans' health and healthcare. The re-election of Trump as president will inevitably have consequences for Australia, more so if the Coalition returns to power in the Australian Government in the same timeframe. The bulwark against the further Americanisation of the Australian healthcare system is dependent on the strength of the reform efforts of the current Labor Government.

But the urgency of these reforms is little driven by American politics. Australia must face the facts, as enunciated by Australian National University academic Professor Frank Bongiorno: the influence of Trumpism in Australia—and specifically in health—has been overstated. Our problems are mostly of our own making and will need our own leadership to resolve them.[99]

III

TRUMP AND THE FUTURE OF DEMOCRACY IN AMERICA AND AUSTRALIA

12
Trump Political Culture
Earthquakes in America, and the Aftershocks in Australia

In the month of June 2022, there were three events—Trump earthquakes—that rocked the body politic in the United States. The House of Representatives Select Committee on the January 6 Attack on the Capitol conducted public hearings on their work to document the insurrection and attempts by Trump to overturn the 2020 presidential election. The Trump Supreme Court began to exercise the power he wanted it to wield by overturning the constitutional right of a woman to access abortion services established by the fifty-year-old precedent in *Roe v Wade*. And the Texas Republican Party met in Houston and adopted the most radical Trump agenda of what their party stood for.

The House Select Committee began to systematically expose a hydra-headed conspiracy, conducted by President Trump, to overturn the 2020 election so that he could stay in office. The constitutional crisis he fomented was not just about the events on that fateful day; it extended on several fronts: a massive disinformation campaign to claim that he had won, that the election was rigged, that there was fraud and that the election had been stolen. It exposed his attempt to decapitate the Department of Justice and put in place a Trump loyalist who would pressure the states to send Trump electors to Washington in place of the Biden electors who had won in those states.

Trump subjected Vice President Mike Pence to immense pressure to take illegal action to overturn the election by refusing to count the electoral votes in several swing states. And there were demands on the secretary of state in Georgia to 'just find me 11,780 votes'[1] so that Trump could be declared the winner in Georgia by just one vote.

Trump's efforts to overturn the election were much deeper and broader than the attack on the Capitol by his mob, who were attempting to prevent the House and Senate from carrying out their constitutional duty to effect the peaceful transfer of power to the winner of the election, Joe Biden.

The vice chair of the House Select Committee, Republican Representative Liz Cheney of Wyoming, stated this plainly in her opening remarks of the first public hearing: '. . . all Americans should keep in mind this fact: On the morning of January 6th, President Donald Trump's intention was to remain President of the United States despite the lawful outcome of the 2020 election and in violation of his Constitutional obligation to relinquish power. Over multiple months, Donald Trump oversaw and coordinated a sophisticated seven-part plan to overturn the presidential election and prevent the transfer of presidential power. In our hearings, you will see evidence of each element of this plan.'[2]

Many people thought the June hearings would be a big nothing-burger, with little impact, but the opposite was true. Television audiences were high—as many as 20 million for the opening prime time session, with strong followership of the subsequent hearings.

Polling showed that 79 per cent of Americans had come to believe that Trump was involved in attempts to overturn the election. Sixty-eight per cent of Americans strongly disapproved of the insurrection. Sixty-five per cent believed that Trump had at least some degree of responsibility for the attack. Forty-one per cent thought he had a lot of responsibility for it.[3]

The hearings coincided with the fiftieth anniversary of the Watergate scandal, which ultimately forced President Richard Nixon to resign. There are uncanny parallels between these two presidency-shaking scandals.

Through the lens of the January 6 House Select Committee hearings in June 2022 we can now understand what January 6 ultimately meant, and it has had a profound effect on American politics.

The overturning of *Roe* was a profound shock: that the Supreme Court actually carried through with the draft opinion sensationally leaked to *Politico* just five weeks earlier—itself an unprecedented occurrence for the Supreme Court that plunged the institution into internal crisis and damaged trust in the court's integrity. Public approval of the court was 60 per cent in July 2021; following the overturn of *Roe*, it fell to 38 per cent.[4] In several state elections following the court's decision, voters, even in conservative states such as Kansas, voted for abortion rights.

The overturning of *Roe* was the first time, in any case of any longstanding significance, that the court had repealed a constitutional right enjoyed by the American people. Many women of child-bearing age when the right to abortion services was established in 1973 were grandmothers when Trump's Supreme Court took that right away, leaving their daughters and granddaughters without the same protection in law they could turn to. As House Speaker Nancy Pelosi said on the day the Supreme Court ruled:

'Today, the Republican-controlled Supreme Court has achieved the GOP's dark and extreme goal of ripping away women's right to make their own reproductive health decisions. Because of Donald Trump, Mitch McConnell, the Republican Party and their supermajority on the Supreme Court, American women today have less freedom than their mothers.'[5]

Trump consistently said he would appoint judges to the Supreme Court who were against abortion, and also who opposed any limits on the Second Amendment right for Americans to 'bear arms'. His appointment of three justices cemented a radical anti-abortion majority on the court.

What was so devastating is that the arc of jurisprudence throughout American history has been, with fits and starts to be certain, to continue to advance freedom, rights and liberty—to go forwards and not backwards in the standing of citizens under the Constitution. In 1857, the Supreme Court ruled in *Dred Scott v Sandford* that slaves were not citizens of the United States and had no standing to sue in court. That ruling was overturned after the Civil War by the Thirteenth and Fourteenth Amendments to the Constitution.

In 1896, the Supreme Court held, in *Plessy v Ferguson*, that 'separate but equal' facilities, including for public schools, for African Americans were legal. This standard, which perpetuated severe discrimination, was ultimately overturned in 1954 in *Brown v Board of Education*, with the court ruling that school segregation was unconstitutional; it ordered that schools across America be integrated 'with all deliberate speed'.

The Trump Supreme Court reversed this trajectory of the evolution of constitutional rights. Linda Greenhouse covered the court for the *New York Times* for decades. The day after the decision to overturn *Roe*, she wrote:

They did it because they could.

It was as simple as that.

What the court delivered ... is a requiem for the right to abortion. As Chief Justice John Roberts, who declined to join Justice Alito's opinion, may well suspect, it is also a requiem for the Supreme Court.[6]

The foundations of America shook when the court struck down *Roe*. The human impact on women is immensely frightening. As Josh Gerstein, the journalist who broke the leaked draft opinion, said at the time: 'And if Justice Alito's draft opinion that we reported and made public on Monday becomes the Supreme Court's final word on this issue, you'd have really a situation of abortion haves and have-nots across the country, where you would have many states where abortion was relatively available and probably about 26 states where abortion is banned or very, very sharply restricted. You would then have women trying to get medication abortions in those states or possibly travel through what might develop as a kind of Underground Railroad to get them out of those states and into other states where they could get legal abortions. It would be a pretty dramatic change in the availability of abortion across the country.'[7]

Gerstein was right. The day after the court's ruling, California, Oregon and Washington opened their borders to women seeking abortions. Canada stated its intention to do the same. In the immediate aftermath of the repeal of *Roe*, the incidence of abortions declined markedly. This is the world the United States has been plunged into by the Trump Supreme Court. Some states responded by enacting legislation restricting abortion, others held referenda, and by the end of 2024, thirteen states had ceased nearly all abortion services and four states had enacted six-week bans.

But there is a deeper tie here to the political culture Trump has so deeply affected. Greenhouse also wrote, 'There will be turmoil now, for sure, as the country's highways fill with women desperate to regain control over their lives and running out of time, perhaps followed by vigilantes across state lines. But the only turmoil that was caused by Roe and Casey was due to the refusal of activists, politicians and Republican-appointed judges to accept the validity of the precedents. Justice Alito's reference to "turmoil" reminded me of nothing so much as Donald Trump's invocation of "carnage" in his inaugural address. There was no carnage then, but there was carnage to come.'[8]

This glaring blindness to the 'validity of precedents' that were accepted and understood to be settled law was seen to be on par with the refusal of Trump and his followers to accept the validity of elections.

Which brings us to Texas.

The Texas Republican Party held its major convention that June too. To say that it was a Trumpist solidarity session would be an understatement. As Axios headlined, 'Texas GOP goes full MAGA ["Make America Great Again"—the Trump motto] at 2022 convention'.[9]

On the outcome of the 2020 election, and the underlying issue of voting rights, the Texas Republicans solemnly declared: 'We believe that substantial election fraud in key metropolitan areas significantly affected the results in five key states in favor of Joseph Robinette Biden Jr. We reject the certified results of the 2020 Presidential election, and we hold that acting President Joseph Robinette Biden Jr. was not legitimately elected by the people of the United States.' They also wanted to tighten the voting rules in Texas—even though under the current law Trump won Texas decisively, and the Republicans have a total grip on the governorship, the legislature, the congressional delegation and their senators.

The Texans minced no words on homosexuality. 'Homosexuality is an abnormal lifestyle choice. We believe there should be no granting of special legal entitlements or creation of special status for homosexual behavior, regardless of state of origin, and we oppose any criminal or civil penalties against those who oppose homosexuality out of faith, conviction, or belief in traditional values. No one should be granted special legal status based on their LGBTQ+ identification.' They opposed all efforts to 'validate transgender identity'.

Texan schools are not properly educating their children. 'Divisive curricula' are to be eliminated, including 'Marxist, anti-American, Critical Race Theory, multiculturalism, or diversity-equity-inclusion courses', with no public funding for 'homosexuality, transgender, or diversity-equity-inclusion centers'.

Environmental stewardship needs to be revoked. 'We oppose the abuse of the *Endangered Species Act* to confiscate and limit the use of personal property and to infringe on a property owner's livelihood. We support the defunding of "climate justice" initiatives, the abolition of the Environmental Protection Agency, and repeal of the *Endangered Species Act*, and we oppose the "America the Beautiful" Initiative.'

For Texas Republicans, memories of the Covid pandemic are raw. 'We call for an addition to the Texas Bill of Rights that explicitly states that Texans have the natural, inalienable right to refuse vaccination or other medical treatment.' And they oppose any 'Nuremberg Code' public health rules that restrict individual freedoms. The Republican Party in Texas sees public health restrictions as the equivalent of Jews being ghettoised and transported to death camps by the Nazis in Germany.

Finally, for Texas Republicans, their state's love affair with the United States may be coming to an end. 'The federal government has impaired our right of local self-government. Therefore, federally mandated legislation that infringes upon the Tenth Amendment rights of Texas should be ignored, opposed, refused, and nullified. Texas retains the right to secede from the United States, and the Texas Legislature should be called upon to pass a referendum consistent thereto.'[10]

The word 'united' in 'United States' may face excision in Texas.

There was one other portentous moment at the convention, which was held just three weeks after the school massacre in Uvalde, Texas, where nineteen children and two teachers were murdered by an eighteen-year-old man-child who was easily able to buy assault weapons and large magazine clips. Those killings, just two weeks after ten people were murdered in a supermarket in Buffalo, New York, finally prompted senators in Washington to begin the first serious and meaningful talks in thirty years to 'do something' on guns. Their efforts ultimately paid off, with President Biden signing a gun safety bill into law. The most significant provision of the new law was that it required deeper background checks on young gun purchasers. It is conceivable, given that a disproportionate number of mass shootings in the United States are committed by eighteen- to 21-year-olds, that tighter screening will save lives. That's the hope. The lead Republican senator in the talks was John Cornyn of Texas. When Cornyn addressed the Texas convention, he was booed lustily. Audience members shouted: 'no red flags' and 'don't take our guns'. This is the state of the gun culture wars in the United States today: citizens of Texas are so fearful of their guns being stripped away by a powerful and intrusive federal police state that they will boo their own senator, a true conservative who was doing his damnedest to stop the blood of *Texas* children from flowing again in classrooms in Texas.

The Texas Republican platform is not just a manifesto for the Lone Star State. It is a distillation of the rivers of ideology and political culture coursing through the Republican Party.

These tremors—three events that occurred in just one month in 2022—defined the platform Trump took to the 2024 election. It is not just a symphony in the key of Trump; it is a clarion call to the future—and to Make America Great Again supremacy.

13
Endangered
American Democracy

There is a growing consensus that the state of democracy in the United States is under extreme stress. It is undeniable: President Biden himself was open about the threat, the stakes and the costs. In his first address to Congress in April 2021, Biden outlined the need to prove American democracy works—and the stakes:

> Can our democracy deliver on its promise that all of us, created equal in the image of God, have a chance to lead lives of dignity, respect, and possibility?
>
> Can our democracy deliver the most—to the most pressing needs of our people?
>
> Can our democracy overcome the lies, anger, hate, and fears that have pulled us apart?
>
> America's adversaries—the autocrats of the world—are betting we can't. And I promise you, they're betting we can't. They believe we're too full of anger and division and rage.
>
> They look at the images of the mob that assaulted the

Capitol as proof that the sun is setting on American democracy. But they are wrong. You know it; I know it. But we have to prove them wrong.

We have to prove democracy still works—that our government still works and we can deliver for our people.[1]

Early on in his tenure, Biden's secretary of state, Antony Blinken, said directly at the UN Security Council: 'We're also taking steps, with great humility, to address the inequities and injustices in our own democracy. We do so openly and transparently, for people around the world to see. Even when it's ugly. Even when it's painful.'[2]

National Security Advisor Jake Sullivan amplified this theme in his press briefing just before a Biden trip to Europe: 'We are in a competition of models with autocracies, and we are trying to show the world that American democracy and democracy writ large can work, can effectively deliver the will of the people. And to the extent that we are not updating, refurbishing, revamping our own democratic processes and procedures to meet the needs of the modern moment, then we are not going to be as successful in making that case to the rest of the world—to China, to Russia, or to anyone else. And so there is a national security dimension to this today, just as there was through the decades of the Cold War.'[3]

Noble words all. But as Australians watched the forensic retelling of the attack on the Capitol and absorbed the palpable fear that the forces unleashed by Trump are not going away, our confidence that American democracy can and will endure is plummeting.

Voices in Australia are clear. There is worry that as authoritarianism becomes the rule in Washington, the discussion has not matured. As historian Emma Shortis asks, 'What happens if all that might falls into the hands of a leader installed by fascists and conspiracy theorists into an office that already has too much power and too little accountability?'4

Shortis notes that Canada and Europe are 'looking warily' at the United States, and then gets to the heart of it all: 'This country [Australia] is, as we have been told repeatedly by successive prime ministers and presidents of all major parties on both sides of the Pacific, the United States' best friend in the world.

'So, what's the plan if the apparently fundamental value of democracy we share with our very best of friends disappears overnight, as it nearly did in January 2021?'

Journalist Stan Grant draws some guidance from history and is similarly fearful: 'America's second president John Adams famously said: "Remember, democracy never lasts long. It soon wastes, exhausts and murders itself. There never was a democracy yet that did not commit suicide."

'. . . More than two centuries after he said that, American democracy is still standing, still offering what another president, Abraham Lincoln, called the "last best hope of Earth".

'But it is wobbling. Americans have lost faith in their democracy. It is a nation riven with tribal political warfare. Division and corrosive, hope-sapping inequality.

'It appears, at times, as a nation ungovernable.

'It is not alone. Democracy is not dead but it is weakened.'

And Grant warns, 'We are not immune. Australia is one of the world's robust democracies but we are falling prey to the American disease of incessant culture wars that inflame passions and obscure reason.'5

When the norms of democracy are trampled, a crevasse opens up. Political commentator Tom Friedman writing in the *New York Times* expanded further on this: 'What is so unnerving to me about the state of the world today is the number of leaders ready to shamelessly, in broad daylight—and with a sense of utter impunity—drive through red lights . . .

'If all those politicians in America who also think that they can run through any red light to gain or hold power succeed. Who will follow our model then?

'. . . I can't think of another time in my life when I felt the future of America's democracy and the future of democracy globally were more in doubt. And don't kid yourself; they are intertwined. And don't kid yourself; they both can still go either way.'[6]

If you add Shortis's and Grant's grave doubts to Friedman's lament of power being exercised solely for the purpose of power, and without any conventions that keep us on course, then violent conflict is near. David Brooks in the *New York Times*, reflecting on Barbara Walter's book (*How Civil Wars Start*), expresses it this way: 'She demonstrates that the conditions for political violence are already all around us: The decline of state effectiveness and democratic norms. The rise of political factions that are not based on issues, but on ethnic identity and the preservation of racial and ethnic privilege. The existence of ferocious splits between urban and rural people. The existence of conflict entrepreneurs—political leaders and media folks who profit from whipping up apocalyptic frenzies. The widespread sense that our political opponents are out to destroy our way of life.'[7]

When truth dies, a civilised society dies with it. J. Michael Luttig, the impeccably credentialed conservative jurist, discussed that consequence in his riveting appearance before the House January 6 Committee: 'These wars that we are waging against each other are immoral wars, not moral ones, being immorally waged over morality itself. We Americans no longer agree on what is right or wrong, what is to be valued and what is not, what is acceptable behavior and not, and what is and is not tolerable discourse in civilized society. America is adrift . . .'[8]

Taking Luttig's sermon to heart, the *Sydney Morning Herald* concluded: 'Australians can only grieve that US democracy is going through such dangerous times. Whether or not Trump is charged, the US needs to end the hyper-partisanship and recommit to shared values and shared institutions. It could start by reforming the antiquated system of counting and certifying elections, where politicians seem to have far too much room for bias and subterfuge. The US should take a look at the Australian Electoral Commission as an example of how to safeguard this most basic machinery of democracy.'[9]

14
Culture Wars
Buttons Are Being Pushed

The decline of America's political culture means that two essential values—truth and trust—are being eroded. If truth is contested all the time, we begin to ask if what we are seeing is true? Is everything extremist political leaders tell us absolutely false? And even when truths and untruths are proved, is there confidence that those judgements will be believed? Is there common ground for political discourse?

Trump's senior media adviser, Kellyanne Conway, packaged the lies that littered Trump's 2016 presidential campaign and formalised their legitimacy in a famous interview she gave to NBC's Chuck Todd on *Meet the Press* two days after Trump became president. Press Secretary Sean Spicer had claimed mammoth crowds at Trump's inauguration. That was not true. The photos of the crowds on the Mall four years earlier at Obama's second inauguration compared with Trump's crowds were conclusive. Conway did not accept that the crowd size they claimed for Trump was not true: 'Don't be so overly dramatic about it, Chuck,' she told *Meet the Press*. 'You're saying it's a falsehood, and they're giving—our press secretary, Sean Spicer, gave alternative facts to that. But the point really is—'

Chuck Todd interrupted her: 'Wait a minute. Alternative facts? Alternative facts? Four of the five facts [Spicer] uttered . . . were just not true. Alternative facts are not facts; they're falsehoods.'

This was the start of a presidency that fact-checkers ultimately certified clocked up over 30,000 lies in Trump's first four years in the White House.[1]

But without truth—and trust—as Tom Friedman has written, 'Everything becomes politics. Normal objects—like masks, vaccines, textbooks in public schools—suddenly become neon signs identifying who you are for and against.'[2]

And when everything is politics because there is no longer any truth or trust, then cultural buttons can be pushed so much more easily—further heightening bitter partisan divides.

Suddenly, mentioning gay rights in schools, the participation of transgender women in sport, scrutiny of what books are in public libraries and school libraries, promotion of academic discussion of racial history, the proper place of prayer in schools and public spaces—all these issues become mediated through politics, campaigns and elections.

More pervasive cultural division enables more poisons to come out from the rocks underneath advanced democratic societies. Under Trump, anti-Semitism increased dramatically. Nazis, with their proclamations that 'Jews will not replace us', have more prominence and reach throughout society, reflecting, as Michelle Goldberg writes, 'A broader cultural breakdown that's leading to an increase in all manner of antisocial behavior.'[3]

The targets of the culture wars become the enemy. Florida Republican Senator Rick Scott has said, 'The militant left-wing in our country has become the enemy within.'[4] Fellow Trump loyalist

Representative Jim Jordan of Ohio says, 'The left doesn't like the country. They don't like people who make things, grow things, move things.'

Most Republicans, up to 70 per cent,[5] believed after the 2020 election that Joe Biden was not the president, that elections are rigged and corrupt, and that the only elections whose outcomes are correct are those which Donald Trump and his loyalist Republicans win. Any elections Democrats win are fraudulent. The enemies of the Republicans have no right to hold power.

There is one glaring contradiction in all these challenges by Trump and his mobs. The ballots that he is contesting weren't just a vote for Trump as president, they were also a vote for House candidates. Trump said that in 2020, Georgia, Michigan, Minnesota and Wisconsin were rigged against him, even though the Republicans won seven new House seats in those states. The ballots that Trump contested are the same ballots that had the names of every other candidate for office in all the states. Neither Trump nor any Republican is saying that those new Republican House seats were won illegitimately, even though they were on the same ballot. The Big Lie was just a trigger for Trump forces to hold sway, to exert great control over elections in order to ensure that 'fraud' is erased and 'integrity' is ensured. Once Trump believed he would win in 2024, he stopped talking abut a rigged election.

Truth is dying. And when truth dies, as Judge Luttig told the House Select Committee on January 6, a political culture is afflicted: 'We Americans no longer agree on what is right and wrong, what is to be valued and what is not, what is acceptable behavior and not, and what is and is not tolerable discourse in civilized society ... America is adrift. We pray that it is only for this fleeting moment that she has not lost her way, until we Americans can once again come to our senses.'[6]

15
The Big Lie
Blunting the Aftershocks in Australia

The aftermath of Australia's May 2022 federal election revealed that core elements of America's culture wars are yet to be fully seen in Australia.

The election outcome, with Labor winning majority government and Anthony Albanese as prime minister, was clear on these issues. Their culture warriors lost. Australians wanted to move on.

Clive Palmer, the biggest Trump imitator and a true billionaire, expropriated Trump's slogan and turned it into 'Make Australia Great Again'. He pivoted off the Covid crisis, with headline calls for no forced lockdowns or vaccine passports, together with populist policies on tax, energy, home loans and exports. Palmer spent upwards of A$100 million to plaster billboards on highways and newspapers across the country, yet his candidates received only 4.7 per cent of the national vote. Palmer's party was left with only one Senate seat from the election.[1]

Unlike the Trumpist in France, Marine Le Pen, whose National Rally party came close to gaining power in 2024, there is no evident road back for Clive Palmer and his United Australia Party. Palmer's terrible showing in the 2022 federal election resulted in his party being deregistered—removed from being a legally constituted party under the election laws—by the Australian Electoral Commission.

In the runup to the 2022 election, as Covid was raging, especially in Sydney and Melbourne, and with Melbourne enduring the most extended lockdowns imposed globally, rebellions erupted in the streets from time to time. Crowds, unmasked, marched and shouted their contempt for health restrictions and the science, adopted by all state governments, that was driving them.

Nick Bryant helped educate American readers to what happened in Australia:

'It was jolting to watch Trump banners that I was more used to seeing in Mississippi and rural Michigan being brandished on the streets of Melbourne. But the Trump paraphernalia, and crowds of Australian protesters that resemble mosh pits of MAGA diehards, have been only a mild form of the sickness. There have been more malign manifestations. Some lawmakers in the state of Victoria who backed tough lockdown measures received death and rape threats. Demonstrations at its assembly building in Melbourne frequently turned ugly. Protesters urinated on the city's most sacred site, its temple-like Shrine of Remembrance. A gallows was even paraded through the streets, upon which was hung an effigy of Victoria's state premier, Daniel Andrews.'[2]

The scenes were powerful. It was frightening to see gallows in the streets of Melbourne in imitation of the gallows erected outside the Capitol to hang Vice President Mike Pence—something Trump appeared to be indifferent about. Was that political cultural virus—the Trump denunciations of science experts, his endorsement of quack treatments and claims that the contagion was just going to disappear—really breaking out in Australia?

Those protestors voted with their feet, but Australians voted with their arms: 95 per cent double vaxxed and 65 per cent triple vaxxed.³ And 'Dictator Dan' Andrews, as he was known to the health anarchists, won re-election for another term as Victorian premier in November 2022, despite the relentless anti-Andrews campaign in the Murdoch media tabloids and on Sky News.

In that state election, rationality prevailed—not extremism. In the course of the campaign, candidates far outside the mainstream who were associated with the Liberal Party in Victoria were expunged or defeated. Bernie Finn, a member of the upper house in Victoria, was thrown out from the party for his anti-abortion views. 'So excited the US is on the verge of a major breakthrough to civilisation. Praying it will come here soon. Killing babies is criminal,' he posted on Facebook.⁴ Independent Catherine Cumming lost her seat in the election after threatening to turn Premier Andrews into 'red mist'—words that triggered a police investigation.

After the federal election, one attempt at The Big Lie did emerge. Two weeks after the election, Liberal Senator Hollie Hughes characterised Labor's clear-majority win this way: 'If we want to consider 32 per cent of the primary vote a mandate we might need to have to review what a mandate looks like.'⁵ The *Saturday Paper*'s lead article called this out immediately: 'Hughes is borrowing an American lie: that the new government is somehow illegitimate. Donald Trump propagated this myth before extremists marched on Washington in January 2021. It is a grievance that undermines democracy and must be condemned. It makes mischief of the preferential voting that put Hughes in office.'⁶

Hughes fired a popgun, not a cannon. Scott Morrison conceded defeat hours after the polls closed and days before it was clear that Albanese had a majority government. There was not a breath in the air of the words 'fraud', 'rigged', 'stolen' or 'corrupt'. This enabled the new prime minister, Anthony Albanese, to be sworn into office and then fly to Japan thirty-six hours after the election to meet with President Biden and the leaders of Japan and India. An astonishingly smooth transition of power.

One of the closest seats in the House of Representatives race was in the electorate of Gilmore. The Liberal candidate, Andrew Constance, lost by 373 votes out of 111,705 cast, to Labor's Fiona Phillips. The loser did not go to court. The loser did not appeal the decision by the Australian Election Commission not to undertake a further recount of the vote.[7]

Mr Constance never said that he won—and everyone accepts that he lost.

Even if the 2022 election was hanging on the seat of Gilmore— that whoever won Gilmore would win government—it is inconceivable that Scott Morrison would call up Commissioner Tom Rogers at the Australian Electoral Commission and say, as Trump did with the secretary of state of Georgia in early January 2021:[8]

> Mr Rogers, we appreciate the time and the call. So we've spent a lot of time on this, and if we could just go over some of the numbers, I think it's pretty clear that we won. We won very substantially in Gilmore. You even see it by rally size, frankly. We'd be getting 250 to 300 people a rally, and the competition would get less than 100 people. And it never made sense . . . And I know you would like to get to the bottom of it, although I saw you on television today, and you said that you found nothing wrong. I mean, you know, and we didn't lose the electorate, Tom. People have been saying that it was the highest vote ever. There was no way. A lot of the political people said that there's no way they beat Constance. So that's it. I mean,

we have many, many times the number of votes necessary to win the electorate. And we won Gilmore, and we won it very substantially and easily ... So what are we going to do here, folks? I only need 374 votes. Fellas, I need 374 votes. Give me a break. You know, we have that in spades already ... So look. All I want to do is this. I just want to find 374 votes, which is one more than we have. Because we won the electorate.[9]

No Australian prime minister could ever make that call and keep his office, and stay out of jail.

Elections in Australia unmarred by racial injustice

In the closing months of 2021, Prime Minister Scott Morrison moved—at first under the radar but at later stages with greater visibility—to impose 'voter ID' requirement 'reforms'.[10] This was straight out of the Trump playbook: make voters show official identification records, such as driver's licences, passports, Medicare cards, proof-of-age cards, account statements from financial institutions and utilities. And write the 'reform' rules in such a way as to ensure that voters of colour—First Nations peoples and immigrants—will have greater difficulty producing such records, resulting in lower numbers of votes legitimately cast by those caught up by the restrictions.

The push for this discriminatory, racially tainted legislation began in 2018, when Trump was president and Morrison was prime minister.[11]

The Australian Election Commissioner, Tom Rogers, testified before the Senate that there was no basis for the legislation. 'Evidence of multiple voting to date is vanishingly small,' he said.[12] In the 2019 election, only 0.03 per cent of the 91.9 per cent turnout involved fraudulent marks. 'One of the things we do at the end of every election is we examine multiple marks in every electorate to make sure that there's never a situation where if there was multiple voting, it was greater than the margin in the election itself. We've said publicly that, if that was the case, we would then go to the Court of Disputed Returns and seek for that result to be overturned and we've never had to do that.'[13]

The voter ID bill died.

In the United States, the heart of the issues over voting—who votes, who counts the votes, who certifies the votes—is race.

White lawmakers in Republican states across the country continue to propose and pass laws making it harder for Blacks and people of colour to vote. In the aftermath of the 2020 election and Trump's prosecution of The Big Lie, at least twenty-one states have passed forty-two laws to tighten voting procedures. The most common elements of these laws were limitations on advance voting, restrictions on the number of ballot drop boxes (which are like post boxes, where voters can deposit their pre-poll completed ballots), shortening the window to apply for mail-in ballots, prohibiting local officials from sending out unsolicited ballots to registered voters, and other similar barriers.

The element of racial discrimination and racial justice is inherently linked to the battles over how voting is conducted in many states in America. In their 2022 book, *100% Democracy*, E.J. Dionne Jr and Miles Rapoport advocate Australia's system of universal voting as essential to healing the wounds afflicting America's democracy. Their book opens with this foreword from Heather McGee: 'Contrary to the lofty goals of the nation's founding, the actual design of our democracy has created a system that has depressed the participation and influence of communities of colour, and is also far less responsive to the needs of all Americans than the democracy we deserve . . . the laws controlling voting have been crafted, in many ways and in many places, to undercut the power of people of colour . . .'[14]

After the Civil War, the Fourteenth and Fifteenth amendments to the Constitution ensured that every citizen could vote. Following decades of repressive practices, such as literacy tests and poll taxes imposed on Black citizens across the South, Congress enacted the *Voting Rights Act* of 1965 that outlawed such discriminatory practices. But two key Supreme Court decisions, in 2013 and 2021, limited the ability of voters and the Department of Justice to challenge state laws that limited voter eligibility.

In the wake of the 2020 election, Democrats in Congress moved to supersede these impediments through legislation named for a great civil rights champion, John Lewis, a disciple of Martin Luther King Jr and one of the most respected members of Congress in his later years. The proposals would restore strict federal scrutiny of changes to voting laws, and whether they repress voting rights. It would also strengthen the ability of citizens to challenge these issues in court. The bill provided for more early voting, voting by mail, and automatic voter registration, and would make Election Day a national holiday. While President Biden and Democratic leaders across the country made passage of this legislation an urgent priority, Republicans attempted to delay the legislation in the Senate and, in scenes reminiscent of the great civil rights battles of the 1960s, blocked approval. The Trump forces, with Republican numbers in the Senate sufficient, because of Senate rules requiring a supermajority of 60 votes to pass legislation in the Senate, have the upper hand in gaming the election system. None of these reforms were law for the 2024 presidential election.

Australia's system of voting is recognised as the gold standard for advanced democracies. While racial discrimination against Aboriginal and Torres Strait Islander people remains pervasive throughout Australian society, as reflected in the failure of the Voice referendum in 2023, race is not inherent in the voting system today. Voting rights for Indigenous peoples were enacted under the Menzies Government in the *Commonwealth Electoral Act of 1962*. All the states in Australia passed conforming legislation by 1965. With the system of compulsory voting established in 1924, the inclusion of women in Commonwealth elections in 1902 (and in the states thereafter), and with passage of the historic referendum of 1967 to include Aboriginal people in the census and enable the Commonwealth to make laws for Aboriginal people, there is no parallel in Australia with the discriminatory and uneven voting rules in US elections for the president and Congress. Indeed, the Australian Electoral Commission makes extra efforts to encourage remote area Aboriginal people to enrol and vote.

Abortion rights

The US Supreme Court decision to overturn *Roe v Wade* divided America, but united Australia. Thousands of women marched across Australia to affirm their belief in a woman's right to control her health and reproductive choices. 'I am really, really scared that [what happened in America] is going to come here in Australia,' a woman in Canberra said. New South Wales Greens MP Jenny Leong was just as firm. 'The rights that were rolled back were chipped away slowly and deliberately for years. That's why we must remain vigilant, keep up the fight for accessible and free abortion care and take to the streets to be clear that our reproductive rights are not up for debate.'[15]

Prime Minister Albanese was clear: Australians, he said, were 'entitled to their own views, but not to impose their views on women for whom this is a deeply personal decision. That is, in my view, one for an individual woman to make based upon their own circumstances, including the health implications. This decision has caused enormous distress. And it is a setback for women and their right to control their own bodies and their lives in the United States. It is a good thing that in Australia, this is not a matter for partisan political debate.'[16] These views were echoed by his cabinet.

However, there were voices in the National and Liberal parties applauding the Supreme Court ruling. Senator Matt Canavan tweeted, 'A wonderful day to protect human life.'[17] By late 2024, others on the political fringes tried to rekindle the abortion debate in Australia, inspired by the success of the long US conservative campaign to weaponise the issue. In October 2024, South Australia's upper house narrowly defeated a proposal to amend abortion laws that would have required people wanting to terminate their pregnancy after 28 weeks to deliver their baby alive.

In the same month, the Katter Australia Party declared during the Queensland state election campaign that it would table a bill to recriminalise abortion in the state. The Liberal National Party won the election by a large margin as predicted, but leader David Crisafulli found himself uncomfortably dodging media questions as to whether he would permit a conscience vote on the issue. Federal Coalition leader Peter Dutton clearly did not see recriminalising abortion as a platform that would benefit his party: he explicitly ruled out abortion policy changes in the federal Coalition platform, and blasted his MPs for stirring debate.

Despite this manoeuvering on the political right, public support for abortion in Australia is broad and strong. But even though abortion has been decriminalised in every state, there is no universal access to abortion for women in Australia. Abortion laws and practices across Australia are uneven, and service availability can depend upon the personal beliefs of individual medical practitioners, leaving some rural regions as 'abortion deserts'.

The end of *Roe* was a shock across America, provoking fierce legislative and cultural divisions that will engulf the country for years to come. It was a shock in Australia too, but it served to reinforce the strong consensus in the community that a ban on abortion is unacceptable and must not become law.

What is lamented in Australia is not that the radical, extremist campaign against abortion by powerful conservative forces in America might leach into Australia, but that Australia and its very close ally have diverged and headed in different directions.

On this issue, Australia rejects the Trump Supreme Court.

Gun control

Three days after Labor won the federal election, with Anthony Albanese sworn in as prime minister, a killer in Texas took the lives of nineteen children and two teachers in a school in Uvalde, Texas. Although the United States was approaching three hundred mass murders in 2022, this was a horror that shook the country and the world. Albanese, who had just met with President Biden in Tokyo, reacted two days later on ABC television with unequivocal condemnation: 'Look this is an atrocity that just keeps happening in the United States. Nineteen children and two teachers slaughtered with a, an automatic weapon. It is just astonishing that it continues to happen. I know that President Biden is very serious about gun law reform. He has made very strong comments. But the US democratic system in their Congress and their Senate needs to act on this. They can't continue to have these tragedies occur. It's far too often. Some of the representatives in Texas seem to be more concerned about people, students wearing masks than they were about students carrying automatic weapons. This is a tragedy. And I reflect on Australia's actions and I give credit to former Prime Minister John Howard. He showed great courage, as did the Nationals Leader at the time, Tim Fischer, in introducing laws after the Port Arthur massacre that have ensured that we haven't seen one of these tragedies occur since then. We were able to do it in a united way, with leadership from John Howard and Tim Fischer and the Labor Leader at the time as well, Kim Beazley. And America does need to act on these issues.'[18]

It takes a lot for a new prime minister, even of a country that has the closest alliance with the United States, to be so blunt. Albanese was reflecting the instinctive horror of Australians at the needless slaughter. The American gun lobby always says that guns don't kill people, people kill people. There is mental illness all around the world, but the American experience with mass murder is not repeated in any other country. Put simply, what is happening in America is simply incomprehensible to Australians.

After the Port Arthur massacre, under Howard's leadership, strict gun controls were enacted. Australia has one of the world's lowest firearm-related death rates, with 1.04 per 100,000 firearm-related deaths per year.[19] This is compared to 12.21 deaths per 100,000 for the United States. There has been only one mass shooting in the nearly thirty years since Port Arthur. According to a University of Sydney study, there are 3.5 million guns registered, but the number of people owning guns, and the number of households where guns are present, has declined markedly— by 47 per cent (gun owners) and 75 per cent (households).[20] With perhaps 100,000 gun owners in a population of 25 million, the presence of guns—intolerable when they are used in gang crimes and murders—is not the epidemic that it is in the United States, where there are more guns than the 330 million people who reside there.

More recently, it was not the carnage in America that prompted a smarter reaction to gun violence in Australia. The Christchurch mosque shootings in March 2019 brought a new, horrifying high-tech component to the massacre because the killer livestreamed the assaults. Almost immediately, Australia's eSafety Commissioner, Julie Inman Grant, insisted that all social media platforms take down video and images from the massacre. New laws to back up those demands were passed by the Australian Parliament. No other country has the equivalent of the eSafety Commissioner, which was established to ensure safe use of the internet—especially to protect women and children from sexual abuse and violence, among many vulnerable populations. After a mass murder in Buffalo, New York, in May 2022, the eSafety Commissioner issued notices carrying penalties of fines for eight platforms to remove the killer's video of the shootings and his manifesto—said to be inspired by the Christchurch killer. Australia now has in place a holistic regime that requires social media platforms to remove 'abhorrent violent material', which includes videos that show terrorist attacks, murders or rapes. Christchurch reinforced the lessons of Port Arthur.

The gun lobby in Australia has well over 200,000 members and is well-financed—enough to donate close to A$2 million in political campaign contributions. Their biggest controversy in recent years was an attempt to approve the importation of a new rapid-fire shotgun. It failed—under a conservative government.

Nothing has shaken the resolve of the vast majority of Australians to maintain the country's gun restrictions.

While there have been ties between the National Rifle Association in America and politicians in Australia, with Senator Pauline Hanson coming under media scrutiny, the gun lobby in Australia does not control the outcome of the decision made on gun control in Australia. This will remain true no matter who is the president in Washington.

Morrison's failed dog whistles on transgender

In the runup to the federal election in May 2022, Scott Morrison and Minister for Immigration Alex Hawke played a massive power game intended to control the pre-selection of Liberal Party candidates for the New South Wales branch of the Liberal Party. It was so convoluted that only the power players had a real clue about what was going on. But in the end, Morrison and Hawke won, enabling Morrison to install candidates for federal parliament without Liberal Party members in certain seats having the opportunity to make the choice by a ballot of members. Candidates in those seats were denied the democracy of a party vote.

Morrison made a shocking choice to appoint Katherine Deves for the seat of Warringah—the seat independent Zali Steggall took from former Prime Minister Tony Abbott. Steggall's victory in 2019 crystallised the Liberal Party's low standing, in certain electorates, due to its policies on global warming and equity for women in their lives and careers. In the months before the 2022 election was officially called, other women independents like Steggall were surfacing in other seats held by Liberals, especially in Sydney and Melbourne. Climate change, equity for women, and ending government corruption were their calling cards. They were running in long-held Liberal seats that were never going to flip to Labor but were ripe for the taking by an independent because Morrison was so unpopular. Many people saw him as tone deaf, or worse, on women's issues, hostile on environmental protection and, perhaps most significantly, not to be trusted in governing truthfully.

The selection of Deves injected another element into this equation. She was exceptionally hostile to transgender women in life and in sport. She believed that transgender children were 'surgically mutilated and sterilised'.[21] She claimed half of all males with trans identities were sex offenders. She likened pro-trans activists to

Nazis transporting Jews to concentration camps in the Holocaust. She claimed a link between transgender people and serial killers.

Morrison refused to distance himself from Deves, and he spurned calls by others in his party for her to be disendorsed for the election. Morrison said that Deves was standing up for something 'really important'. He added: 'Katherine is an outstanding individual. And she's standing up for things that she believes in, and I share her views on those topics. This is just about common sense and what's right. And I think Katherine's right on the money there.'[22] Morrison invoked the intolerance of the cancel culture; he was not going to tolerate it. 'She is a woman standing up for women and girls and their access to fair sport in this country,' he said. 'I am not going to allow her to be silenced.'[23]

The method in his madness was a play to push this culture war button to appeal to religious voters in other suburban seats held by Labor, seats that Morrison and his strategists believed could be taken away from Labor—and thereby offset at least some of the Liberal losses that were going to go to the new wave of independents.

But the method reeked. There was solid polling three weeks before the election that the strategy was failing—especially in crucial seats in greater Sydney, including Parramatta and Wentworth.

Matt Kean, the New South Wales Treasurer, was clear that Deves was not 'fit for office'. And more tellingly: 'I do not believe that she is aligned with the values of the Liberal Party.'[24]

The Liberals lost thirteen seats in Sydney and Melbourne. Deves was certainly a factor. Morrison was incredibly stubborn in prosecuting his belief that this issue—transgender women—would help save the election, or at least some of the furniture.

Morrison died on the transgender hill. As a result, the issue is discredited as a potent, pervasive political factor in Australia—principally because, as Liberal Matt Kean concluded, such an issue does not fit with the beliefs and principles of the Liberal Party. This diverges markedly from the Republican Party in America. The politics of transgender identity is growing in America as conservative Republicans continue to gain strength in state legislatures, and as conservative judges appointed by Trump stand ready to narrow the rights of gay and transgender Americans. Trump used it among his many slurs against Democrat presidential candidate Kamala Harris, claiming she 'cared more for trans rights than struggling Americans'.

Conservatives in Australia are no longer trying to take that hill.

Truth won and lying lost

By the Saturday of the 2022 federal election, Scott Morrison had been deemed, by a critical mass of Australian voters across several political parties and movements, a liar. It was a characterisation that stuck, and that contributed significantly to his party's defeat.

Writing in *The Atlantic* before the election, Aussie-returned-home Nick Bryant unloaded on Morrison: 'A small-*t* Trumpism has also found a home in Canberra, the nation's capital. Although Prime Minister Scott Morrison has a wholly different persona from the former U.S. president—more banal suburban dad in an Aussie soap opera than Fifth Avenue tycoon starring in prime-time reality TV—there are similarities nonetheless. During his three and a half years in charge, this former marketing executive has earned a reputation as a serial political liar and peddler of "alternative facts." In a polity famed for plain speaking, maybe we should look upon him as Australia's first post-truth prime minister.'[25]

Morrison was asked in a radio interview if he had ever told a lie in public life. 'I don't believe I have, no. No.'[26]

The maelstrom that unleashed the charge that Morrison was a serious, serial liar was his failure to front when the bushfires exploded across New South Wales in December 2019. His office tried to hide the fact he was actually holidaying in Hawaii, and he appeared to return to the country under duress. Morrison insisted he did not lie about letting Anthony Albanese know he was overseas—but that is not how Albanese heard it.

On Covid, Morrison lied about Australia being 'head of the queue'[27] for vaccines, when he and his team botched discussions with Pfizer, leaving Australia months behind in deliveries of the medicine. Morrison said that fighting Covid was 'not a race'.[28]

Morrison said electric vehicles would 'end the weekend'[29]— a powerfully misleading statement about the capabilities of EVs.

But there were two terrain-shifting events that occurred later in 2021 that left a clear impression with voters that this emperor had no clothes. On 31 October, Bevan Shields of the *Sydney Morning Herald* asked Emmanuel Macron, President of France, about Morrison and the collapse of Australia's contracts with the French for submarines. That deal was upset when Morrison shifted Australia into AUKUS, with US nuclear submarines replacing the deal with France. 'Did he lie to you?'

Macron replied, 'I don't think, I know.'[30]

The next day, 1 November, Sean Kelly's portrait of Scott Morrison, *The Game*, was published. In a stunning dissection of the man, his character and his politics, the book made a deep impression to the political class—especially on the issue of Morrison's character and his capacity to lie. Morrison would never concede he had lied and has certainly never apologised for any lies. In discussing how he approached Morrison, Kelly wrote: 'The fact he seemed boring wasn't an obstacle: it was the opening. Here was a man who was on display all the time, yet we knew so little about him—and nobody seemed to want to know more. And he had become prime minister! How had he pulled off this trick?'[31]

These two events, taken together, were a thunderclap that

legitimised for the political class—the politicians, their staffs, the media, business leaders, trade associations, lobbyists, civil society and NGOs, academics—and through their reactions, for much of the public, the removal of the burden of proof that Morrison was a liar. Who do you believe: Morrison or Macron? Who has control over the narrative: Morrison or Kelly? In the course of the campaign, members of Morrison's own party, sitting in Parliament, would call him a bully and a liar, a hypocrite, a horrible person, a person who could not be trusted. Shocking public denunciations for which Morrison paid the ultimate price.

Albanese had a good start after winning the election. He is seen as honest. There was a sharp increase in the sense that the country was on the right track.[32] Albanese did not reverse policy on any of his campaign platform, and mostly seemed to say, and be seen as saying in very straightforward terms, what he is doing and why.

Albanese followed the Biden paradigm: running for the top job in order to defeat a man who corrupts the processes of government, a man who is dividing the country, a man who does not tell the truth, a man who cares more about himself and his power than the people he serves.

The difference on this issue of political culture in Australia and America is that Trump and his followers in the Republican Party, with tens of millions of voters across the country, believe in The Big Lie, campaign on The Big Lie, and destroy his enemies with The Big Lie. And as a result, the United States remains profoundly divided.

In Australia, The Big Lie helped destroy Morrison.

Truth won in Australia in 2022, because Australians, taken as a whole, did not believe in The Big Lie when spouted here.

16
Race

Trump's Voice versus the Voice

Australia, with its historically pervasive atmosphere of fear around Indigenous aspirations, is fertile territory for Trump and his rhetoric on race—just as America is, with its embedded fear of the aspirations of Black people, immigrants and people of colour.

Trump's engagement with racism has a long history—decades before he entered politics. Trump sensationalised the 'Central Park Five', in which five Black and Latino men were wrongly accused and convicted of raping a white jogger in 1989. The reported attack was huge news at the time, sending tremors of fear across the nation of crime by young Blacks. When the men were arrested, Trump took out full-page ads in New York's major newspapers supporting the death penalty. 'Roving bands of wild criminals roam our neighborhoods, dispensing their own twisted brand of vicious hatred on whomever they encounter. At what point did we cross the line from the fine and noble pursuit of genuine civil liberties to the reckless and dangerous permissive atmosphere which allows criminals of every age to beat and rape a helpless woman and then laugh at her family's anguish?'[1] The ad was signed with the vertical cursive style that would become famous when, as president, Trump signed bills and sweeping executive orders ... Even after the young men's convictions were overturned in 2002, after exposure of an extraordinary miscarriage of justice, Trump stood by his claims.

That was perhaps the most sensational example of Trump wallowing in racist fears. There have been many more such transgressions. In the 1970s the Trump Management Company was sued for racial discrimination in one of their housing projects. Trump attacked a Native American Tribe casino competitor as a 'group accused of drug smuggling, money laundering, trafficking in illegal immigrants and violence'.[2] Trump expressed views that Blacks have only themselves to blame for their struggles, and Jews are 'only in it for themselves'.[3]

Nearly two years after leaving office, Trump had a spectacular falling out with Jewish Americans and leaders of the Jewish community following his now-infamous November 2022 dinner at Mar-a-Lago with Kanye West, whose anti-Semitic views are expressed in plain daylight (West wrote that he wants to go 'to death con 3 on Jewish People'),[4] and Nick Fuentes, a notorious white nationalist and Holocaust denier. The head of the Zionist Organization of America said, 'Donald Trump is not an anti-Semite. He loves Israel. He loves Jews. But he mainstreams, he legitimizes Jew hatred and Jew haters. And this scares me.'[5] But Trump does not apologise, recant or retreat. And Trump's power and base remained so strong that most Republican leaders in Congress, who condemned West and Fuentes, refused to directly criticise or repudiate Trump for dining with them. Most Republican leaders, trapped by their fear of Trump's power, condemn the extremists, but not the man who willingly accepts the support they give him.

Jonathan Greenblatt, head of the Anti-Defamation League, said, 'The normalization of anti-Semitism is here.'[6]

Trump's approach to Israel and the politics of the Middle East in America is marked by cognitive dissonance. Trump has expressed support for right wing anti-Semites in the US even as he claims that no one has done more for Israel than Trump. Although Israel's prime minister Benjamin Netanyahu is the kind of strongman Trump favours and has called Trump the 'best friend Israel has ever had in the White House',[7] Trump doesn't support Israel without question. In October 2024, Trump met with Netanyahu and reportedly told him to 'wrap up the war in Gaza by the time he returns to office'.[8] Meanwhile, the majority of Jewish American voters maintained their usual preference for the Democrats in the election.[9]

Trump knows how to push the fear button on race. To curb unrest in the cities, he wants the next president to have the power to override the governors and send in the National Guard—something Trump could not do in his first term. 'The next president needs to send the National Guard to the most dangerous neighborhoods in Chicago until safety can be restored,' he said.[10] Trump means using armed force to suppress residents in the inner cities. 'Inner cities' is code for 'not white'.

Trump does not dog whistle. He shouts it from the podium with throngs of supporters behind him. In his second term, Trump will continue to exploit racial themes whenever he can—which will be often.

What he says is heard in Australia, because the culture wars prosecuted by Trump have a parallel presence in Australia.

Stan Grant penned a very powerful essay in the runup to the 2022 federal election. 'The culture wars [in Australia],' he wrote, 'have also stopped us reaching a settlement on the greatest issue of Australian virtue: a just reconciliation with First Nations people. Each advance is met with resistance. Not based on rational argument, but fanning fear. Land rights were meant to take away Australians' backyards. Didn't happen. The Mabo decision would threaten mining and agriculture. We found a way through.'

In their lived experience, Black Americans and Black Australians are profoundly burdened. 'We should ask why,' Grant insists, 'after two centuries, in one of the richest countries on earth, Indigenous people are the most imprisoned and impoverished in the country.'[11]

The gap between Black and white Australians is roughly parallel to that between Black and white Americans, in incarceration rates, economic status and poverty, and life expectancy. Australia is a mirror image of what is experienced by African Americans.[12]

	Australia		United States	
	Indigenous Australians	Non-Indigenous Australians	Black Americans	White Americans
Incarceration rate (per 100,000 adults of representative group)	2368	204	1134	218
Median household income (per year)	A$25,428	A$40,560	US$48,297	US$77,999
Life expectancy (years at birth)	73.6	81.8	70.8	76.4

On the surface, Black Lives Matter in America and Black Lives Matter in Australia have converged. The shocking persistence of Aboriginal deaths in custody, the seemingly routine beatings and neglect of Indigenous prisoners in the country's jails—which we tend to know about only because of closed circuit TV recordings that come out when families of the victimised demand it—keep occurring.

As do the killings in encounters between Indigenous Australians and the police. In 2019, Kumanjayi Walker, a Warlpiri man, was shot three times by Constable Zachary Rolfe after resisting arrest and stabbing the constable with a pair of scissors in the remote community of Yuendumu in the Northern Territory. Rolfe was charged and acquitted of murder. A subsequent inquest was established to examine issues that might be pertinent to the killing.

In October 2022, Cassius Turvey, a fifteen-year-old Noongar-Yamatji boy, was ambushed and beaten with a metal pole when he was walking home from school near Perth. Turvey died from his wounds several days later. Turvey's thirteen-year-old companion was also beaten and his walking sticks were taken away by the assailants. Prime Minister Anthony Albanese was moved to say, 'This attack, that clearly is racially motivated, just breaks your heart. We are a better country than that, and my heart goes out to the family and the friends.'[13] Memorial and protest vigils were held across the country.

Since the Royal Commission into Aboriginal Deaths in Custody was completed and its report issued in June 1991, there have been over 500 Indigenous deaths in custody. The majority have been prison deaths, but in more recent times, most deaths have been the result of custody-related operations. In 2020–21, the death rate for Indigenous prisoners was 0.09 per 100 compared to a non-Indigenous rate of 0.18 per 100.[14] As of June 2018, Aboriginal and Torres Strait Islander Australians account for 2 per cent of the overall population, but 28 per cent of the prison population. Indigenous adults are fifteen times more likely to be imprisoned; and Aboriginal juveniles are twenty-six times more likely than non-Indigenous youth to be imprisoned.

In October 2022, ABC's *Four Corners* revealed that 'at least 315 First Nations women have either gone missing or been murdered or killed in suspicious circumstances since 2000'. In Australia, *Four Corners* reported, 'Australian Aboriginal women are among the most victimised groups in the world, murdered up to twelve times the national average.'[15]

The casual racism in some police departments is ugly. In October 2022, a whistleblower leaked to *Guardian Australia* audio tapes of officers in the Brisbane police watchhouse talking about Blacks in Australia and immigrants from Africa. 'There are fucking black fellas running around everywhere. I said to my cousins, "What the fuck?" They wait outside fucking supermarkets and they'll follow ya and they'll fucking try and rob ya and I'm thinking . . . just get 'em and beat the fuck out of them and bury them. Just bury them. Mate, no one would know.'[16]

Six years after *Four Corners*' shocking report on the Don Dale Youth Centre in the Northern Territory, which held children as young as ten years old, and placed children in solitary confinement, in November 2022 the program again exposed horrific conditions in youth detention centres. Children in detention were being brutalised by guards using methods of restraint that are illegal in many jurisdictions. One of them is the 'folding-up technique' that contorts and immobilises the victim's body. One child cries out, 'I can't breathe, I can't breathe motherf***ers.'[17]

Looking across the Pacific to the United States to absorb these terrible crimes and attitudes is like looking into a mirror.

The murder in Minneapolis in 2020 of George Floyd—who cried out twenty times that 'I can't breathe',[18] all captured on video that ricocheted around the world—sealed the prominence of the Black Lives Matter movement in the United States, years after so many similar horrific encounters faced by Blacks.

Before that, Trayvon Martin was killed in Florida by a white 'neighborhood watch' volunteer. In 2023, President Obama shared his thoughts: 'You know, when Trayvon Martin was first shot I said that this could have been my son. Another way of saying that is Trayvon Martin could have been me thirty-five years ago. And when you think about why, in the African American community at least, there's a lot of pain around what happened here, I think it's important to recognize that the African American community is looking at this issue through a set of experiences and a history that doesn't go away.

'There are very few African American men in this country who haven't had the experience of being followed when they were shopping in a department store. That includes me. There are very few African American men who haven't had the experience of walking across the street and hearing the locks click on the doors of cars. That happens to me—at least before I was a senator. There are very few African Americans who haven't had the experience of getting on an elevator and a woman clutching her purse nervously and holding her breath until she had a chance to get off. That happens often.'[19]

Trayvon's killer was acquitted of manslaughter.

In 2020 in Louisville, Kentucky, Breonna Taylor, an emergency medical technician, was shot to death when police, acting under a no-knock warrant for narcotics, broke into her apartment while Breonna and her partner were sleeping. Her boyfriend fired at the intruders with his weapon. The police fired dozens of bullets indiscriminately, killing Breonna. One officer who was criminally charged was acquitted. More than two years later, the Department of Justice filed civil rights charges against the officers involved in seeking the warrant that led to this killing. 'Breonna Taylor should still be alive,' Attorney-General Merrick Garland said.[20]

Also in 2020, a young Black man, Ahmaud Arbery, was jogging in a suburb of Atlanta, Georgia. Three white men hunted him down, cornered him and killed him. They were found guilty of murder and each was sentenced to life in prison. The three men were also convicted of committing a hate crime, the first-ever verdict of this kind in the state's history.

All these events received huge coverage in Australia. These terrible acts are the threads that tie Black Lives Matter and the search for justice together in both countries. The echo from America's injustices resonates deeply in Australia. Atrocities continue to be committed, and awareness of their occurrence is growing.

But beneath the surface of these parallel experiences by Black Australians and Americans are profoundly different historical contexts. First Nations peoples in Australia are living with the impact of invasion and forced dispossession of their land, and the tragedies that flow from it; to this day, it weighs on First Nations peoples and Australian society. African Americans are living with the legacy of slavery. The oppression that flows from the weight of history has a common character, but the original sins were different, with different consequences. And this informs how the echo chamber in Australia will absorb Trump's rhetoric, policies and actions on race.

In a discussion for this book, James Blackwell, a research fellow in indigenous diplomacies at the Australian National University, said, 'The race story in Australia is different to the race story in America.'

Both political cultures are vulnerable to Trump on race issues—but in significantly different ways. As Blackwell explains, 'Australians are not as conservative as the right is in the US. The country is more moderate. They do not like Trumpist behaviour, message and approach. Trump will not push the Australian right on race to the point where they mimic what Trump does. But Trump's attitudes towards minorities in the US will harden racial attitudes of the right here. It will help the right see a way to use Trump in the rhetoric and positioning on racial issues.'

Jeff McMullen, veteran journalist and advocate for Indigenous Australians, put it this way: 'What Trump elevated is—he takes the most dangerous words out of the closet. "These groups are taking away your rights." This is creeping into Australia.'

It can even creep into Parliament. In October 2018, just two months after Scott Morrison became prime minister, Pauline Hanson tabled a motion in the Senate proposing that the Senate recognise 'the deplorable rise of anti-white racism and attacks on Western civilisation' and that 'it is okay to be white'.[21] The resolution was defeated, but all the Coalition senators voted for it. 'The government condemns all forms of racism,' one Liberal senator said as she voted to support Hanson. It took a day of intense pressure, driven by anger across the country and international headlines of what had happened in the Senate, for Morrison to say that the votes of government senators were 'regrettable'. Attorney-General Christian Porter said there had been an 'administrative error' in his office that did not pick up the offensiveness of the Hanson language. Senators were given another vote the following day to go on record opposing Hanson. But the blind spot on race from the most senior ministers in the government was glaring—and it was not cured three years later in another Hanson episode on the Senate floor.

On the first day of the new Parliament in 2022, Pauline Hanson stormed out of the Senate chamber because she objected to the Acknowledgement of Country—an acknowledgement of Australia's First Nations peoples that is routine every day the Senate is in session. Hanson literally makes the Senate an echo chamber for Trumpist views.

The intersection of these forces in America—the expression and pursuit of racism in the political culture—is over voting rights.

As discussed, at the heart of the right to vote is the determination of who votes and who is able to vote. And the heart of who votes is racial identity.

In Australia, the heart of racial equity is over dispossession, and ensuring that First Nations peoples have a guaranteed place in Australia's democracy.

Sometimes, the most electrifying and inspiring documents in our histories are among the shortest. The Bill of Rights in the United States Constitution consists of 566 words. The Treaty of Waitangi in New Zealand is 578 words. The Uluru Statement from the Heart, adopted in 2017, is 444 words. It contains these:

> Our Aboriginal and Torres Strait Islander tribes were the first sovereign Nations of the Australian continent and its adjacent islands, and possessed it under our own laws and customs . . . This sovereignty is a spiritual notion: the ancestral tie between the land, or 'mother nature', and the Aboriginal and Torres Strait Islander peoples who were born therefrom, remain attached thereto, and must one day return thither to be united with our ancestors. This link is the basis of the ownership of the soil, or better, of sovereignty. It has never been ceded or extinguished, and co-exists with the sovereignty of the Crown. How could it be otherwise? . . .
>
> With substantive constitutional change and structural reform, we believe this ancient sovereignty can shine through as a fuller expression of Australia's nationhood. Proportionally, we are the most incarcerated people on the planet. We are not an innately criminal people. Our children are aliened from their families at unprecedented rates. This cannot be because we have no love for them. And our youth languish in detention in obscene numbers. They should be our hope for the future.

These dimensions of our crisis tell plainly the structural nature of our problem. This is the torment of our powerlessness. We seek constitutional reforms to empower our people and take a rightful place in our own country. When we have power over our destiny our children will flourish . . . We call for the establishment of a First Nations Voice enshrined in the Constitution . . . We seek a Makarrata Commission to supervise a process of agreement-making between governments and First Nations and truth-telling about our history. In 1967 we were counted, in 2017 we seek to be heard.[22]

The beauty of the Uluru statement is its simplicity in cutting to the heart of the issue: the dispossession of the land can only be redressed through securing equity in constitutional recognition.

But in the initial days and months after the proclamation of the Uluru statement, a cacophony of wilful misrepresentation of what Uluru was—and was not—unfolded with a vengeance. A vengeance driven by fear of Aboriginal aspiration. Malcolm Turnbull's cabinet rejected the statement shortly after it was issued. It was 'neither desirable nor capable of winning acceptance at referendum,' he said.[23] Attorney-General George Brandis and Minister for Indigenous Affairs Nigel Scullion jointly said that the Voice to Parliament 'would inevitably come to be seen as a third chamber of Parliament'.

This was not, and is not, true. But it was immensely destructive of prospects for the statement to move forwards promptly. Most of the country could not understand or properly absorb what Uluru was, and what it truly meant, when the statement emerged from the convention at Uluru in 2017. Given that lack of substantive knowledge on what Uluru was or said, when a prime minister declares in response that the statement was unworkable as a constitutional instrument, that it fundamentally altered the functioning of Parliament by creating a new chamber in addition to the House and Senate—a structure known and understood for over a century—that cut-through judgement will have an enormous impact. And it did.

A year later, Turnbull's successor, Prime Minister Scott Morrison, was equally emphatic that Uluru created a third chamber. Morrison said he didn't support a 'third chamber' of parliament. 'It really is. People can dress it up any way they like—but I think two chambers is enough. The implications of how this works, frankly, lead to those same conclusions and I share the view that I don't think that's a workable proposal.'[24]

These distortions, the twisting of the truth, the button-pushing of fear were so intense that it would take the 2022 election outcome—with the Labor leader, Anthony Albanese, taking every opportunity he had in the campaign to make the case of Uluru, and to say repeatedly that he was determined to see Uluru adopted and that the country has to travel this road together with the country's First Nations peoples—to change the polarity of the debate. This was reflected in the first words of Albanese's victory speech on election night, 21 May: 'I begin by acknowledging the traditional owners of the land on which we meet. I pay my respects to their elders past, present and emerging. And on behalf of the Australian Labor Party, I commit to the Uluru Statement from the Heart in full.'[25]

Indeed, five years after the Uluru Statement from the Heart was born, Malcolm Turnbull reversed his earlier judgement that the Voice would in effect create a 'third chamber' of Parliament. 'The voice will not be a third chamber of parliament in the way the Senate is the second chamber,' he wrote. 'But on matters relating to Indigenous Australians, it will be politically very challenging, although legally possible, to pass a law that the voice opposes especially when its members are united. The voice will become a very influential and politically powerful part of our democracy—that is the whole point of the exercise.'[26]

Mark Leibler, an eminent lawyer and advocate for social justice and reconciliation, who has laboured for decades with distinction to help effect reconciliation across Australia, wrote about the new consensus that was forming around Uluru: 'Active support for a yes vote is there for the asking from the business community, the trade union movement, professional bodies, welfare organisations, schools and universities ... Representatives of the Catholic, Uniting and Anglican churches, the Australian National Council of Imams and the Executive Council of Australian Jewry, together with Australian Sikhs, Buddhists and Hindus, gathered at Barangaroo to endorse the Uluru Statement from the Heart.'[27]

At the opening of the new Parliament after the federal election in 2022, Paul Girrawah House delivered the Welcome to Country. He placed the Uluru Statement at the forefront by going to the heart of the issues of recognition and equity. 'Evidence of our occupation, ownership and nationhood can be seen everywhere throughout our country. Our signature is in the land, not just in our DNA,' House said that day. 'We should reflect for a moment on the significance of this occasion by honouring the heroes among our First Peoples, who, over 234 years have maintained the integrity of our ancient connection to our lands against relentless forces to extinguish us by successive generations of colonisers.'[28]

Australia is immersed in, and haunted by, racism. But Australia does not have to be trapped on the course it chooses for the future because of a Trump return to the presidency. Jeff McMullen explains why: 'Australians should be concerned that "Trumpist" views on race may fan the flames of racial intolerance in Australia, rejecting the calls by First Peoples for a constitutionally guaranteed Voice to Parliament. Trump pointedly supports and defends Americans who openly attack those seeking their rights including African Americans and migrants from south of the US border. It is enlightening to consider that in the USA and Australia we have never truly reconciled those perceived as "whites" and "Blacks". Trump behaves as if the gulf is unbridgeable whereas Australia still has the potential to enter a season of truth-seeking, negotiation and careful collaboration that could build on the ancient and fundamental multicultural nature of Australia's diverse Indigenous nations.'

Prime Minister Albanese attempted to bring Australia together on the issue of the Voice to Parliament, not to counter Trump, but to transcend the Trumpism that exists in Australia that has frustrated First Nations' aspirations. His 2022 Garma address was emphatic:

The Uluru Statement is a hand outstretched, a moving show of faith in Australian decency and Australian fairness from people who have been given every reason to forsake their hope in both.

I am determined, as a Government, as a country, that we grasp that hand of healing, we repay that faith, we rise to the moment.

To work with you in lifting the words off the page and lifting the whole nation up:
- With a new spirit of partnership between government and First Nations people
- Through the work of Makarrata, treaty-making and truth-telling
- And by enshrining a Voice to Parliament, in the Constitution.

We approach these tasks and the work of constitutional change, with humility and with hope.

Humility: because over 200 years of broken promises and betrayals, failures and false starts demand nothing less.

Humility because—so many times—the gap between the words and deeds of governments has been as wide as this great continent.

But also hope.

Hope in your abilities as advocates and campaigners, as champions for this cause.

And hope because I believe the tide is running our way. I believe the momentum is with us, as never before.

I believe the country is ready for this reform.

I believe there is room in Australian hearts for the Statement from the Heart.[29]

Dr Chris Sarra, educator and Director-General, Department of Aboriginal and Torres Strait Islander Partnerships for the Queensland Government, commented, 'We have people here who are Trump-like—those types of characters are emboldened by a Trump in the world ... And Australia always falls in behind the US— is this an issue if Trump is in power expressing his view on race issues? Will it make erecting that firewall even harder?'

In his powerful Boyer Lectures in 2022, Noel Pearson was insistent and unequivocal: 'Let me point out what is incontrovertible: Australia doesn't make sense without recognition. Until the First Peoples are afforded our rightful place, we are a nation missing its most vital heart ... Constitutional recognition of Indigenous Australians is not a project of identity politics, it is Australia's longest standing and unresolved project for justice, unity and inclusion.'[30]

In the end, the political truism that referendums fail in Australia if they don't get bipartisan support was proven correct yet again.

Well-funded conservative lobby group Advance and Opposition Leader Peter Dutton harnessed Australian racism to devastating effect to ensure the failure of the Voice referendum in October 2023. Profound damage was done to the aspirations of First Nations people and their supporters, and it is unclear when the country may be able to return to the Uluru agenda. The failure of the Voice deeply damaged Albanese's political credibility, and empowered Peter Dutton and his supporters to continue on a Trumpist path.

17
Media
Will 'The Enemy of the People' Prevail?

By the time he ran for president in 2016, Trump was well known across the American media; not only in newspapers, and on TV and radio, but online as well. For three decades he had milked the tabloids in New York with his fear-mongering on criminal gangs and the tantalising tales of his affairs and marriages. (The *New York Post*'s cover, 'The Best Sex I've Ever Had', attributed to Marla Maples, is one for the record books.[1])

But it was Trump's run on NBC with *The Apprentice*, and its spin-offs, that occupied valuable prime-time real estate from 2004 to 2017. The reality TV show presented Trump as a very wealthy, authoritative, astute and commanding CEO, accountable to no one but himself. A man who knew how to assess people and wield executive power with abandon. Tens of millions of viewers were exposed to Trump and the virtues millions saw in him.

When Trump decided to pursue the presidency, he tapped into something deeper—the tie between popular culture, especially television, and the political culture—that he instinctively knew a lot about, and that he knew was under-appreciated at the time.

In September 2016, the *Washington Post* was told by Leonard Steinhorn, a professor at American University teaching a course on communications and the election: 'He [Trump] had a lifetime of experience with TV, and he understands the power of the medium in a way that many presidents have not. Donald Trump set out in this campaign to dominate the [TV] experience, to keep people glued in and to define the parameters of how we all experience this election.'[2]

To be sure, we see the real-world White House for what it is. But we are also seeing it through the lens of our entertainment culture. What does everyone say after they see a terrible, violent tragedy in real life, such as a terror attack, a building exploding, an aeroplane crash? 'It was just like a movie.' No, it was just like real life.

In addition to the TV series, Americans saw Trump through the lens of motion pictures where actors exhibit presidential virtues, save the country, and sometimes the planet: *The American President*, *Air Force One*, *Independence Day*, *Deep Impact*, *Primary Colors*, *Dave*, *In the Line of Fire* and *White House Down*. And TV series such as *The West Wing*, *Veep*, *Commander in Chief* and *Designated Survivor*.

The issue is not just that Trump's 2016 candidacy resembled a reality television show; it was something deeper, which even provoked President Obama to comment about the presidential election: 'This is a serious job. This is not entertainment, this is not a reality show. This is a contest for the presidency of the United States. What that means is every candidate, every nominee needs to be subject to . . . exacting standards of genuine scrutiny.'

One answer to the nagging question of Trump and why he got so far in 2016 is that America's entertainment culture, in the way it portrays the presidency, legitimised even a Donald Trump as a serious contender for the highest office in the land.

As Obama's former speechwriter Jon Favreau told the *New York Times* that September, before it was clear Hillary was failing to put Trump away and Trump was attaining critical mass to win: 'I worry that if those of us in politics and the media don't do a lot of soul-searching after this election, a slightly smarter Trump will succeed in the future. For some politicians and consultants, the takeaway from this election will be that they can get away with almost anything.'[3]

Favreau's future arrived on election night 2016. Trump's secret to success was not simply being identified with celebrity. Presidents have associated with Hollywood and entertainment since motion pictures were born. Kennedy hung out with Marilyn Monroe, Peter Lawford, Dean Martin and Sammy Davis Jr. Ronald Reagan, an actor himself, was close with Sinatra, Elizabeth Taylor, Jimmy Stewart and dozens of Hollywood moguls and powerbrokers. Bill Clinton with Streisand and Sheryl Crow. Obama with Beyoncé, Oprah, Stevie Wonder, Paul McCartney, Springsteen and so many more.

The real issue in 2016 was not presidential candidates and celebrity. The issue was not reality television. The issue was that both phenomena played a role in the public's awareness of Trump and how he projects himself in the media. From his first day as a candidate for president, Trump made it clear he would never back down to the media, never apologise for words he said, never concede he was wrong. Jared Kushner, Trump's son-in-law and senior adviser, relates in his memoir, *Breaking History*, that when Trump announced his campaign in 2015, there was a wall of hostile reaction to Trump's vicious characterisation of Mexican immigrants. 'They're bringing drugs, they're bringing crime.

They're rapists.' Ivanka Trump recommended to her father that he pull back on those words with an op-ed. Trump refused: 'I haven't said anything wrong, and the media knows that I haven't said anything wrong,' Kushner quotes Trump as saying. 'I don't plan to follow their rules, and they just want me to apologise for entering this race. There is no way I am doing that.'[4] Trump has been true to his word ever since.

Trump was determined to change the political culture further by changing how the public views the media, and especially the mainstream media elite that dominated political journalism from World War II through to the Obama presidency.

Margaret Sullivan, formerly a longstanding columnist on the media for the *Washington Post*, captured this succinctly: 'From the start of his presidential bid, Donald Trump took full advantage of the public's growing mistrust of the mainstream press. The journalists tirelessly chronicling the near-daily scandals erupting from his White House were "scum," he taunted. They were dishonest, he insisted. They were "the enemy of the people." His adviser Stephen K. Bannon memorably called the media "the opposition party." Plenty of Americans agreed: These days, even local TV reporters are likely to be blasted as "fake news" as they try to cover school board meetings.'[5]

Trump started using the term 'fake news' in the first few days of his presidency.[6] The term goes beyond denial; it is meant to discredit a source of news that contradicts or threatens the standing of a public official. Trump never has to lie to say that news being reported on him is untrue. He simply has to say it is 'fake' without engaging on any substance. Today, in Australia as well as in the United States, when a politician wants to dismiss any reporting he or she does not want to face, it is simply labelled 'fake news'—and no more credence needs to be given to it. The resort to employing this term, as veteran journalist and writer Michael Brissenden says, 'has given a licence to government and politicians not to be accountable to the media—"fake news" gives Trump and his politicians more flexibility on their accountability' because they deny journalists their legitimacy. Politicians now use 'fake news' when they don't want to rebut the truth about a story.

But it is Trump's use of the phrase 'enemy of the people' in targeting journalists that is especially dangerous and frightening. Stalin used the term against his enemies in the Soviet Union, and was responsible for executing a million of the Soviet Union's citizens, with up to 9 million more dying from forced relocation, starvation, imprisonment and other atrocities. After Stalin's death, Soviet leader Nikita Khrushchev gave a secret speech to the Communist Party in 1956 in which he demanded a reckoning with Stalin's legacy. 'Stalin originated the concept "enemy of the people",' Khrushchev said. 'This term automatically made it unnecessary that the ideological errors of a man be proven. It made possible the use of the cruellest repression, against anyone who in any way disagreed with Stalin, against those who were only suspected of hostile intent, against those who had bad reputations.'[7] By the end of his 2024 campaign, Trump even talked about reporters ('the fake news') being shot, a dangerous suggestion from a populist leader in a country awash with guns.[8]

What Trump was really doing was channelling his inner Richard Nixon. The Watergate tapes captured a 1972 conversation in the White House between Nixon, National Security Advisor Henry Kissinger and General Alexander Haig. 'Never forget,' Nixon said. 'The press is the enemy, the press is the enemy. The establishment is the enemy, the professors are the enemy, the professors are the enemy. Write that on a blackboard 100 times.'[9]

This is why being labelled 'the enemy of the people' is

exceptionally threatening for so many in the media in America (and many of those writing during Trump's presidency began their careers covering Nixon and his crimes).

Throughout his first presidency, at Trump rallies, Trump would wave his finger at the enclosed pen at the rear of the hall or stadium that held the press and their cameras, pointing them out to the crowd and decrying them for fake news and often calling them the 'enemy of the people'. Throughout his campaign and presidency, reporters were booed, shoved and assaulted by crowds egged on by Trump's abusive rhetoric.

In August 2022, Trump debuted his first serious television commercial to signal his 2024 presidential campaign and flag his issues. Highly produced, with rich cinematic quality, the video opens with black and white film of Trump decrying the state of America today as he sees it, and then blossoms into rich colour for his hopes for the future. A core message is his hatred for the media:

> We are a nation that no longer has a free and fair press. Fake news is about all you get. We are a nation where free speech is no longer allowed, where crime is rampant as never before. Where the economy has been collapsing. Where more people died of Covid in 2021 than died in 2020. We are a nation that in many ways has become a joke. It is time to start talking about greatness for our country again.[10]

Trump intends to dominate the media in the same way he intends to dominate the United States. And to dominate the media, he is impelled to be the great disruptor, the enemy of mainstream media—another dimension of the powerful political leader who can, to the delight of his base, kick over the tables of power in Washington and engineer an unprecedented way of ruling.

For Trump, this has meant aligning himself with the upstarts, the agitators, the new media enterprises that would break down the influence and market share of the legacy media behemoths with their liberal pedigrees. Trump's primary targets were the three major commercial television networks CBS, NBC and ABC, the leading newspapers such as the *New York Times* and the *Washington Post*, and the cable news operations run by the old guard including Time Warner (CNN) and Comcast (MSNBC). Trump would instead align himself with the radical media revolutionaries of the populist right, help build up their audiences and ensure that everyone immersed in Trump's politics had to pay attention to those outlets and platforms and what they were saying and doing 24/7. For Trump this meant Rupert Murdoch's Fox, Twitter and the far-right website Breitbart among others. And he did it very effectively.

While there is great irony that NBC made Trump a star with *The Apprentice*, it was Fox News, started by Rupert Murdoch and Roger Ailes, that was indispensable to the making of Donald Trump as a public, and ultimately a political, figure. Trump's biggest defenders and champions in the media have been on Fox: Sean Hannity, Tucker Carlson, Laura Ingraham, Jeanine Pirro, Steve Doocy—even though many of them were quite scorching of Trump when his campaign got underway in 2015. Roger Ailes told Steve Bannon on the Sunday before the election that Trump was doomed to lose: 'It will be over by 8 o'clock.'[11]

By the 2020 election, Fox had killer ratings from Trump, with 4.9 million viewers in prime time, way ahead of CNN and MSNBC. Tucker Carlson commanded 3 million viewers a night, the biggest audience on cable.

Nicole Hemmer, an American historian at Vanderbilt University, is unequivocal: 'The relationship between Donald Trump and

Fox News is distinctly different, bringing the channel closer to state television than anything the United States has ever known.'[12]

The intersection between the network and the Trump White House was deep. Bill Shine, a former co-president of Fox News, became White House director of communications and deputy chief of staff to President Trump. When he was president, Trump worked to ensure his regulatory agencies took positions favourable to Murdoch, including trying to block AT&T's merger with Time Warner, which owned CNN.

The interplay between Fox News on-air hosts and Trump's decision-making as president was hidden in plain sight. Trump would be swayed on signing or vetoing major spending bills based on what he saw on the Fox News screen. When Fox commentators decried the absence of money to build Trump's promised wall with Mexico in the overall government spending bill that would keep the government funded and operating, Trump vetoed the bill and government services ground to a halt, triggering the largest government shutdown in US history. Trump paid a heavy political price in public opinion for that debacle.

Murdoch's business genius and why it was valuable to Trump was captured in an interview with Reed Hundt, chairman of the Federal Communications Commission, by Jane Mayer in 2019. Hundt recalled Murdoch discussing (in the 1990s) his thinking on what would become the Fox network: 'What he was really saying was that he was going after a working-class audience. He was going to carve out a base—what would become the Trump base. This person's made a huge mark in two other countries, and he had entered our country and was saying, "I'm going to break up the three-party oligopoly that has governed the most important medium of communication for politics and policy in this country since the Second World War."'

Blair Levin, who worked with Hundt at the FCC, added, 'Fox's great insight wasn't necessarily that there was a great desire for a conservative point of view. The genius was seeing that there's an attraction to fear-based, anger-based politics that has to do with class and race.'

Hundt completed the circle: 'Murdoch didn't invent Trump, but he invented the audience. Murdoch was going to make a Trump exist. Then Trump comes along, sees all these people, and says, "I'll be the ringmaster in your circus!"'[13]

And he was—until election night in 2020 and its aftermath. Murdoch was reportedly close with Trump throughout the presidency, but was especially close with Jared Kushner. Trump pressed Kushner to call Murdoch on election night 2020 to try to get Fox to reverse its call that Arizona had gone for Biden—a very serious blow at a crucial moment to Trump's chances of emerging victorious on election night itself. 'There is nothing I can do,' Murdoch said.[14]

The Murdochs changed their strategic settings and began, in mid-2022, to turn the page on Trump. Trump went for over one hundred days in 2022 without an interview on Fox. Fox was no longer broadcasting his campaign rallies live. Ron DeSantis, governor of Florida and a leading contender for the Republican presidential nomination for 2024, was interviewed on Fox hundreds of times in 2021 and 2022. The formal trigger of change for the Murdoch newspapers was the blockbuster hearings by the House Select Committee on the January 6 attack on the Capitol, which presented a devastating picture—painted by Trump's Republican staff, Republican politicians in Congress and Republican political supporters—of a president who refused to stop the insurrection as it was unfolding. A president who did not lift a finger to stop a mortal threat that day to his vice president.

Two Murdoch mastheads issued their severe decree. On 22 July 2022, the *Wall Street Journal* editorialised: 'The brute facts remain:

Mr. Trump took an oath to defend the Constitution, and he had a duty as Commander in Chief to protect the Capitol from a mob attacking it in his name. He refused. He didn't call the military to send help. He didn't call Mr. Pence to check on the safety of his loyal VP. Instead he fed the mob's anger and let the riot play out. Character is revealed in a crisis, and Mr. Pence passed his Jan. 6 trial. Mr. Trump utterly failed his.'[15]

On the same day, the *New York Post* also editorialised: 'As his followers stormed the Capitol, calling for his vice president to be hanged, President Donald Trump sat in his private dining room, watching TV, doing nothing. His only focus was to find any means—damn the consequences—to block the peaceful transfer of power. It's up to the Justice Department to decide if this is a crime. But as a matter of principle, as a matter of *character*, Trump has proven himself unworthy to be this country's chief executive again.'[16]

A romance of convenience and necessity ended at that moment. This was re-affirmed when Trump-endorsed candidates for the 2022 midterms led the Republicans to a disastrous result. Murdoch's *Wall Street Journal* rejected what it called the 'Republican Party's biggest loser': 'Since his unlikely victory in 2016 against the widely disliked Hillary Clinton, Mr. Trump has a perfect record of electoral defeat. The GOP was pounded in the 2018 midterms owing to his low approval rating. Mr. Trump himself lost in 2020. He then sabotaged Georgia's 2021 runoffs by blaming party leaders for not somehow overturning his defeat ... Now Mr. Trump has botched the 2022 elections, and it could hand Democrats the Senate for two more years. Mr. Trump had policy successes as President, including tax cuts and deregulation, but he has led Republicans into one political fiasco after another.

'"We're going to win so much," Mr. Trump once said, "that

you're going to get sick and tired of winning." Maybe by now Republicans are sick and tired of losing.'[17]

The story with Twitter is not dissimilar: a platform that benefited enormously from Trump but ultimately was forced to turn on him.

Has there ever been a more powerful voice on Twitter than Trump's?[18] In his first thirty-three months in office, he posted 11,000 tweets. Ultimately, he would tweet more than 20,000 times in his 1461 days in office. By Inauguration day in January 2017, he had 20 million followers. He left office—and the platform when Twitter banned Trump for the January 6 attack on the Capitol— with 88.9 million users.

It was quite a ride.

Trump conducted everything by tweet: hirings, firings, foreign policy, declassifying top secret information and photos, sending demarches to Congress, instructing the bureaucracy, making and breaking trade deals with China and others, regularly influencing the stock market to goose it higher, targeting businesses who opposed what he wanted, providing a running commentary on all things Hollywood and TV, persecuting his enemies and praising himself. His go-to favourite tweet was to attack his enemies and opponents, often with denigrating nicknames such as 'Little Rocket Man' (North Korea's Kim), 'Pocahontas' (Senator Elizabeth Warren), 'The Failing New York Times', 'Crazy Nancy' (House Speaker Nancy Pelosi) and 'Crying Chuck' (Chuck Schumer, the Democratic Leader in the Senate).

Trump turned to Twitter when he was under pressure, especially during the investigations by FBI Director Robert Mueller for Trump's alleged ties to Russia, and when the House Committees were seeking his impeachment. Trump excoriated the media he did not like, particularly CNN, the *New York Times*, and media owners such as Amazon's Jeff Bezos, who publishes the *Washington Post*. He is not shy about attacking minorities and immigrants when he can associate them with crimes, as well as women Members of Congress of colour, whose families came to America (they should 'go back' where they came from).

He fired his chief of staff, his national security adviser, his secretary of state and acting secretary of homeland affairs, among others, by tweet. The 2020 election was not the first presidential election Trump attacked for being 'rigged': he used Twitter to make the case that the 2016 election was rife with fraud—even though he won.

There is a degree of irony that Trump used a Big Tech platform to attack Big Tech for being hostile to conservatives.

> Google search results for 'Trump News' shows only the viewing/reporting of Fake News Media. In other words, they have it RIGGED, for me & others, so that almost all stories & news is BAD. Fake CNN is prominent. Republican/Conservative & Fair Media is shut out. Illegal? 96% results on 'Trump News' are from National Left-Wing Media, very dangerous. Google & others are suppressing voices of Conservatives and hiding information and news that is good. They are controlling what we can & cannot see. This is a very serious situation—will be addressed![19]

Trump was true to his word but was unsuccessful in getting Congress to change the law and make Big Tech responsible for what is posted by others on their platforms.

Trump could be viciously personal and mean. When MSNBC's morning TV hosts Mika Brzezinski and Joe Scarborough became huge Trump critics, Trump went into the gutter. ('Low I.Q.

Crazy Mika' had been 'bleeding badly from a face-lift' at a party at Mar-a-Lago.[20]) In a 2015 presidential debate, after Fox News' Megyn Kelly asked Trump a tough question about his views and treatment of women (she asked Trump about his calling women 'fat pigs, dogs, slobs, and disgusting animals'), Trump said on CNN, 'You could see there was blood coming out of her eyes. Blood coming out of her wherever.'[21] He never apologised to either woman.

A *New York Times* study found that 65 per cent of Trump tweets made news stories. Trump was the largest driver of misinformation on Covid. He was also the largest driver of false and misleading information on elections in the United States and how they are conducted.

The great virtue of Twitter for Trump was that he could use it anytime, anywhere, to speak directly to his supporters. It was an unparalleled channel of Trump Unplugged allowing him to reach those loyal to him—and everyone else who was paying attention—with what he felt, what he wanted, who he excoriated for opposing him and how unfairly he was being treated.

The loss of his audience on Big Tech platforms since the January 6 attack—Trump was also banned from Facebook, Instagram and YouTube—resulted in a decline of Trump mentions on social media through mid-2022, with some surveys indicating a fall off of up to 90 per cent.[22]

But this did not hurt Trump's overall approval rating among all voters, which held steady at 40 per cent or so—although he remained underwater with 55 per cent disapproval. Among Republicans in mid-2022, after the FBI raids on his home in Florida, Trump's approval rating was close to 60 per cent—with a similar margin of Republicans saying they would vote for him again for president in 2024.[23]

When his Twitter megaphone was taken away, Trump's voice was diminished. But his MAGA base still received his messages, and they remained loyal. Some followed him to his new personal platform Truth Social, but he never gathered the massive following there that he had on Twitter. Eventually the new owner of Twitter (rebadged as X), Elon Musk, invited Trump to return in August 2023.

Australia continued to hear from him, even out of power. Most mornings, the lead international news story is from the United States. And the leading story out of the United States is often about Donald Trump. Trump news and views enter the Australian media echo chamber.

While Trump's resumption of the presidency means a return to the noise of the statements he will make every day, Australia most decidedly is not the United States in the structure of its media industry and the Trump tidal wave of news cannot have the same effect here.

In one sense, Australia is an easy target for Trump. It has one of the most concentrated media markets in the world for an advanced democracy. That concentration is driven by News Corporation, now in the hands of Rupert Murdoch's son Lachlan, and the outlets he controls in Australia. As documented by the Senate Environment and Communications References Committee 2021 report on 'Media Diversity in Australia': 'News Corporation . . . controls about two-thirds of metropolitan daily newspaper circulation, including monopolies in Brisbane, Adelaide, Hobart and Darwin; regional daily monopolies in a range of cities including Cairns and Townsville; substantial chains of suburban and rural newspapers; [and] the only subscription television news service, Sky News—which also operates as a free-to-air channel in regional areas.'[24]

Former Prime Minister Kevin Rudd testified before the committee that News Corp's dominance 'cripples the conversation' on major issues, from climate to China. Former Prime Minister Malcolm Turnbull testified: '. . . We also see the impact of the way in which News Corp has evolved from being a traditional news organisation, or journalistic organisation, to one that is essentially like a political party but it's a party with only one member. You see the way in which it is used in an aggressive, partisan way to drive particular agendas, whether it is fermenting antagonism and animosity towards Muslims . . . [or] whether it is the campaign against effective action on climate change, which has been where Murdoch is the principal amplifier and promoter of that in the English speaking world, at a huge cost to all of us, and to the planet—the whole world.'

Rod Tiffen, Emeritus Professor in Government and International Relations at the University of Sydney, told the committee: 'The Foxification of News has manifested itself in several ways—a stable of columnists whose market appeal is their stridency, and whose main mission is to grab attention and to reinforce prejudices. It is also evident in its news priorities, such as its double standards in stories about the right and left in Australian politics. It is especially apparent in the way they report on global warming, a determined lack of coverage of scientific reports, including one a couple of months ago on damage to the Great Barrier Reef.'

The committee cited these and other stakeholder views as expressing a concern that, 'The concentration and polarisation of news content has had a "corrosive" effect on politics, and reduced the trust that the general public had towards government.'

The University of Melbourne's Centre for Advancing Journalism told the Senate Committee: 'Murdoch's Sky News subscription television service in Australia requires a licence to operate. [As of] early December 2020 this channel was engaged in outright lying about the outcome of the 2020 US presidential election. Two of its presenters, Rowan Dean and Alan Jones, continued to propagate the lie that the election was rigged or stolen, the same lies as those being inflicted on the American people through Murdoch's Fox News. There are no constraints on this crude abuse of media power or dissemination of disinformation.'[24]

Murdoch-owned Sky News Australia has poor ratings for free-to-air TV relative to the ABC and the three other commercial television networks[25] (none of which are owned by Murdoch), but it has grown a substantial international subscriber base on YouTube. It does not set the agenda here as Fox does in America. But the audience reach of News Corp, through its newspapers, radio and Sky News, is significant enough to create a major presence for Trumpian news and views.

There are also new entrants in Australia's media markets that dilute Murdoch's dominance. *Guardian Australia* and the *Saturday Paper* have significant circulations in print and online, and expand the contours of debate with their strong, progressive editorial style. Seven West Media's recently launched digital newspaper *The Nightly* has a growing readership. The *New York Times* and the *Washington Post* have both opened bureaus in Sydney, and even though their local online audiences are modest, the impact of Australian news reaching the political class in Washington and across the United States means that the 'embarrassments' of news events that reflect badly on the country—such as the treatment of women and First Australians, environmental threats and national security failures such as with the Solomon Islands—get prime time attention in the United States.

Nevertheless, 'People in Australia are listening to Trumpist media,' says Michael Brissenden, who was the ABC's Washington correspondent for several years, and who has written extensively on the United States. Indeed, through Murdoch and News Corp, Trump had a platform in Australia. 'This does embolden many Australians but it does not have the same political impact as in the US,' Brissenden continues. 'It does drive the political narrative, and it deepens divisions in our society. It hardens the National Party and conservatives in the Liberal Party on issues like climate and immigration. So views on issues like that are angrier, louder.'

Trump and Trumpism will also continue to heavily use the social media platforms in Australia. Even if Trump remains barred from Facebook and chooses to remain off Twitter, his allies are not. The misinformation and disinformation propagated in America will be fully utilised here.

In an interview for this book, a deeply experienced expert in digital platforms and social media issues outlined the impact across the social media landscape in Australia: 'Trump's is a singular voice. And not just Trump—he also has acolytes. They amplify the misinformation and the haters. He recognises the power of propaganda—and his chosen acolytes do the same.

'The truth matters—and we're experiencing a desensitisation to accuracy and lies. We have no effective way to counteract that. We are assaulted on a daily basis.

'What Trump intends—and is able to do—is chip away at peoples' belief in democracy and its institutions. It is designed to undermine and tear at the fabric of democracy.

'The Big Tech platforms have not looked at Jan 6 and then made changes to do things differently. We need government agencies to work together on these issues here.

'To be sure, the issues here are not of the same degree as in the US. Online safety has been bipartisan here. But Trump will trigger rising tensions online.'

Australia's government agencies need to understand the digital hurricane hitting these shores, and sharpen the tools to deal with it.

There is a deeper, darker dimension to this, which Australian writer and *Guardian* columnist Van Badham explored—and exposed—in *QAnon and On*, her masterful, thorough and forensic dissection of QAnon, the American political conspiracy movement. As Badham has documented, 'QAnon is an American invention but it has become a global plague.'[26] In Australia, QAnon leached into the mainstream. United Australia Party's Senator Ralph Babet and One Nation politicians spruik QAnon style rhetoric. Prime Minister Scott Morrison did not condemn Trump's role in the January 6 insurrection—an omission that was seen by QAnon believers as filial support for the movement. During the Covid pandemic, Australia had one of the highest social media penetration rates— per capita access to social media platforms—globally. The Institute for Strategic Dialogue reported that after the United States, Britain and Canada, Australia was the fourth-largest producer of QAnon content worldwide. Australia created more QAnon content than Russia.

In the runup to 2024, just as Trump refused to break his ties with white nationalists and anti-Semites, he deepened his ties to QAnon. 'I don't know much about the movement, other than I understand they like me very much,' Trump said in 2020.[27] But as he prepared to enter the 2024 presidential race, Trump took to publishing QAnon posts and wearing the Q pin embroidered with the words 'The Storm is Coming'—which meant that Trump would be restored to power and his enemies would be executed. Trump has posted messages portraying himself as a martyr fighting the Deep State.

The Trump–QAnon cult alliance reaches into Australia's cyber atmosphere as well.

Dr Kristy Campion, a leading Australian expert in terrorism and right-wing extremism, has written extensively on the fertile environment for these movements and the threat they pose. The 2019 Christchurch massacre, carried out by an Australian, was the tip of this iceberg. She writes: 'There were—and are—individuals and groups in the Australian community who harbour the desire to threaten, harm or kill those who do not conform to their exclusionary ideals. Second, they were—and still are—capable of doing so. In the three years since Christchurch, the threat has not diminished—but has instead endured.'[28]

Campion says it is essential, if Australia is to effectively take on these white supremacist extremists, to establish 'a transparent national database that captures the diverse array of hate crime, politically motivated violence and terrorism, and other politically motivated incidences associated with the extreme Right. Through such a database, we could better understand the ongoing development of the threat, its geographic spread, activities, resources, and transnational links.'

Based on how elections have played out in Australia since Trump lost in 2020, the scope and depth of these threats, as disturbing as they are, appear to be in check. Until something happens.

The strongest counterbalance to extremism in Australia's media is the ABC. At A$1.1 billion per year annually, it is well-funded (although its journalists and ABC's most fervent supporters will never concede that). Total US public television and radio revenues are approximately US$4 billion per year. On a per-capita basis, the ABC is funded at A$40 per person, and US public television and radio at US$12.50 per person. The ABC's programming depth on television, radio and online far exceeds what is available through the United States' Public Broadcasting Service (PBS) and National Public Radio (NPR) and their local stations, which have nothing comparable in the digital television capacity of the ABC and the multiple radio networks on both AM and FM. Relative to what public broadcasting can deliver to the American people, the ABC is a heavyweight in the media landscape in Australia.

Trump gets plenty of attention in Australia from the mainstream media, the right- and left-wing media and all stripes of social media. Experienced journalist Mark Kenny now at the Australian National University says, 'The existence of hyper partisan media has a huge enabling effect that benefits Trump. Trump needs the revving up of the base and the ridicule directed at the opposition—and hyper partisan media enables that. This means you can tough out just about any crisis. The foghorns will vindicate almost any behaviour and de-legitimise against whom it is targeted. At some point, the breach of proper standards will not be sufficiently condemned. Everything—no matter what is committed—becomes contestable.'

Such as the legitimacy of an assault on the Capitol. Such as whether Joe Biden won the 2020 election.

But, so far, those poisons have not seriously corrupted debate on such issues in Australia.

The leadership of the ABC is fully cognisant of the threat, and of their responsibility to the Australian people. In her Andrew Olle lecture in 2022, ABC chair Ita Buttrose said, 'Australians will only rely upon the mainstream media as part of our civic and democratic life'—and make no mistake, the ABC is absolutely core to the mainstream media in Australia—'if they can trust we are able to expose the spin and the lies and misinformation, and deliver the facts and the truth. All the facts. All the truth. With fragile press freedom, democracy is at risk. Without a free press, democracy dies.'[29]

Through much of the decade of the last Coalition Government, there was great tension between the ABC and the government, with budget cuts imposed by Tony Abbott, Malcolm Turnbull and Scott Morrison. Then newly-elected ALP Prime Minister Albanese, speaking on the ABC's ninetieth birthday, showed he understands the threats posed by anti-democratic sentiments that ricochet through the political culture, and what needs to be done to insulate against them:

> Confidence in our democratic system is underpinned by strong public organisations contributing accurate information and well-informed, carefully reasoned analysis. That has to be delivered in an atmosphere of independence, without any form of intimidation—no matter how subtly applied. And one of those organizations has to be the ABC.
>
> Democracy is not something we can afford to take for granted. As we look around the world, we see democracy under sustained attack—either through direct assault or a more insidious erosion. A strong ABC is an insurance policy against the misinformation and disinformation chipping away at what we hold dear . . .
>
> A government that chooses to attack the public broadcaster does so motivated by either ideology or fear—or a toxic cocktail between the two. No government should fear the ABC—unless it fears the truth . . .
>
> The ABC must always be a public broadcaster, never a state broadcaster.

Albanese established five-year funding terms for the ABC—a very advanced funding cycle designed to ensure continuity and stability for the ABC—with a boost to funding levels, and pledged to explore other options that will deliver a higher degree of financial stability in order 'to safeguard against political interference'.[30]

It may well be needed for the balance of this decade.

18
Is Trump an '-ism'?

Is Trump an '-ism?' Is Donald J. Trump truly comparable to some of the enduring personality -isms: Leninism, Stalinism, Reaganism? There are not many -isms in American political history. Not the two greatest American presidents—Washington, Lincoln—have been deemed worth of an -ism. Not Kennedy, and his New Frontier. Not Harry S. Truman, and his Fair Deal. Not Lyndon B. Johnson, and his Great Society. Not Richard Nixon, even with his historic conduct of foreign policy, especially the opening to China. (But his name is used often as a term of the darkest, likely criminal political arts: 'Nixonian'.) Not even Franklin D. Roosevelt, whose New Deal forged a paradigm of American government and social policy for three generations, became an -ism.

One -ism in American history is named for a senator: Joseph McCarthy of Wisconsin. McCarthyism was born in the senator's 'red scare' hunt for Communist subversives within the State Department and other government agencies, over time extending to Hollywood and other sectors of American life. McCarthy generated an enormous base of support, and was so feared by his colleagues within the Republican Party that not even President Eisenhower could bring himself to publicly break with McCarthy. McCarthyism had an offshoot in Australia, in the Petrov affair, when a Soviet diplomat and his wife sought asylum in Australia.

'Reaganism' has emerged as a concise but comprehensive world view of what government should be and stand for: individual liberty, smaller government, lower taxes, less regulation, less welfare, and immigration to build the country. On foreign policy, it requires an assertive and muscular US military, with a presence around the world to defend freedom, build alliances, stare down totalitarianism and terrorism, and promote a world order that celebrates those values.

Reagan was wildly popular in the Republican Party, enjoying two terms and leaving his mark on the orientation of government to the American people. His aggressive posture of defence spending is credited with helping to bring on the fall of the Berlin Wall and dismantlement of the Soviet Union. But he became a true -ism when the most successful Democrat after him, Bill Clinton, could declare before Congress in his 1996 State of the Union address—a year in which Clinton himself was seeking re-election, making it imperative that he struck a winning note with his speech that night outlining his goals and vision—that 'The era of big government is over.'[1] Clinton immediately cautioned, 'But we cannot go back to the time when our citizens were left to fend for themselves. Instead, we must go forward as one America, one nation working together to meet the challenges we face together. Self-reliance and teamwork are not opposing virtues; we must have both.' What Clinton was doing was calling an end to the era of Roosevelt's New Deal, which Reagan had supplanted. There is no doubt that Reagan, still alive at that time, enjoyed that moment immensely.

For now, Trump leaves no written text of ideology. No Little Red Book. No memoirs yet, just a picture book, *Our Journey Together*, of his time in the White House.[2] All we know of 'Trumpism' is what comes out of his mouth, and what he posted on Twitter and, after being evicted from that platform, on Truth Social. So all we have from Trump is dicta.

Trump's speeches, bearing, posturing and demands have five core '-ism' themes: *populism, nationalism, protectionism, nativism and unilateralism.* If there is a Trumpism, those ideological drivers capture it. America First at home and abroad, bring manufacturing jobs to the heartland, go to war on trade with countries who take advantage of America economically; attack the establishment, the Deep State, and woke intellectual and cultural elites; ban Muslim immigration, build the wall with Mexico, and deport undocumented migrants; weaken the United Nations and NATO, dial down US support for South Korea; exit the World Health Organization, the Paris climate agreement and the Iran nuclear deal.

Reaganism endured for decades before Trump broke his mould. And there is no doubt that Reagan would have really disliked Trump and seen him as crushing Reagan's vision within the Republican Party. Stuart Spencer, one of Reagan's closest and most trusted advisers, said in 2021, 'He would be sick. Not just the issues out there, but the personal things [Trump] has done. The way he treated women. All those people he robbed of money.[3] He couldn't fathom that stuff. [Trump's] behavior would have upset him the most.'[4] Another of Reagan's senior staff said that the former president would have supported a primary challenge against Trump in 2020.

In American party politics, there is no fixed ideology that anchors the party for years, or decades. It is so unlike Australia's Labor Party or Menzies' vision for the Liberal Party. In American politics, what the party is, and what it stands for, depends on the views of the presidential nominee in any given election year. The candidate writes the platform, and uses it to campaign on and guide at least the beginning of their presidency. Trump has dominated the Republican Party so that its entire platform for the 2020 election was a one-page document that simply said: We are for whatever Trump is for.

> *RESOLVED*, That the Republican Party has and will continue to enthusiastically support the President's America-first agenda;
>
> *RESOLVED*, That the 2020 Republican National Convention will adjourn without adopting a new platform until the 2024 Republican National Convention.[5]

The 2024 Republican party's platform was in the full spirit of Make America Great Again. Specifically:

1. SEAL THE BORDER, AND STOP THE MIGRANT INVASION
2. CARRY OUT THE LARGEST DEPORTATION OPERATION IN AMERICAN HISTORY
3. END INFLATION, AND MAKE AMERICA AFFORDABLE AGAIN
4. MAKE AMERICA THE DOMINANT ENERGY PRODUCER IN THE WORLD, BY FAR!
5. STOP OUTSOURCING, AND TURN THE UNITED STATES INTO A MANUFACTURING SUPERPOWER
6. LARGE TAX CUTS FOR WORKERS, AND NO TAX ON TIPS!
7. DEFEND OUR CONSTITUTION, OUR BILL OF RIGHTS, AND OUR FUNDAMENTAL FREEDOMS,

INCLUDING FREEDOM OF SPEECH, FREEDOM OF RELIGION, AND THE RIGHT TO KEEP AND BEAR ARMS
8. PREVENT WORLD WAR THREE, RESTORE PEACE IN EUROPE AND IN THE MIDDLE EAST, AND BUILD A GREAT IRON DOME MISSILE DEFENSE SHIELD OVER OUR ENTIRE COUNTRY—ALL MADE IN AMERICA
9. END THE WEAPONIZATION OF GOVERNMENT AGAINST THE AMERICAN PEOPLE
10. STOP THE MIGRANT CRIME EPIDEMIC, DEMOLISH THE FOREIGN DRUG CARTELS, CRUSH GANG VIOLENCE, AND LOCK UP VIOLENT OFFENDERS
11. REBUILD OUR CITIES, INCLUDING WASHINGTON DC, MAKING THEM SAFE, CLEAN, AND BEAUTIFUL AGAIN
12. STRENGTHEN AND MODERNIZE OUR MILITARY, MAKING IT, WITHOUT QUESTION, THE STRONGEST AND MOST POWERFUL IN THE WORLD
13. KEEP THE U.S. DOLLAR AS THE WORLD'S RESERVE CURRENCY
14. FIGHT FOR AND PROTECT SOCIAL SECURITY AND MEDICARE WITH NO CUTS, INCLUDING NO CHANGES TO THE RETIREMENT AGE
15. CANCEL THE ELECTRIC VEHICLE MANDATE AND CUT COSTLY AND BURDENSOME REGULATIONS
16. CUT FEDERAL FUNDING FOR ANY SCHOOL PUSHING CRITICAL RACE THEORY, RADICAL GENDER IDEOLOGY, AND OTHER INAPPROPRIATE RACIAL, SEXUAL, OR POLITICAL CONTENT ON OUR CHILDREN

17. KEEP MEN OUT OF WOMEN'S SPORTS
18. DEPORT PRO-HAMAS RADICALS AND MAKE OUR COLLEGE CAMPUSES SAFE AND PATRIOTIC AGAIN
19. SECURE OUR ELECTIONS, INCLUDING SAME DAY VOTING, VOTER IDENTIFICATION, PAPER BALLOTS, AND PROOF OF CITIZENSHIP
20. UNITE OUR COUNTRY BY BRINGING IT TO NEW AND RECORD LEVELS OF SUCCESS IN THE HOUSE AND SENATE

As Trump continued his hold on the Republican party even while out of office, increasingly candidates needed to be Trumpists. All of Trump's opponents in the 2024 Republican primaries voiced support for this platform.

Trump chose J.D. Vance, his strongest acolyte in the Senate, to be his vice president. Trump had no interest in uniting more traditional conservatives like Nikki Haley. He wanted to double down on everything he stood for so that his values dominate the Republican party for at least the next generation.

19
Trump 2024
We Know What We're Getting This Time

It was so different from seven years earlier, when Trump glided down the escalators in Trump Tower in New York City, his wife Melania at his side, a crowd augmented by actors paid to be there and to look enthusiastic.

Trump's words then are best remembered for his bedrock anti-immigration theme. 'When Mexico sends its people, they're not sending their best. They're not sending you. They're not sending you. They're sending people that have lots of problems, and they're bringing those problems with us. They're bringing drugs. They're bringing crime. They're rapists. And some, I assume, are good people.'[1]

Building the wall to keep out immigrants from Mexico was the centrepiece. 'I would build a great wall, and nobody builds walls better than me, believe me, and I'll build them very inexpensively. I will build a great, great wall on our southern border. And I will have Mexico pay for that wall.'

But Trump went much deeper. He decried America's standing in the world . . .

'Our country is in serious trouble. We don't have victories anymore. We used to have victories, but we don't have them. When was the last time anybody saw us beating, let's say, China in a trade deal? They kill us. I beat China all the time. All the time.'

And he said that America had become terribly weak . . . 'Our enemies are getting stronger and stronger by the way, and we as a country are getting weaker. Even our nuclear arsenal doesn't work. And that the election of a great and strong leader was needed then more than ever . . . Now, our country needs—our country needs a truly great leader, and we need a truly great leader now. We need a leader that wrote *The Art of the Deal*.

'We need a leader that can bring back our jobs, can bring back our manufacturing, can bring back our military, can take care of our vets. Our vets have been abandoned.'

And the country also needed a cheerleader. 'We need somebody that can take the brand of the United States and make it great again. It's not great again. We need—we need somebody—we need somebody that literally will take this country and make it great again. We can do that.'

Trump outlined his support for gun rights, building infrastructure, winning new trade deals, finding generals who will 'take that military and really make it work', getting rid of the Iran nuclear deal, reducing the debt, and taking care of veterans. His verdict was harsh and searing: 'Sadly, the American dream is dead. But if I get elected president I will bring it back bigger and better and stronger than ever before, and we will make America great again.'

In 2022, Trump's words in announcing his renewed quest for the presidency were a distillation of his 2016 vintage of America First with all the same elements—immigration, energy, crime, Washington's corruption—underscored by Trump's four years in the presidency, and his building of the 'greatest economy in the history of the world'. But his message was darker, and more apocalyptic.

> ... Now, we are a nation in decline. We are a failing nation. For millions of Americans, the past two years under Joe Biden have been a time of pain, hardship, anxiety and despair ...
>
> Joe Biden has intentionally surrendered our energy independence. There is no longer even a thought of dominance and we are now begging for energy help from foreign nations, many of whom find us detestable ...
>
> Our southern border has been erased and our country is being invaded by millions and millions of unknown people, many of whom are entering for a very bad and sinister reason, and you know what that reason is ...
>
> The blood-soaked streets of our once great cities are cesspools of violent crimes which are being watched all over the world as leadership of other countries explain that this is what America and democracy is really all about. How sad. The United States has been embarrassed, humiliated, and weakened for all to see.
>
> The decline of America is being forced upon us by Biden and the radical left lunatics running our government right into the ground. This decline is not a fate we must accept. When given the choice, boldly, clearly and directly, I believe the American people will overwhelmingly reject the left's platform of national ruin and they will embrace our platform of national greatness and glory to America, glory.
>
> But just as I promised in 2016, I am your voice. I am your voice. The Washington establishment wants to silence us, but we will not let them do that.[2]

Less than a month later, Trump erupted again on how the 2020 election was stolen, and how it had to be rerun and overturned. Notwithstanding that he took an oath of office to 'preserve, protect and defend the Constitution of the United States', Trump insisted that 'with the revelation of MASSIVE & WIDESPREAD FRAUD & DECEPTION in working closely with Big Tech Companies, the DNC, & the Democrat Party, do you throw the Presidential Election Results of 2020 OUT and declare the RIGHTFUL WINNER, or do you have a NEW ELECTION? A Massive Fraud of this type and magnitude allows for the termination of all rules, regulations, and articles, even those found in the Constitution. Our great "Founders" did not want, and would not condone, False & Fraudulent Elections!'[3]

We see more clearly now Trump's insipid, ranting nonsense. We did not fully understand, in 2016, what was coming; how much Trump would captivate the media and amass enough support to slice the Republican Party into sushi-like slivers that he could devour one by one.

Even though the Republicans went backwards at the November 2022 midterm elections, Trump calculated that he could do it again.

How? Why? To Carlos Lozada, former book editor for the *Washington Post* and currently a columnist for the *New York Times*, Trump's words from a September 2022 campaign rally in Ohio were revealing. Trump, he wrote, 'reiterated his commitment to the lie. "I ran twice. I won twice," he declared. For a moment, when bragging about how many more votes he won in 2020 than in 2016, the veil almost fell. "We got 12 million more and we lost," Trump said, before recovering. "We didn't lose," he continued. "We lost in their imagination." It was a classic Trumpian projection: The lie is true and the truth is fake.'[4]

Trump wins with 'truth' that is fake. He wanted to do it again. Trump thought he could win again because he believes he never loses. Much to the surprise of many political observers, he turned out to be right, with the Republican sweep of presidency, the Senate and the House in November 2024.

Other autocrats in formerly democratic countries are aligned with Trump and his bedrock nativist themes. We know that Trump's entire political being inspired Hungary's leader, Viktor Orbán, to proclaim at the CPAC, the Conservative Political Action Conference, a major force in Republican politics, just months before Trump announced his campaign: 'We have to be brave enough to address even the most sensitive questions: migration, gender, and the clash of civilisations. Don't worry: a Christian politician cannot be racist. So we should never hesitate to heavily challenge our opponents on these issues.'[5]

Trump met with Orbán after the speech. 'We discussed many interesting topics—few people know as much about what is going on in the world today,' Trump reported.[6] Orbán articulates what Trump excels at: white Christian nationalism, which is the most powerful identity politics in play today.

We know what is coming in Trump's second term, because Trump made it clear when he endorsed *Hillbilly Elegy* author and populist J.D. Vance in the Senate race for Ohio. Vance is 'strong on the Border, tough on Crime, understands how to use Taxes and Tariffs to hold China accountable, will fight to break up Big Tech, and has been a warrior on the Rigged and Stolen Presidential Election'. To which Vance replied: 'He was an incredible fighter for hard working Americans in the White House. He will be again, and I'll fight for the America First Agenda in the Senate.'[7] Vance won his election in Ohio, and at the behest of billionaire tech investor Peter Thiel, Trump anointed Vance his vice-presidential running mate.

We know Trump will always be obsessed with his enemies because he is never free from his enemies, and he insists to his base that they are under attack too. At that same event in Ohio: 'The people behind these savage witch hunts have no shame, no morals, no conscience, and absolutely no respect for the citizens of our country. Our cruel and vindictive political class is not just coming after me. They're coming after you, through me.'[8]

After twice leading the impeachment of President Trump, House Speaker Nancy Pelosi knows what Trump will do. 'One of the things that the previous occasional occupant of the White House would do was ... undermine the credibility of the press, undermine the credibility of institutions of government. It was very clever. It was very authoritarian, autocratic.'[9]

Trump is a double-barrelled authoritarian: he uses autocratic means to undercut democratic ends, and he uses the tools of democracy to bury democracy. The press understands this even better than Pelosi. Jonathan Karl of the ABC, and a former president of the White House Correspondents' Association, asks, 'How do you cover a candidate who is effectively anti-democratic? How do you cover a candidate who is running both against whoever the Democratic candidate is but also running against the very democratic system that makes all of this possible?'[10]

The overall political morbidity that emanates from Trump is frightening. It is not hidden. It is plain as day even to someone half a world away from Mar-a-Lago who simply follows the news at a Perth radio station. In a 2022 on-air interview with me, ABC Radio Perth *Drive* host Geoff Hutchison said at the outset, 'Any of us who have long admired the United States or visited the United States ... will acknowledge it is getting harder and harder to recognise today's version of it. Its much-vaunted democratic ideals seem fractured and corrupted. Its political and public debate is partisan and angry. Cracks in the United States seem to be widening, and dangerously so. Is the United States flirting with fascism?'

A major study by the *New York Times* of the threats that afflict American democracy focuses on several evident factors that are consistent with fascism: a growing conviction inside the Republican Party not to accept the results of any election that a Republican loses—that any win by any Democrat is presumptively illegitimate; and a growing power to set government policy—such as abortion—that is not supported by mainstream public opinion.

In the 2022 midterm elections, it seemed as though these dark forces were pushed back. The Republican candidate for governor in Wisconsin said that, if elected, the Republican Party 'will never lose another election in the state'.[11] He lost 51 per cent to 48 per cent. The Republican nominee for secretary of state in Arizona—a state that Biden carried in 2020, much to Trump's continuing rage—is an election denier. He was defeated 53 per cent to 47 per cent in 2022.

Such resistance occurs within a growing dominance of institutions—such as the electoral system itself—that are undemocratic, and that enable presidential candidates who lose the popular vote to become president. Two of the last five presidential elections—2000, with Bush and Gore, and 2016, with Trump and Hillary Clinton—have been so decided.

We know, from the superb reporting of Australian-born journalist Jonathan Swan for Axios (he is now with the *New York Times*), what is coming from Trump. 'Former President Trump's top allies are preparing to radically reshape the federal government if he is re-elected, purging potentially thousands of civil servants and filling career posts with loyalists to him and his America First ideology. The impact could go well beyond typical conservative targets such as the Environmental Protection Agency and the Internal Revenue Service. Trump allies are working on plans that would potentially strip layers at the Justice Department—including the FBI, and reaching into national security, intelligence, the State Department and the Pentagon.'[12]

As the 2024 election campaign progressed, these plans acquired a name and a blueprint: Project 2025. The 2025 Presidential Transition Project was a political initiative published by the American conservative think tank the Heritage Foundation in 2023. J.D. Vance has close connections to Project 2025 and wrote a foreword to a book by Kevin Roberts explaining the policy blueprint, *Dawn's Early Light: Taking Back Washington to Save America*.

Immediately upon his election, Trump started to nominate super loyalists for key roles throughout the government and the bureaucracy. A panel of experts has warned that he will govern without the formal advice and consent of the Senate for approval of presidential appointments.[13] Trump will use the military within the borders of the United States to promote his political power. These excesses will have calamitous effects—including higher prospects for civil war.

Trump will ensure that only loyalists hold the top policy jobs, control the military, and dominate the law enforcement and security agencies, and he will refuse to submit to court orders. There will be no more Trump obstructionists inside the White House, at the Department of Justice, or among the Joint Chiefs of Staff. He made sure he wouldn't have another vice president like Mike Pence, who broke with him—who Trump believes betrayed him.

Peter Baker, co-author of *The Divider*, the first definitive history of the Trump presidency, knows what is coming. 'The point is that, in a second term, a lot of things that held him back, that constrained him in the first term wouldn't be there. He wouldn't hire John Kelly. He'd only hire a Mark Meadows. He wouldn't be captive to the people who are slow-walking him or resisting him.

He would be much more aggressive and certain of his own ability. And he wouldn't have a re-election to worry about, to think about. He could do what he thought was the right thing or the thing he wanted to do most, without being constrained.'[14]

A Trump return to power is not just a comeback—it's retribution. A Trump campaign adviser told Bob Woodward and Robert Costa for their book, *Peril*, on Trump's final year in office, 'I don't think he sees it as a comeback. He sees it as vengeance.'[15]

Former Australian Prime Minister John Howard has reached a grave judgement about what lies ahead. 'Trump's atrocious behaviour after losing the 2020 election . . . has surely made him unfit to return to the White House. It was dumbfounding to me, and I am sure to many others, that the party should have chosen him as its candidate in 2016. He lacked public grace, a huge deficiency for an American president, who is both head of state and head of government. He had little respect for his party organisation, despite the support it gave him during the presidential campaign. I am not any fan of Trump. His behaviour since losing the election has been disgraceful and I just hope, pray, that the Republicans will find somebody else to get behind because he has behaved terribly.'[16]

What does all this angst mean in real terms? Emeritus Professor of political science Clement Macintyre of the University of Adelaide told me, 'The election of Trump would reinforce—give legitimacy—to the tactics and behaviour of the last several years: lies, arrogance, trashing of norms of governance and institutions.

'Trump's election would mean that he was rewarded for that. It gives a licence to established players to have less regard for our constitution and institutional arrangements, that is, some parties could push the boundaries on some practices like pork barrelling. In a world where Trump is the norm, government becomes emboldened to stare down objections to Trumpian practices.

Trump normalises bad behaviour. The processes of integrity can get undermined. If Trump is rewarded in 2024 by being elected again after all he did—anything is possible.'

Kim Hoggard, who worked in both the administrations of presidents Ronald Reagan and George H.W. Bush, knows what this means for Australia: 'The US may remain an economic and military superpower, but it will no longer be a superpower in terms of democracy. It has lost its status as a role model and symbol of a well-functioning democracy.'

IV
THE DEMOCRACY GUARDRAILS IN AUSTRALIA

20
The Safeguards of Australia's Democracy

Can Australia's democracy withstand the assault Trump will make on America's democracy?

Yes.

Australia has in place guardrails, both in law and long-established norms and traditions of governance, that will ensure the continuance of democracy in Australia as we know it today.

Compulsory voting

In 2016, Trump came from outside the political system to conquer the Republican Party, and then ride his nomination to the presidency. In office, Trump exercised raw power to overturn long-established rules and norms of governance, corrupting the political system and how it operated. In seeking re-election in 2020, Trump sought to overturn the orderly counting and certification of the vote itself. Trump sought the imposition of new rules and restrictions that would limit the ability of millions of citizens to vote, and which would also affect how their votes are counted and certified.

The core of these efforts by Trump and the Republicans in power in Washington, and especially in state legislatures across the country, was to pass new laws targeting the voting rights of people of colour. These measures no doubt contributed to his successful re-election in 2024.

In their book, *100% Democracy*, E.J. Dionne Jr and Miles Rapoport highlight Australia as the gold standard for securing democracy through universal voting. 'Twenty-six countries around the globe, in multiple continents, with functioning democracies, actually require participation in elections. And one of them—Australia—has been doing it for one hundred years! The chapter in this book on Australia is an eye-opening tour. Australia adopted universal voting nationwide in 1924, after several Australian states began to use it in the years before that. Turnouts in Australia have been off the [U.S.] charts, consistently around 90 per cent of registered voters, and well over 80 per cent of eligible voters, year in and year out. The requirement to vote in Australia has been accompanied by a system that makes registration and voting itself easily accessible. And Australia has succeeded in creating a culture of celebration around elections as full-community affairs.'[1]

Australia's model works for three fundamental reasons. First, Australians do not have to vote. Their responsibility—legal and civic—is to simply show up every polling day and say, 'Present!' Dionne Jr and Rapoport are insistent that what Australia requires of its citizens is not 'compulsory voting' but 'civic duty voting'. In Australia, we are not forced to vote for anyone. We can deface the ballot in any imaginable manner. But we, as citizens, have to participate because of our obligations as members of Australian society.

Second, if you have to vote, you will inevitably come to the conclusion, through some process of osmosis that can span talks with family and friends to what you hear at the pub or from parents at children's football games to online sources from Google to TikTok, that you need to tune in at least a few days before election day to help you decide how you will cast your ballot. This means that the degree of political literacy among the population in Australia is higher than in the United States.

Third, universal voting promotes cleaner—and much less expensive—elections. In the United States, most of the money raised and expended (over US$14 billion in the 2020 presidential and congressional elections[2]) is spent by candidates to get their voters just to turn out to vote on election day. In Australia, all the voters are already out—especially on a Saturday. In the United States, Tuesday voting in elections is a huge burden for citizens to fulfil. This means that Australian elections are structurally cheaper and freer of special-interest manipulation. A 2022 paper by the United States Studies Centre documented that, in per capita campaign expenditure adjusted for the exchange rate, in its 2019 federal election Australia spent US$11.84 per voter, while in 2020 the United States spent US$27.41 per voter.[3]

Former Prime Minister Julia Gillard is a fierce advocate for compulsory voting. In a 2013 newspaper interview, she said, 'Compulsory voting is a precious, precious thing and it makes our politics, the politics of the mainstream.'[4] Gillard told a California audience in 2018: 'Australian politics at election time is about capturing the political centre. Small, highly motivated minority groups can campaign but ... they cannot disproportionately dictate the result. That mattered for gun control. Even though gun supporters mobilised at huge rallies, politicians knew that the vast majority of voters wanted change and it was delivered. Now I don't expect compulsory voting to suddenly emerge here in America but I think the moral of the story is big problems can be addressed if the large mass of the community get involved and are all in.'[5]

Mandatory voting means the outside radical fringe will stay outside.

In terms of winning and taking power, it is impossible in Australia for an outsider like Trump to vault the system and become prime minister. Neither Clive Palmer nor Pauline Hanson can, or will, do it. They may win seats in Parliament, but they will never get a majority vote in Parliament to serve as prime minister. Trump can never be replicated in Australia.

While many observers and analysts believe there is a creeping Americanisation of Australia's political system because of the 'presidential style' of federal election campaigns here, with an increasing focus on the personality, media presence, and degree of physical presentation and style of the prime minister and opposition leader, the fact is that there is not a direct popular vote for the prime minister. Every vote cast is for deciding who will be the local member of parliament. The vote-winner is a member of a political party, and when a party wins a majority of seats in the House of Representatives, it forms government. A majority of that party's caucus then determines who is their leader, and consequently prime minister. The two major parties generated six prime ministers over five elections between 2010 and 2022. The parties—not the prime ministers—are dominant.

The integral partner to mandatory voting in Australia is the Australian Electoral Commission.

The heart of the Trump challenge to democratic norms in an election is his challenge to the legitimacy of the outcome of any election involving him. It has been part of his modus operandi from the very beginning. Even when Ted Cruz won the Iowa caucus Republican presidential primary in 2016—a key early victory that gave Cruz momentum—Trump claimed the vote was rigged. 'Ted Cruz didn't win Iowa, he illegally stole it,' Trump wrote in a tweet. 'That is why all of the polls were so wrong any [*sic*] why he got far more votes than anticipated. Bad!'[6] A month before the 2016 election with Hillary Clinton, Trump tweeted, 'Of course there is large scale voter fraud happening on and before election day. Why do Republican leaders deny what is going on? So naive!' and 'The election is absolutely being rigged by the dishonest and distorted media pushing Crooked Hillary—but also at many polling places—SAD ... Election is being rigged by the media, in a coordinated effort with the Clinton campaign, by putting stories that never happened into news!'[7] Months before the 2020 election, Trump decried mail-in voting and said the November election should be postponed because it would be rigged. 'You never even know who won the election.'[8]

The existence and vigilance of the Australian Electoral Commission ensures that any similar words from a candidate in an election in Australia would have absolutely no standing or legitimacy. The maintenance of the electoral rolls; the processes for counting, reporting and certifying the votes; the deliberate care taken to ensure that every vote is counted through the cooperative work of the 'scrutineers' from all the parties who monitor the vote counting—these all work to emphasise the integrity of Australia's elections.

Every voter, wherever they are across Australia on election day, is treated equally in terms of access to the polls and how their votes are counted. This is a profound contrast with the United States, where each state and territory establishes their own rules for how voting is conducted, where the polls are located, how and when early voting is possible, whether there is online voting and drop boxes for early voting ballots to be returned. There are more than fifty presidential elections in the United States every four years: each state counts its own votes by its own rules. In Australia there is one election, with one standard of voting, every three years. It is impossible to rig or manipulate the votes and how they are counted in any separate state in an attempt to influence the outcome.

A second AEC electoral guardrail is in how electorates are drawn. In the United States, the drawing of electoral lines for each congressional district is undertaken every ten years after the national census. Each state controls the drawing of its congressional seats, with the mapping done by the state legislature in a bill that must be approved by the governor. Where one party controls the legislature and the governor's mansion, the entire process is a political monstrosity. In recent years, some states, such as California and Colorado, have adopted independent commissions that have the power to draw congressional districts, significantly reducing political imbalances.

In Australia, the AEC conducts the redistribution of parliamentary electorates in a transparent and objective process, with all parties acceding to the agency's expertise. There is no gerrymandering.

Taken together, these AEC practices ensure that there is no discrimination against voters as they exercise their right to vote, nor is there any inherent political imbalance that would skew a party's representation in any state's delegation to Parliament.

These are precisely the pressure points that political parties in America seek to exploit. The Democrats are no less culpable than Republicans in seeking to gerrymander seats in the House of Representatives. But there is no fiercer actor than Trump in seeking to use these political processes to suppress the votes of people of colour in order to ensure maximum Republican power in elections.

It will take an enormous amount of work to make the voting system in the United States less susceptible to political interference. In 2022, a majority of Republican nominees for Congress were deniers of the outcome of the 2020 election. In 2022, there were many Republican candidates for state offices that administer elections. The Republican running for secretary of state in Nevada said while campaigning: 'When my coalition of secretary of state candidates around the country get elected, we're gonna fix the whole country and President Trump is going to be President again in 2024.'[9] He was defeated. But he and his like-minded election deniers will be back. Officials who count the votes are under increasing harassment and threats of violence. Training and security for poll workers are not uniform. Finally, however, as one of its last acts before adjourning in December 2022, Congress passed important corrective reforms to the certification by Congress of the presidential election. This new law prevents any effort to make the final official counting of the Electoral College by the House and Senate nothing more than a ceremonial act.[10]

Westminster rules

Australia operates under the Westminster system. As outlined in a paper from the Australian Parliament:

> Parliamentary government means that the Executive Government comes from within the Parliament; responsible government means that the Executive Government is responsible to the Parliament. This is the central feature of a Westminster-style government following the United Kingdom model—in contrast to other systems of government where the Executive is quite separate and not directly answerable to the Legislature—for example, in the United States of America.[11]

The ramifications of this model are profound.

The hostile takeover by Trump of the Republican Party cannot be effected here. The cabinet in Australia cannot be controlled by political outsiders. In the United States, members of the cabinet are nominated by the president and confirmed by the Senate. The president can nominate any person—but not a sitting Member of Congress—to the cabinet. Presidents use these appointments so that the cabinet reflects the president's policies and political objectives. The persons confirmed by the Senate run their assigned government department—from the Pentagon to health and everything in between.

In Australia, the cabinet is drawn from the parliamentary party that has a majority in the House of Representatives. This has two crucial effects on the degree of politicisation of the government. Members of Parliament are not business executives, labour leaders or community activists. They may have come from those backgrounds, but they are in Parliament because they have won an election after being pre-selected for their seats. They are absolutely political but how they vote as a member of the House or Senate is governed by their party's policies on issues—that outweighs any personal, outside interest.

Members of Parliament are bound in their cabinet responsibilities by the conventions, norms and traditions that have evolved over the more than 120 years since Federation. As the Parliament House paper states, 'Some of the central features of Australia's system of government (described as parliamentary, or responsible government) are not set down in the Constitution but are based on custom and convention.' These informal rules govern their conduct and accountability to Parliament. To be sure, there are politics galore on every issue, and standards are stretched in every government, but ministers in Canberra are under a tighter leash than cabinet officers in Washington. Ministers serve Parliament and the cabinet serves the president. In Australia, the executive is within Parliament. In the United States, the executive is a *separate and co-equal* branch of the government and is far less directly accountable to Congress than cabinet in Australia is to Parliament.

This means that the chances for monstrous abuses of power by an Australian prime minister and cabinet in Canberra are less likely than those by a president and cabinet in Washington.

We learned in the Trump presidency how precious and essential to the functioning of a democracy norms of governance are. It is a lesson absorbed because he stomped on them so viciously.

The former president's biggest atrocities included, among a long list of abuses of power, unprecedented violations of decades of practice and traditions. Trump attempted to reverse the results of the 2020 presidential election. He used his office to enrich his businesses by channelling government activities to his hotels and resorts. Trump withheld foreign aid from Ukraine unless that government helped to find dirt on his political opponent, Joe Biden. Trump attempted to obstruct and subvert investigations of his activities by Congress and the Department of Justice. Two of his raw exercises of power—pressuring Ukraine to serve his personal political interests, and his attempts to overturn the results of the 2020 presidential election—resulted in his impeachment.

After the 2022 election in Australia, it was revealed that Prime Minister Scott Morrison had secretly assumed several ministerial posts. This act was executed between the prime minister and the governor-general with no public record or announcement. In most instances, not even the affected ministers knew their departments were being jointly governed by the prime minister.

This violation of norms of governance by Morrison was truly shocking. As Prime Minister Anthony Albanese said, we are absorbing 'an unprecedented trashing of democracy'.[12] It triggered a firestorm of concern about an abuse of power.

What made this sting so sharply was that, when revealed, what could be seen was a prime minister wielding power of Trumpian proportions. Throughout his presidency, Trump wanted immense, direct control of the executive branch. Instead of making appointments to the cabinet and having them duly confirmed to their office by the Senate as prescribed in the Constitution, Trump resorted more and more to making the highest officials in key agencies 'acting' secretaries or directors. This meant he could put his people in power without the ratification of Congress. Even his chief-of-staff in the White House was 'acting'.

The biggest difference between Trump and Morrison's actions is that Trump acted in broad daylight to control his government through these 'acting' officials, knowing that Congress could not force him to do otherwise. The Morrison assertion of control was done in secret. This secrecy is what made the breach of Westminster so offensive.

The revelations about Morrison's secret ministries provoked special inquiries into exactly what transpired and when these secret deeds were done. The real-world effect of these arrangements may have been relatively incidental compared with the breadth of Trump's abuses, but the corrosion of democratic values and the bruising of Australia's democratic institutions and processes were exceptionally high. Indeed, this was the conclusion of Virginia Bell AC, a former High Court justice, who conducted an official review of these matters for the government. 'The lack of disclosure of the appointments to the public was apt to undermine public confidence in government,' she concluded. 'Once the appointments became known, the secrecy with which they had been surrounded was corrosive of trust in government.'[13]

The House of Representatives voted overwhelmingly, 86–50, to censure Scott Morrison for his actions on 30 November 2022. The censure resolution stated that Morrison has 'fundamentally undermined the principles of responsible government' and that this worked to 'undermine public confidence in government' and was 'corrosive of trust in government'.[14] It was the first time a former prime minister had been censured.

The Liberals—defeated in the May 2022 federal election and with a disgraced former PM now on the back bench—voted 'No' on the motion to censure. Only one Liberal member crossed the floor to vote with Labor and independent members.

Like the Republican Party in the aftermath of the attack on the Capitol, the Liberals dug in behind a failed leader, even if it meant they run a significant risk of continued defeat at the polls.

By censuring Morrison, the Parliament in Australia did what Congress failed to do. Although Trump was impeached for his role in the January 6 insurrection and attack on the Capitol, he was not convicted in the Senate.

Australia's political system was able to respond in a way the United States did not. As a returned president, we can expect Trump to continue to repeat all of his abuses in office, with minimal accountability. No future prime minister here could repeat Morrison's appropriation of several cabinet portfolios without full accountability.

The High Court and the Reserve Bank

For nearly the past four decades in Washington, the president's nomination of a Supreme Court justice has provoked a firestorm of controversy as the nominee is examined, pursuant to the Constitution, to the 'advice and consent' of the Senate. In 1987, President Ronald Reagan nominated Robert Bork, a federal judge, to the court.[15] An extreme conservative, Bork had an extensive track record of opinions that were hostile to mainstream settled law regarding civil rights, voting rights, privacy rights and gender equality. Senator Ted Kennedy, a member of the judiciary committee conducting the confirmation process, said, 'Robert Bork's America is a land in which women would be forced into back-alley abortions, blacks would sit at segregated lunch counters, rogue police could break down citizens' doors in midnight raids, and schoolchildren could not be taught about evolution.'[16] The Bork confirmation hearings were exceptionally heated and resulted in his confirmation being rejected by the Senate, 58 to 42—the largest such margin against a nominee to the court. The entire process became a verb: 'to bork' a nominee, or to say that a nominee was 'borked'. Clarence Thomas, nominated to the court by President George H.W. Bush in 1991, was 'borked' over allegations of sexual harassment of one of his associates, Anita Hill. Thomas barely survived his confirmation hearing and was approved by the Senate 52 to 48.

This heavy politicisation of the process of nominating and confirming justices to the Supreme Court came to be centred on one of the issues that dominated the Bork confirmation hearings—abortion—and how any nominee would affect the balance of the court on the question of whether to continue or limit or repeal the constitutional right of a woman to abortion services. Every nominee since Bork has been assessed with this question uppermost.

This fight over the ideological balance of the Supreme Court reached its climax during the Trump presidency. In his 2016 campaign, Trump was unequivocal: he opposed abortion rights and pledged to appoint Supreme Court justices who would repeal *Roe v Wade*.

Currently, except for two women Republican senators, there are no Republican senators who support the abortion rights established by *Roe*. In February 2016, Justice Antonin Scalia, a staunch 'pro-life' conservative, died. Senator Mitch McConnell, the Republican leader in the Senate, declared that he would prevent any nominee by President Obama from being confirmed to fill the court vacancy until after that year's presidential election—and then only if the Democrat won the presidency. The successful delay in preventing Obama from filling the Scalia seat meant that with Trump's 2016 victory the Republican Senate could approve a Trump nominee (in this instance Neil Gorsuch) who was strongly anti-abortion. McConnell used the same tactics to ram two more Trump nominees, Brett Kavanaugh and Amy Coney Barrett, through the Senate on the eve, respectively, of the 2018 midterm and 2020 presidential elections.[17] This savage exercise of raw political and parliamentary power was unprecedented. These three new members of the court ensured there was a solid majority to overturn the *Roe* precedent on abortion.

This history shows that the process of appointing and confirming judges—not only to the Supreme Court, but to all federal courts—has been infected by the hyper-partisan politics that has engulfed America's political culture. Presidential campaigns become referenda on the political composition of the courts and how they will rule on the culture war issues—abortion, immigration, gun control, voting rights—that are in play in any given year.

This is decidedly not the case in Australia. There is no Senate confirmation of justices appointed to the High Court. The prime minister does not make High Court appointments. It is the attorney-general who exercises this responsibility. There are no public hearings in Parliament of a judge being considered for the High Court. There is instead a norm, a tradition, a process of consultation undertaken by the attorney-general before such a momentous decision.

For appointments to the High Court, the attorney-general conducts wide consultations to fill a vacancy. As Nicola Roxon, a former attorney-general in Prime Minister Gillard's cabinet, explained to me, 'There are very wide consultations, designed to ensure we have visibility on who would be good. There is very little ideological vetting. The process identifies the expertise needed.' And importantly: 'Expertise is valued more than politics.'

This is a completely different culture than exists in Washington. George Brandis, attorney-general in the cabinets of Tony Abbott and Malcolm Turnbull, was equally clear. 'Unlike the US, we haven't politicised appointments to our highest court—and that's something to celebrate ... Unlike the United States, the appointment of members of Australia's highest court is seldom controversial. That is because, with rare exceptions, attorneys-general from both sides of politics recommend eminent men and women in whom the public can have complete confidence.

'The most important consultations are with the senior members of the judiciary ... While there are many eminent judges and QCs, like any profession, the best of the best are generally acknowledged as such by their peers.'[18]

These conventions were also followed by the current attorney-general, Mark Dreyfus. His first appointment of Judge Jayne Jagot to the High Court received universal acclaim—and her ascension gave the High Court a majority of women justices, a first.

An additional factor that depoliticises the High Court in Australia is that its justices face mandatory retirement at age seventy. Nicola Roxon observes, 'The age retirement limit is so important. The randomness flowing from the age limit is a protection. It removes tying appointments to who will be in government.'

This culture of wide-ranging consultation reduces the intensity of a political calculus on making appointments to such an important institution.

21
Futureproofing Australia's Democracy

Trump's assault on the media in America will, as discussed earlier, continue to spawn more extremist media expression in Australia. The shape of the alignment between Trump and Fox will continue to influence Murdoch outlets here, from Sky News to the tabloids. Whatever the style of extremism of Trump, it will find hospitable Australian media petri dishes to grow in.

While there is always high drama within the ABC, there should be no doubt, while the Albanese Government is in place, that the national broadcaster's mission is intact and that the ABC has sufficient funding to fulfil it. However, the Coalition has a history of attacking the ABC, and a Coalition Government is likely to cut ABC funding again.

The political environment that enabled the Murdoch media to have such a powerful presence during its endless attacks on the Rudd and Gillard Governments, especially on climate and immigration issues, collapsed in the 2022 election. It was eclipsed, at least for a time, by the will of the people.

To be sure, as Stephanie Brookes, a lecturer in journalism at Monash University, wrote to me, 'News Corp does have a significant impact on how certain conversations play out ... I think the impact here is on the daily, mundane shaping of political and public discourse over time, especially in media markets where few alternatives exist. Australia's media policy, and the whittling away of some elements of cross-media ownership and other restrictions over time, have made this kind of concentration possible.'

As author and feminist Anne Summers has observed, there is a disconnect at present between the dominance of the Murdoch media in key markets and its current degree of influence. 'The Murdoch media has been demonstrated to have failed to have influenced the 2022 federal election and in Queensland and South Australian state elections (one newspaper towns) and is likely to fail in Victoria and New South Wales.' Richard Whittington, a former adviser to Prime Minister Gough Whitlam, agrees: 'Murdoch here is not as powerful as his enemies portray him to be.'

But News Limited, like Arnold Schwarzenegger's character in *The Terminator*, tells us, 'I'll be back.'

And it will. The success of the Murdoch business model depends on a comeback.

Kim Hoggard, who served in the Reagan White House and George H.W. Bush State Department, wrote to me: 'The ABC is a source of trusted information. It serves as a central source of information in times of crisis or importance. This helps to educate and inform all Australians. This is critical to a well-functioning democracy. In America, too many sources of disinformation are rampant. It is more important than ever to have the national broadcaster available at all levels, including regional and rural, and to have funding restored in order to continue to provide quality information. The threat to Australia's democracy is not Trump but the disinformation, the conspiracy theories, the internet rabbit holes.'

The best protection for a strong Australian media to stand up to the pollution of Australia's political culture that will occur from Trumpist media in the United States—its Gatling gun of lies, misinformation and inflammatory and hurtful commentary and coverage—is to ensure the ABC is strong.

This will keep the ABC fully capable of fulfilling its charter 'to provide within Australia innovative and comprehensive broadcasting services of a high standard as part of the Australian broadcasting system consisting of national, commercial and community sectors and, without limiting the generality of the foregoing, to provide: (i) broadcasting programs that contribute to a sense of national identity and inform and entertain, and reflect the cultural diversity of, the Australian community; and (ii) broadcasting programs of an educational nature.'[1]

This is the best shield against what will be felt here from Trump's war on mainstream media and his political enemies in the United States.

Combating extremism in social media platforms

A real and growing threat to the nature of political discourse is the propagation of misinformation, deliberate distortion and lies about issues and news coverage in political campaigns. One state, South Australia, and one territory, the ACT, have 'truth in advertising' laws, which make it against the law for false or misleading political advertisements to be published. These empower the state election commission to order political parties to desist from advertisements that make false claims in election campaigns. The ACT banned false political advertising in 2020. In South Australia, Labor, running to unseat the government in 2020, was ordered to remove ads that contained false characterisation of the ambulance service in the state.

Other states are looking at similar laws—and expanding them to capture more false political content on social media platforms. In Victoria, a parliamentary committee has recommended effective measures to remove political content that is out of bounds. 'The Committee has also recommended some changes to legislation to specify platforms' responsibility to remove illegal content once they have been alerted to it,'[2] and recommendations to work with tech platforms to augment their policing of misinformation and disinformation.

These measures are very popular in the community. To be certain, these restrictions in the ACT and South Australia would not last a New York minute in the United States with its First Amendment right to free speech. But they are an effective tool in Australia in curbing a toxic political atmosphere. A federal law patterned on the South Australia and ACT models should be adopted by Parliament.

Measured but powerful suasion can also get the job done. The Australian Electoral Commission has a robust social media presence across platforms. When it sees material that threatens the integrity of the election process, the AEC goes on social media to urge content changes, often with humour. The AEC monitors prominent social media threads that may be promoting incorrect information, and will jump in to correct it and discourage further lines and memes. Much more often than not, it works. And it makes Australia's democracy safer.

In the 2022 federal election, the AEC put in place a systematic campaign to educate voters to help them better understand disinformation and misinformation in political advertising. The result: an election unthreatened by any semblance of denial of the result.

Campaign finance reform

There is a further guardrail for Australia's political structure that should be erected to better protect the integrity of political campaigns here: full and prompt disclosure of political contributions.

In the United States, the financing of political campaigns is out of control. There is virtually unlimited money available to candidates and groups supporting candidates, with minimal disclosure of sources and expenditures. The Supreme Court has ruled in the *Citizens United* case in 2010 that corporations have the same free speech rights under the First Amendment as individuals have—and therefore their 'political speech' cannot be limited by capping their campaign contributions. At the same time, the amount of political contributions by an individual to a candidate is limited. This results in huge distortions throughout the political system, with corruption by special interests rife. As the Brennan Center for Justice argues: 'Today, thanks to Supreme Court decisions like *Citizens United*, big money dominates U.S. political campaigns to a degree not seen in decades. Super PACs ['political action committees', which are established to finance political campaigns] allow billionaires to pour unlimited amounts into campaigns, drowning out the voices of ordinary Americans. Dark money groups mask the identities of their donors, preventing voters from knowing who's trying to influence them. And races for a congressional seat regularly attract tens of millions in spending. It's no wonder that most people believe the super-wealthy have much more influence than the rest of us.'[3]

Australia is on the cusp of going down a similar path. Under current rules, both individuals and corporations can give to campaigns in Australia. The amount that can be donated is not capped. For federal elections, the source of any donation under A$14,500 does not have to be disclosed. Indeed, in the 2022 federal election, ten independent candidates—most of them the Teal women who won election—spent A$12.2 million on their political campaigns, including nearly A$5 million from Climate 200, an environmental advocacy group, led by Simon Holmes à Court. Climate 200 raised A$13 million for that election cycle. But none of this was disclosed until months after the election. In 2016, one month after the federal election, the media reported that Prime Minister Malcolm Turnbull had donated A$1 million to his party's 2016 election campaign—which Turnbull barely won. Turnbull only confirmed the full amount, A$1.75 million, in 2017.

An authoritative official accounting and disclosure by the AEC covering Turnbull and the Climate 200 donations, and all the donations from special interests—corporations and labour, lobbies and activists—would be of strong interest to the public. There is no reason why voters should not know, when they go to the polls, who is backing the names on the ballot. It will help them make more informed judgements about candidates seeking their vote. Disclosure will also help eliminate the prospect of any hidden influencers putting their finger on the polling booths.

Two simple reforms would have a major impact on preventing Australia from going further down the road of dark money poisoning the integrity of the country's elections. First, lower the disclosure threshold to A$1000, indexed for inflation. Second, require the disclosure of any campaign contribution within twenty-four hours of its receipt. All Australians can have immediate online access to their bank transaction records within minutes of using their credit card, so there is no reason why political contributions cannot be made public on the same day they are made.

As Kim Hoggard said to me, 'Australia is well-positioned to withstand another possible Trump term because it has a strong democracy underpinned by an election infrastructure that is non-partisan and independent.'

Let's make sure it stays that way.

V
TRUMP'S RETURN

22
The Existential Question for Australia

The most tangible flashpoints between Australia and the United States for Trump's return to the presidency in 2025 are foreign policy and trade: Trump's isolationism and penchant for autocrats will cripple, if not destroy, the existing architecture across the Indo-Pacific that helps ensure and promote Australia's security and prosperity. As we have seen, there is a powerful consensus among several leading foreign policy, defence, trade and intelligence officials that the best way to protect Australia's national security and trade interests against Trumpist policies and interventions is to promote Australia's presence, reach and commercial ties across the region. Australia, they counsel, should have a commanding posture of engagement throughout the Indo-Pacific. This is the lesson from China's trade war with Australia and the rotten fruits of years of Australia's strategic neglect of the region.

The Albanese Government fully appreciated these imperatives and has made impressive progress in re-establishing Australia's influence in the region. Creative diplomacy with a strategic intent is the order of the day. As Peter Hartcher reported in the first weeks of the Albanese Government, 'A functioning Pacific Islands Forum is itself a vital diplomatic asset for Canberra—while Australia and New Zealand are members, China is not . . . Beijing inevitably will seek to counter and outmanoeuvre. Albanese, and Australia, had a good [start]. It's one moment in a struggle without end.'[1]

Albanese and Foreign Minister Penny Wong stabilised the relationship with the Solomon Islands soon after they took government. They attended multiple summits across the region, from the Pacific Islands Forum to the Association of Southeast Asian Nations (ASEAN), with a renewed emphasis on climate change. Albanese increased Australia's foreign aid commitment to Indonesia and Papua New Guinea. He was also a prime participant in the G20 leaders' meeting in Bali in November 2022—notwithstanding Putin's attendance. Strengthening Australia's relationship with Japan has also been a prime focus. Albanese had four meetings with Prime Minister Fumio Kishida in his first five months in office, which resulted in a joint declaration on security cooperation. At the Australia–US Ministerial Consultations (AusMin) meetings in December 2022, Australia and the United States moved to integrate Japan into their joint military activities.[2]

This high-level, steady diplomacy is fully consistent with the guidance of Peter Varghese, a former secretary of the Department of Foreign Affairs and Trade, in terms of the strategic competition with China: 'Instead of primacy we should focus on a balance that favours our interests. We should be looking for a new strategic equilibrium that improves our room for manoeuvre, and engages and constrains China. We should build up collective mechanisms, such as the Quad, that signal that China does not have a clear run at re-creating its version of the Middle Kingdom.

'We should deepen our strategic relationships in Southeast Asia and consolidate our position as partner of first choice in the South

Pacific. We also should see what we can salvage of regional institutions because, notwithstanding the deepening strategic fault lines, we also face common regional challenges.

'None of these objectives rests on US primacy. Australia should support a strong, enduring US commitment to the Indo-Pacific.'

Varghese then turned to the Australia–US alliance, and advised: 'And we should hold firm to the US alliance, not because it will come to our rescue in all circumstances but because it can help us in the defence of Australia. The alliance has value as a deterrent, a source of sophisticated defence technology and intelligence, even if the US is no longer the predominant power in our region.'[3]

This is wise, not only in recognition of the decades of partnership between Australia and the United States, not only for the immense challenges posed by China and its increasingly aggressive posture, but also because of the urgency to embrace a potential reality.

All of this was captured by Foreign Minister Penny Wong in a major speech following the AusMin meetings in Washington. 'We are doing this by investing in our diplomatic power, renewing Australia's closest partnerships, and advancing our interests and values. We are bringing more to the table. Supporting the region's aspirations for economic development, critical infrastructure and the clean energy transition. Returning to a constructive role on climate change. Supporting the Pacific's priorities in law enforcement and security. Making major new investments with development assistance and through loans that don't impose unsustainable debt burdens. Developing Australia's economic strategy for Southeast Asia for the next two decades. We are supporting regional partners to become more resilient, so they have less need to call on others. In all these ways, we are making Australia stronger and more influential—working to make Australia a partner of choice for the countries of our region. And the value of our engagement in the region is central to the value we add in our alliance with the United States.'[4]

Australia is now engaging more thoroughly across the Asia-Pacific. The US alliance is rock solid. AUKUS is proceeding apace and with firm resolve. Even cooperation with France on Indo-Pacific strategy has been renewed. All of this is exactly what is needed at this time.

But what happens to this urgency with Donald Trump's return? What happens if Trump, erecting his force fields of isolationism and protectionism, wants to get a trade deal with China and signals an abandonment of Taiwan in exchange? What happens if the tariffs he imposes on US imports distort world trade? What happens if Trump acts on his long-held impulse to withdraw US forces from South Korea? What happens if Trump demands hundreds of billions of dollars from Japan for the privilege of having US troops on its soil? What if Trump demands impossibly high prices if Australia is to purchase US nuclear submarines, and decrees that all the manufacturing, servicing and maintenance will be done in US ports, and not in Adelaide? What happens if the Five Eyes intelligence sharing agreement Australia relies on so heavily is undermined by Trump's isolationism and willingness to share sensitive intelligence with Putin?

In other words, what happens if there is a breakdown in the existing strategic consensus between Washington and Canberra on what the Indo-Pacific looks like today and should look like in the decades ahead? What if the two countries disagree on what they need to do jointly to rise to the challenge, manage the issues and prevail in engaging with China?

To be sure, the emergence of stresses between Washington and Canberra would not be unprecedented in the more than seven decades' history of the alliance. On at least three occasions over the past sixty years, very serious differences and rifts have erupted in relations between the two countries—and the alliance survived.

Vietnam tore at the fabric of society in both countries. But for most of that war's duration, the prime ministers in the Lodge—Harold Holt, John Gorton and William McMahon—and presidents Lyndon B. Johnson and Richard Nixon in the White House were aligned.

Gough Whitlam, however, broke with Nixon over Vietnam. In his book, *Years of Upheaval*, Henry Kissinger wrote that Nixon was 'scathing in his comments about the new, leftist Prime Minister Gough Whitlam, whose uninformed comments about our Christmas bombing [of North Vietnam] had made him a particular object of Nixon's wrath'.[5] The relationship went into a very deep freeze—but it was not broken. Whitlam continued to allow US intelligence facilities to maintain their operations on Australian soil. What was astonishing is that both men came to share the same outlook that it was imperative to establish direct diplomatic relations with the People's Republic of China. Whitlam shocked Australia—and the West—in his historic trip to China in July 1971. Just days later, Whitlam's judgement was vindicated when the White House announced that Nixon would be travelling to China for a breakthrough visit.

In 1976, Malcolm Fraser reacted furiously to adverse treatment of Australian beef exports under policies being considered by the Ford administration. Fraser wrote to the president: 'I must say to you that the Australian Government could not accept, and the Australian people will not be able to understand, any decision which penalises, or appears to penalise, Australia for failure on the part of others. Any such discriminatory action against Australia would be incomprehensible to us and would provoke very strong reactions.'

WHAT TRUMP'S SECOND TERM MEANS FOR AUSTRALIA

The president's National Security Council staff in Washington backed off, advising, 'Australia is an important US ally. Thus we hope that we can resolve this problem in a way which will not jeopardise our strong bilateral relationship.'[6] That is exactly what happened.

In 2003, the decision to go to war in Iraq was immensely controversial. In Parliament, the House of Representatives approved a resolution supporting the impending military invasion by the United States, but Labor was opposed. The Senate did not approve such a resolution. But action by the House was deemed sufficient by Prime Minister Howard to proceed.

Once again, the Australian prime minister and the American president, in this instance George W. Bush, were aligned on the merits of invading another country.

In both Vietnam and Iraq, a very high cost was paid in terms of Australian popular sentiment on the justification and moral correctness of these wars. But there was no decisive, collective Australian sentiment to break with the United States.

In contemplating Trump's return to the presidency, two immediate issues present.

Can the Australian prime minister work with President Trump? Yes, of course the PM can. It is incumbent on anyone who becomes prime minister to forge a constructive working relationship with the president—even if they despise each other. Macron of France, Trudeau of Canada, Merkel of Germany: they all 'worked' with Trump even under the most trying and provocative circumstances. The huge diplomatic, military, intelligence and business superstructure each of those countries have with the United States continued to operate, even under extreme conditions—just as Australia did with respect to Vietnam, trade issues and the Iraq war.

There were grave differences, but those relationships did not break.

Prime Minister Albanese and Australia's diplomatic, military and intelligence services will figure out how to keep the alliance as stable as possible. The bonds between the countries are also underscored by the commercial and business ties and by the US–Australia Free Trade Agreement.

But what if those efforts are not enough? What happens if Trump cripples, perhaps even works deliberately to destroy, NATO and the United Nations, executes an alliance with Putin and Russia, surrenders Taiwan to China, drops support for Ukraine, and withdraws troops and naval forces from the Asia-Pacific?

How does Australia weigh the prospect that its island continent is home alone?

Answers to this scenario can be conjured: NATO has become more united than ever before in the wake of Russia's invasion of Ukraine. Trump will likely renew his efforts to destroy NATO. NATO will want to endure for its own security in a world more fraught than ever, with menace from Russia, China—and now America. Australia served shoulder-to-shoulder with NATO in Iraq. The United Kingdom is part of AUKUS, and France wants back into security arrangements for the Indo-Pacific. Both countries are integral to NATO. If the United States effectively exits Asia and NATO under Trump, perhaps Australia should enter into a formal alliance with NATO in order to promote stability, security and peace in its home region. Japan and South Korea may well be interested in this arrangement as well.

Australia's best strategic minds will do their best to find answers.

With Trump redux, however, there is also an existential question: *Can Australia—should Australia—continue its alliance with the United States if the United States is no longer the United States?*

Australia's alliance is with the United States. It is with a country that stands for freedom, democracy, liberty, and human and civil rights.

What happens if Trump dismantles America's democracy?

In his 'closing argument' speech before the November 2022 midterm elections, President Biden said:

> Democracies are more than a form of government. They're a way of being, a way of seeing the world—a way that defines who we are, what we believe, why we do what we do.
>
> Democracy is simply that fundamental.
>
> We must, in this moment, dig deep within ourselves and recognize that we can't take democracy for granted any longer.
>
> With democracy on the ballot, we have to remember these first principles. Democracy means the rule of the people—not the rule of monarchs or the monied, but the rule of the people.
>
> Autocracy is the opposite of democracy. It means the rule of one: one person, one interest, one ideology, one party.
>
> To state the obvious, the lives of billions of people, from antiquity until now, have been shaped by the battle between these competing forces: between the aspirations of the many and the greed and power of the few, between the people's right for self-determination and the self-seeking autocrat, between the dreams of a democracy and the appetites of an autocracy.
>
> What we're doing now is going to determine whether democracy will long endure. It, in my view, is the biggest of questions: whether the American system that prizes the individual, bends toward justice, and depends—depends on the rule of law—whether that system will prevail.
>
> This is the struggle we're now in: a struggle for democracy, a struggle for decency and dignity, a struggle for prosperity and progress, a struggle for the very soul of America itself.[7]

Days after Biden's speech, Representative Jim Clyburn, at the time the third-ranking Democrat in the House, was even more blunt on Fox News Digital: '... I said this in 2018, it caught a lot of hell from a lot of people for having said it. It was true then and it's true now. This country is on track to repeat what happened in Germany when it was the greatest democracy going, when it elected a chancellor that then co-opted the media that this past president called the press the enemy of the people. That is a bunch of crap and we know it. And that's what's going on in this country.'[8]

What if that struggle for democracy and the soul of America fails with Trump's return? What happens if Trump declares martial law, if military troops are deployed to cities across the country to put down protests and detain ten million undocumented immigrants in concentration camps, if Trump ignores court orders to cease and desist acting under the authority of his executive actions, if Trump ignores laws passed by Congress, if Trump orders the detention and imprisonment of his political enemies, if Trump cancels elections, if Trump has journalists arrested and jailed and shuts down certain media outlets, if Trump directs the regulatory agencies in the Executive Branch to promulgate orders that render targeted companies uncompetitive or puts certain companies out of business, if he acts to instigate tax audits by the Internal Revenue Service, and to prevent companies deemed unfriendly to the president from merging or entering new markets?

What if Trump sets about completing his efforts to destroy the electoral process by installing his supporters at the state and precinct (booth) level to count the votes, and empowers the officials to certify the votes to be responsive to him? What if he pressures Republican legislatures in states with decisive clout in the Electoral College to have the power to overturn the popular vote in their states and to substitute and certify the result deemed best by that legislature?

As the *New York Times* has editorialised, 'The task of safeguarding democracy does not end with one election. Mr. Trump and others looking to pervert the electoral process are full of intensity and are playing a long game.'[9]

Bob Woodward wrote for his audiobook of his twenty hours of interviews with Trump, '[His] voice, almost whispering and intimate, is so revealing. I believe that is Trump's view of the presidency. Everything is mine. The presidency is mine. It is *still* mine. The only view that matters is mine. "The Trump Tapes" leaves no doubt that, after four years in the presidency, Trump has learned where the levers of power are, and full control means installing absolute loyalists in key cabinet and White House posts. The record now shows that Trump has led . . . a seditious conspiracy to overturn the 2020 election, which in effect is an effort to destroy democracy. Trump reminds [us] how easy it is to break things you do not understand—democracy and the presidency.'[10]

What if the United States becomes more like Hungary and less like America?

Comprehensive polling conducted by the United States Studies Centre in the second half of 2022 revealed that Australians are very anxious about the state of America's democracy. At least half of Australians are 'very concerned' about American democracy, the degree and dangers of political misinformation that has infected US politics, and prospects for political violence in the United States.[11]

If American democracy is destroyed, the American continent will no longer be populated by united states.

The country will no longer be constituted of united states.

The country will no longer be the United States.

With respect to Australia's foreign policy and national security interests, Australia is committed to an alliance with a country that first and foremost is a democracy, and a country that supports free trade and global institutions that promote security, freedom, prosperity, arms control and global health.

With Trump's return to the presidency—at least for four years—the United States no longer stands for those things.

The deeper dimension of this existential question is: *Does Australia want to stay in alliance with the disunited states under Trump?*

In an interview for this book, Emma Shortis, an expert in the history and politics of the United States now at the Australia Institute, said: 'Our understanding of how delicate the situation is in the US needs to be deepened. We need a public debate on what Trump might do—and that asks Australia on whether—or how—to support him and the US.'

Anne Summers was even more direct with me. 'The Australian government has to make clear that ... the relationship with the United States will change in consequential and irreversible ways. We can't condone what he will do now nor can we risk the contagion in Australia of what he will do.'

The guardrails of democracy Australia has do not exist in the United States. America's democracy remains in more peril than at any time since the Civil War.

Australia has never faced such an existential question posed regarding its alliance with the United States.

The Australian Government, the media and the business sector need to start engaging with the existential issues posed by the new Trump presidency immediately. He is a clear and present danger to Australia and its future.

Australia's democracy will survive Trump. But the alliance with America may not.

Epilogue
A Letter to Australia from an American Friend

Norman J. Ornstein

When I first visited Australia decades ago, I felt very much at home. With the vastness of the country, the history of its peoples, the boisterousness of its politics and people, the obsession with sports and the humour, Australian culture seemed to parallel that of America. But the more time I spent in the country, the more I observed its politics and governing structures, the more I also saw the differences.

Like my colleagues Tom Mann and E.J. Dionne Jr, we saw the benefits of the Australian system of mandatory attendance at the polls (Kim Beazley cautioned us not to use the term 'mandatory voting'.) We learned the lesson, and the marvellous and compelling book aimed at Americans by Dionne Jr and Miles Rapoport is called *100% Democracy*. We had long lamented an American voting system where the burden of registering to vote was placed on the citizen, not the state; where there were regular imposed barriers to voting, with attendance often barely over 50 per cent for presidential contests, a third of eligible voters in midterms, and often much less than that for many primaries.

American elections had come to be shaped by party strategies aimed at ginning up the party base while depressing that of the opposition. That means scaring to death your own base voters, and using 'wedge' issues such as abortion and guns to motivate them, while using the same issues to target vulnerable candidates on the other side. What struck me most about the Australian system of mandatory attendance at the polls was not simply the increase in turnout percentages—after all, given that the former Soviet Union had 98 per cent participation, it is not a clear reflection of democratic health—it was that politicians, knowing that the voters from their base were going to turn out, as were the voters from the base of the opposition, had every incentive to avoid controversial wedge issues and fiery rhetoric, and to make appeals to persuadable voters on the issues that matter most to them.

There were other elements of the Australian political system that left us American observers envious. Election administration—like that in most Western democracies—is handled by nonpartisan experts unchallenged by political actors in any party. Elections are run smoothly, and without any charges of rigging or bias. In the United States, elections are run by partisan officials, a bit like a footy match between the Tigers and Giants where the referees own a share of one of the teams. And in Australia, voter registration, with the burden on the state, is sharply different from the United States, where the onus is on the voter. That, in turn, opens up chicanery over voter eligibility, and gives more traction to the kind of voter suppression that is entirely absent Down Under.

The visions of Australia's two major parties have long been different, but for a long time we saw, with centre-right leaders such as

WHAT TRUMP'S SECOND TERM MEANS FOR AUSTRALIA

Malcolm Fraser and Malcolm Turnbull, and centre-left ones such as Kevin Rudd and Julia Gillard, governance that stayed somewhere close to the middle. It was striking, as an American, to see John Howard take on the issue of guns, and even argue the case for strict gun control in the conservative *Wall Street Journal*. The guns themselves make a stark difference between our two countries, and that has implications that go well beyond random incidents of deadly violence. In the United States, where a quarter or more Americans say that violence is an appropriate remedy if one's way of life is threatened,[1] there are 400 million guns in private hands, including over 20 million military-style assault weapons. Australians have 0.01 per cent of the guns that Americans have, with few or any assault weapons after the mandatory buyback.

Of course, as in other established democracies, we have seen political polarisation in both countries. With the Liberals, we have seen a sharp move to the populist and more extreme right, but with significantly less breadth and depth in its extremism than we have seen in America. And, of course, Australia had its own succession headaches, whether over ideology, for the Liberals, or personality, for Labor. Overall though, as Bruce Wolpe has pointed out in this masterful book, the safeguards built in to Australia's political system, provided by the Westminster model, the election laws and rules, and the norms baked into the country's culture, have left guardrails in place that make it unlikely that Australia could flirt with autocracy or devolve into sectarian strife.

But there are still plenty of dangers. The political polarisation in America, as our parties came more and more to resemble parliamentary parties and moved away from broad ideological coalitions, was in process for decades, starting in the 1960s. But the move to tribalism—seeing political opponents not as legitimate and worthy adversaries but as enemies trying to destroy one's way of life—required demagogic leaders in the 1990s, such as former House Speaker Newt Gingrich, 'the man who broke politics' and ended a reliable tradition of bipartisanship in Congress, and the rise of tribal media such as Murdoch's Fox News. The Murdochs, through Fox and their other properties such as the *New York Post*, have contributed substantially to the most corrosive elements of this. What Gingrich started in Washington, beginning in 1979, quickly metastasised to the states and the public at large.[2]

The rise of social media added a multiplier, with the ability to form affinity groups; spread misinformation, disinformation and conspiracy theories; and build business models that thrive on division. And adversaries such as China and Russia have developed sophisticated strategies to use social media to sow division. Donald Trump was an accelerant, but if Trump disappeared tomorrow, Trump-style tribalism, with its open racism, nativism and authoritarianism, and its premise that any election Republicans lose must be rigged, will still be a dominant feature of the American political system and culture. Australians know all about the Murdochs and their use of their media platforms.

And here we have the deeply cautionary notes: guardrails or not, the American experience has troubling implications for Australia. First is the reality of the damage the Murdochs have caused in America, Britain and Australia already. The inflammatory, racist, nativist, pro-Russian and pro-insurrection frame of Tucker Carlson and other Fox hosts has contributed significantly to the divisions in the United States. One can make the case that Brexit never would have happened without the stance and distortions of Murdoch publications in Britain. And the role of the Murdochs in combating Australian efforts at mitigating the destructive impact of climate change is clear.

Genuine free expression is a hallmark of a democratic society; we can see the opposite side in the pernicious efforts of dictators such as Orbán, Erdoğan, Xi and Putin to silence dissent or criticism of them by destroying opposition press or imprisoning its editors and owners. But the willingness of media moguls to exploit the system in ways that undermine it in return for personal gain is a deeply dangerous side effect in a free society. The tactics and approaches used by Fox and talk radio in the United States can easily be emulated or exported.

As a regular user of Twitter, I am thrilled with the positive side of social media—getting first-person news in real time, reading insightful articles recommended by trusted individuals I follow that I would not otherwise see, and building relationships with people I would not otherwise know. But the downside is enormous. Racist and insurrectionist people and groups are able to connect in ways they could not before. Dylann Roof, who killed nine Black people in a church in Charleston, South Carolina, was an isolated individual with racist beliefs until he found a Facebook group of white supremacists who confirmed and amplified the legitimacy of his views and the need for action.

For social media such as Facebook, making more money depends on getting more hits, and an algorithm that emphasises division and conflict has been shown to work better at accomplishing that goal. That has meant more traffic for sites promoting anti-vaxx views and other conspiracy theories. Those algorithms are not limited to America, and the sophisticated techniques that lure people down into rabbit holes can work in any culture. One truly frightening result in the United States has been that a large share of Republicans believes partly or wholly in QAnon conspiracy theories.[3]

There is nothing to prevent conspiracy theories from crossing borders, or from savvy people adapting those theories to other countries and cultures. And, of course, some of the savviest actors are in China and Russia, with malign intent and major resources for what is asymmetric warfare. As we saw with the tragic Christchurch mosque shootings in New Zealand in 2019, individuals with deep-seated extremist views or who are unhinged can also be triggered by social media posts, and can in turn trigger copycat actions. Those may be individual and isolated acts, but they can accumulate, and in turn influence votes. A sense of danger in a society, with the fear that accompanies it, can give traction to political actors who promise stability via strongarm tactics.

More generally, the American experience shows that any society, no matter longstanding norms, can slide towards authoritarianism and deep and irreconcilable internal divisions. The combination of ruthless demagogues, a pliant or complicit mainstream press, pernicious tribal media and manipulated social media can create conditions that lead to a slow movement in a bad direction. No society, including Australia, should be complacent.

Norman J. Ornstein is an Emeritus scholar at the American Enterprise Institute and co-author of the *New York Times* bestsellers, *It's Even Worse Than It Looks: How the American Constitutional System Collided with the New Politics of Extremism* and *One Nation After Trump: A Guide for the Perplexed, the Disillusioned, the Desperate, and the Not-Yet Deported.*

Acknowledgements

Over Christmas in 2021, Malcolm Knox got in touch to discuss Allen & Unwin's interest in my working for them on a book with a tie to American politics—but addressing those issues in an Australian context. We discussed and settled on a book focused on Trumpism in Australia, centred on the issues and questions discussed in this book. We contemplated that even if Trump did not run, or if another candidate defeated Trump in the Republican primaries, Trumpism now ran so deep in the Republican Party that a Trumpist would almost certainly be the Republican nominee in 2024, with good prospects to win. So the same issues and challenges would remain even if the wattage was lower.

I am so grateful and appreciative of Malcolm for initiating this conversation with me, and for our talking through all the issues, and for his wisdom and guidance throughout. He was also the bridge to Elizabeth Weiss, the publisher, who has been superb in helping me shape and hone the writing. She knew exactly where we needed to go. Tom Bailey-Smith was terrific in guiding me through the editing process. Deonie Fiford edited with unerring precision and suggestions. I am thankful to her and proofreader Dannielle Viera for all their efforts.

ACKNOWLEDGEMENTS

I was so pleased that Victoria Cooper, a scholar at the United States Studies Centre, agreed to be editorial and research assistant on the book. Fabulous is an understatement. She went through mountains of materials to help me analyse and present the issues essential to this book and worked through every draft to convey her thinking, edits, comments and advice. Victoria's work ethic and writing skills are formidable and excellent. I look forward to her future endeavours. I know American politics will be a big part of them.

I am so grateful to Lesley for supporting the book from the very outset, and especially for her outstanding chapter on the pandemic, Trump and Australia. It's an indispensable contribution. Lesley not only tolerated but encouraged my writing at length at home in Balmain and when we were spending extended time at our home in Colorado and while we were on the Pacific coast at Sea Ranch in California. Great settings for the writing to be done.

Norm Ornstein was enthusiastic from the very beginning when I proposed he write the epilogue. Norm is simply one of the most outstanding scholars of US politics, and a most profound human being. He cares so deeply about democracy and its future. It is a special honour and privilege to be friends with him, and to join daily with colleagues Thomas Mann, E.J. Dionne Jr, Larry Sabato and Alan Abramowitz in discussing all manner of politics and issues in the United States—and Australia too. E.J.'s book with Miles Rapoport on Australia's voting system, *100% Democracy*, helped set the tone for what is examined here.

In addition to all the members of the 'AusMin Chorus' in both Australia and the United States, who will remain in secure locations, I am grateful for the support, advice, thoughts and good wishes for this book from Michael Brissenden, Michael Cassel, Josephine Linden, Judyth Sachs, Kim Hoggard, Jeff McMullen,

ACKNOWLEDGEMENTS

David Lipson, Stephen Loosley, Steve Coffin, Patti Shwayder, Mark Best, Margaret Wigglesworth, Lawrence Deyton, Jeff Levy, Catherine Liddell, Anne Summers, Stephanie Brookes, Nicola Roxon, Clem MacIntyre, Peter Jennings, Emma Shortis, Richard Whittington, Mark Kenny, Mark Scott, Chris Sarra, Kara Hinesley, James Blackwell, Gorana Grgic, Susannah Patton, Stephen Bartholomeusz, Percy Allen, Jennifer Westacott, Amelia Adams, Stephen Koukoulas, Jared Mondschein, Stephen Kirchner, Craig Emerson, John Lee, Julie Steiner and Lucie McGeoch.

As needs to be warranted in this business, this author fully owns all errors and deficiencies in these pages.

Thank you, dear readers, for taking time with this book and thinking a bit about the issues we face.

For the new 2025 edition I'd like to again thank Elizabeth Weiss, who has always given her strongest support to my book. I am deeply grateful for all her encouragement and guidance. Special thanks also to Tom Bailey-Smith for his superb editing. Lesley Russell Wolpe's further invaluable expertise and insights on public health—in the US and Australia—are unimpeachable. Thanks also to Victoria Cooper for her editorial assistance and expert review.

Once again, these pages were conceived and written independently of my position as a non-resident senior fellow at the United States Studies Centre at the University of Sydney. This book is not a USSC publication, and the views expressed herein should not be attributed to USSC. I fully own all errors and deficiencies in these pages.

Notes

Foreword
1 https://www.nytimes.com/2024/11/06/us/politics/trump-america-election-victory.html
2 https://www.nytimes.com/2023/06/10/us/politics/trump-georgia-north-carolina.html
3 https://abcnews.go.com/Politics/trump-told-supporters-retribution-now-im-indicted/story?id=100386551
4 https://www.pbs.org/weta/washingtonweek/video/2024/11/washington-week-with-the-atlantic-full-episode-111524
5 https://www.thebulwark.com/p/donald-trump-is-dead-serious-about
6 https://apnews.com/article/gabbard-trump-putin-intelligence-russia-syria-a798adaf9cd531a5d0c9329f7597f0f6
7 https://time.com/7176696/gabbard-russia-connection-trump-intelligence/
8 https://www.reuters.com/world/us/how-trump-presidency-could-lead-purge-pentagon-2024-11-10/
9 https://www.cbsnews.com/news/can-trump-run-again-2028/
10 https://www.scotusblog.com/2024/07/justices-rule-trump-has-some-immunity-from-prosecution/
11 https://www.theaustralian.com.au/nation/politics/albanese-backs-in-rudd-as-us-ambassador/news-story/709be4b12691b844e46833c5fdaf2c47
12 https://www.brookings.edu/articles/which-provisions-of-the-tax-cuts-and-jobs-act-expire-in-2025/
13 https://www.budget.senate.gov/chairman/newsroom/press/extending-trump-tax-cuts-would-add-46-trillion-to-the-deficit-cbo-finds
14 https://www.news.com.au/finance/economy/world-economy/incredibly-stupid-trumps-tariffs-set-to-cost-consumers-2600/news-story/3d3c4e3965321f6b5a554ee8e71c22ed
15 https://www.nytimes.com/2024/11/13/business/economy/trump-immigration-inflation-prices.html
16 https://www.nytimes.com/2024/11/18/us/politics/trump-economy-immigration-inflation-fed.html
17 https://www.dfat.gov.au/publications/countries-economies-and-regions/deepening-engagement-southeast-asia
18 https://www.abc.net.au/news/2024-11-15/apec-climate-donald-trump-albanese/104603996
19 https://www.insurancenews.com.au/life-insurance/covid-effects-far-from-over-swiss-re-warns

NOTES

20 https://scholar.harvard.edu/files/cutler/files/long_covid_update_7-22.pdf
21 https://www.mja.com.au/journal/2024/221/4/public-health-and-economic-burden-long-covid-australia-2022-24-modelling-study
22 https://www.medpagetoday.com/opinion/parasites-and-plagues/112936
23 https://www.cdc.gov/media/releases/s1116-california-first-clade.html
24 https://www.cdc.gov/measles/data-research/index.html
25 https://publichealth.jhu.edu/2023/lyme-disease-isnt-the-only-tickborne-disease-to-watch#:~:text=The%20annual%20number%20of%20tickborne,improved%20tracking%20of%20these%20diseases%20.
26 https://www.ncei.noaa.gov/access/billions/
27 https://www.commonwealthfund.org/publications/scorecard/2024/jul/2024-state-scorecard-womens-health-and-reproductive-care
28 https://www.commonwealthfund.org/publications/fund-reports/2024/sep/mirror-mirror-2024
29 https://www.washingtonpost.com/politics/2024/03/24/trump-2020-better-off-covid/
30 https://www.nbcnews.com/politics/donald-trump/project-2025-trump-heritage-foundation-what-know-rcna161338
31 https://www.forbes.com/sites/alisondurkee/2024/11/06/how-trump-could-affect-social-security-and-medicare-group-warns-funds-could-run-out-in-6-years-under-his-plans/
32 https://edition.cnn.com/2024/10/26/politics/fact-check-trump-rogan-children-gender-affirming-surgeries/index.html
33 Opinion | There's never been a presidential transition like this one—*The Washington Post*
34 https://www.forbes.com/sites/brucelee/2024/11/02/trump-states-hell-let-rfk-jr-go-wild-on-health-food-medicines/
35 https://www.independent.co.uk/news/world/americas/us-politics/trump-rfk-jr-fluoride-water-vaccines-election-b2640915.html
36 https://www.cbsnews.com/news/trump-robert-f-kennedy-make-america-healthy-again/
37 https://static.project2025.org/2025_MandateForLeadership_CHAPTER-14.pdf
38 https://www.pmc.gov.au/resources/covid-19-response-inquiry-report
39 https://www.abs.gov.au/articles/deaths-due-covid-19-influenza-and-rsv-australia-2022-september-2024
40 https://www.health.gov.au/sites/default/files/2024-11/covid-19-vaccine-rollout-update-8-november-2024.pdf
41 https://www1.racgp.org.au/newsgp/clinical/australian-child-vaccination-rates-continue-to-fal
42 https://www.kirby.unsw.edu.au/news/sexually-transmissible-infections-are-rise-australia-syphilis-rates-tripling-over-decade
43 https://www.abc.net.au/news/2024-11-08/whooping-cough-surge-record-cases-2024-pertussis/104474394
44 https://www.health.gov.au/ministers/the-hon-mark-butler-mp/media/delivering-an-australian-cdc?language=en

NOTES

45 https://www.fda.gov/international-programs/australias-robust-strategy-regional-and-global-medical-product-engagement
46 https://www.aph.gov.au/Parliamentary_Business/Committees/Joint/Foreign_Affairs_Defence_and_Trade/FADTandglobalpandemic/Report/section?id=committees%2Freportjnt%2F024552%2F73973
47 https://www.politico.com/news/2021/12/01/trump-america-first-covid-523604
48 https://www.politico.com/news/2020/08/06/trump-sign-buy-american-drugs-order-392247
49 https://www.who.int/emergencies/disease-outbreak-news/item/2024-DON544
50 https://www.cdc.gov/global-measles-vaccination/data-research/global-measles-outbreaks/index.html
51 https://www.nytimes.com/2017/03/06/us/politics/travel-ban-muslim-trump.html
52 https://www.smh.com.au/politics/federal/2001-the-year-howard-drew-a-line-in-the-sand-and-transformed-australia-20211223-p59jwv.html
53 https://www.nbcnews.com/politics/2024-election/trump-says-immigrants-are-poisoning-blood-country-biden-campaign-liken-rcna130141; https://www.npr.org/2023/11/17/1213746885/trump-vermin-hitler-immigration-authoritarian-republican-primary
54 https://www.npr.org/2024/10/13/nx-s1-5150093/kamala-harris-voting-rights-trump
55 https://www.news.com.au/national/queensland/politics/how-abortion-debate-impacted-the-queensland-election-campaign/news-story/e19071b16657e1db9c950bf430c4b3a0
56 https://www.theguardian.com/us-news/2024/mar/12/trump-january-6-pardons
57 https://www.abc.net.au/news/2024-10-23/refugee-rally-disrupted-by-far-right-protesters/104504672; https://www.abc.net.au/news/2023-12-04/ballarat-white-supremacy-march-investigated/103183616
58 https://www.onenation.org.au/fact-check-is-fake-news
59 https://www.theguardian.com/us-news/2023/sep/25/trump-nbc-msnbc-comcast-country-threatening-treason
60 https://www.reuters.com/legal/trump-sues-cbs-over-kamala-harris-interview-2024-10-31/; Trump cannot take away any license from CBS. Under US communications law, it is television stations—not networks—that are licensed to serve their communities.
61 https://www.npr.org/2024/10/22/nx-s1-5161480/trump-media-threats-abc-cbs-60-minutes-journalists
62 https://www.axios.com/newsletters/axios-am-104b5380-a530-11ef-8ebe-9d37d9289490.html?utm_source=newsletter&utm_medium=email&utm_campaign=newsletter_axiosam&stream=top
63 https://www.youtube.com/watch?v=S95hLpGDcKU
64 https://www.2gb.com/abc-hijacked-peter-dutton-takes-aim-at-laura-tingle/
65 https://abcnews.go.com/Business/trump-role-setting-interest-rates-economists-bad-idea/story?id=112773679

NOTES

66 https://www.wsj.com/economy/central-banking/powell-trump-fed-firing-ac7088e6
67 https://www.smh.com.au/world/north-america/trump-signals-support-for-aukus-pact-in-meeting-with-morrison-20240516-p5jdzt.html
68 https://www.nytimes.com/2024/02/29/opinion/project-2025-trump-administration.html

Prologue: Growing Up with Kennedy, Surviving Trump

1 https://www.nytimes.com/2016/11/19/us/mike-pence-hamilton.html
2 https://www.npr.org/2010/01/18/122701268/i-have-a-dream-speech-in-its-entirety
3 William Goldman, *All the President's Men*, Wildwood Enterprises, 1976
4 James L. Brooks, *Broadcast News*, Gracie Films, 1987
5 https://www.washingtonpost.com/lifestyle/style/i-sat-next-to-donald-trump-at-the-infamous-2011-white-house-correspondents-dinner/2016/04/27/5cf46b74-0bea-11e6-8ab8-9ad050f76d7d_story.html
6 https://www.ncregister.com/news/pope-on-trump-person-who-thinks-only-about-building-walls-not-building-bridges-is-not-christian
7 https://www.theguardian.com/us-news/2016/feb/18/donald-trump-pope-francis-christian-wall-mexico-border?CMP=fb_gu
8 https://www.wsj.com/articles/BL-WB-60252
9 https://www.nytimes.com/2016/08/10/us/politics/donald-trump-hillary-clinton.html
10 https://www.npr.org/templates/story/story.php?storyId=94087570
11 Barack Obama, *A Promised Land*, Crown, 2020, pp. 170, 195
12 https://nymag.com/intelligencer/2016/10/barack-obama-on-5-days-that-shaped-his-presidency.html
13 https://www.quarterlyessay.com.au/essay/2016/09/enemy-within
14 https://www.washingtonpost.com/politics/2021/01/24/trumps-false-or-misleading-claims-total-30573-over-four-years/
15 https://www.washingtonpost.com/politics/trump-takes-office-vows-an-end-to-american-carnage/2017/01/20/4b2677d8-df4e-11e6-acdf-14da832ae861_story.html
16 https://www.wsj.com/articles/nixons-example-of-sanity-in-washington-seriousness-maturity-discipline-supreme-court-civil-war-activism-11648764052
17 https://www.nytimes.com/2022/09/06/opinion/biden-speech-maga-republicans.html?smid=nytcore-ios-share&referringSource=articleShare
18 https://www.washingtonpost.com/outlook/2022/06/05/woodward-bernstein-nixon-trump/
19 https://www.forbes.com/sites/andrewsolender/2021/09/15/poll-finds-most-americans-think-an-election-will-be-overturned-over-partisan-sour-grapes/?sh=5d3ffc723171
20 https://www.nytimes.com/2022/02/02/opinion/trump-republicans-2025.html
21 https://www.quarterlyessay.com.au/essay/2022/09/uncivil-wars

NOTES

1. Trump: America First Abroad
1. https://www.politico.com/story/2017/01/full-text-donald-trump-inauguration-speech-transcript-233907
2. https://www.nytimes.com/2022/09/14/us/politics/trump-greenland.html
3. https://www.reuters.com/article/us-trump-china-idUSKCN1GG015
4. https://www.politico.com/story/2017/05/24/trump-rodrigo-duterte-call-transcript-238758
5. https://www.newsweek.com/donald-trump-world-war-3-woodward-1115426
6. https://www.nytimes.com/2019/01/14/us/politics/nato-president-trump.html
7. https://www.washingtonpost.com/politics/trump-renews-attacks-on-media-as-the-true-enemy-of-the-people/2018/10/29/9ebc62ee-db60-11e8-85df-7a6b4d25cfbb_story.html
8. https://www.washingtonpost.com/news/retropolis/wp/2018/01/16/why-trumps-enemy-of-the-people-bluster-cant-be-compared-to-stalins-rule/
9. https://ustr.gov/tpp/Summary-of-US-objectives#:~:text=Our%20goal%20in%20the%20TPP,in%20the%20Asia%2DPacific%20region.
10. https://www.pbs.org/newshour/world/how-the-world-is-reacting-to-trumps-use-of-shole
11. https://www.reuters.com/article/us-usa-trump-cabinet-idUSKCN1P00IG
12. Malcolm Turnbull, *A Bigger Picture*, Hardie Grant, 2021, p. 442
13. https://www.sbs.com.au/news/article/donald-trump-praises-morrisons-great-win/9otegvg2t
14. https://www.washingtonpost.com/politics/youre-a-bunch-of-dopes-and-babies-inside-trumps-stunning-tirade-against-generals/2020/01/16/d6dbb8a6-387e-11ea-bb7b-265f4554af6d_story.html

2. China: Transactional and Unpredictable
1. https://asialink.unimelb.edu.au/stories/australia-and-the-indo-pacific-an-address-by-prime-minister-scott-morrison
2. https://www.cfr.org/in-brief/us-australia-alliance-what-know
3. https://www.abc.net.au/news/2019-09-25/donald-trump-scott-morrison-on-unity-ticket-criticism-of-china/11545546
4. https://www.theaustralian.com.au/nation/politics/scott-morrisons-state-visit-takes-on-flavour-of-campaign-rally/news-story/c2eacc89b0edf4f6e083c333d4b5f895
5. https://www.nytimes.com/2020/04/28/world/asia/coronavirus-china-compensation.html
6. https://www.theguardian.com/australia-news/2021/jan/11/australias-acting-pm-says-capitol-attack-unfortunate-and-condemns-twitter-censorship-of-trump
7. https://www.smh.com.au/world/north-america/just-not-going-to-happen-us-warns-china-over-australian-trade-stoush-20210316-p57b4l.html
8. https://www.washingtonpost.com/politics/at-mar-a-lago-trump-to-welcome-chinas-xi-for-high-stakes-inaugural-summit/2017/04/06/0235cdd0-1ac2-11e7-bcc2-7d1a0973e7b2_story.html

NOTES

9   https://www.theguardian.com/us-news/2017/apr/12/trump-xi-jinping-chocolate-cake-syria-strikes
10 https://www.businessinsider.com/xijinping-trump-meeting-2017-4
11 https://www.reuters.com/article/us-trump-asia-china-bromance-idUSKBN1D91C8
12 https://abcnews.go.com/Politics/trump-dont-blame-china-us-china-trade-imbalances/story?id=51030935
13 Bob Woodward, *Rage*, Simon & Schuster, 2021, p. 333
14 https://ustr.gov/phase-one
15 Woodward, *Rage*, p. 331
16 https://www.scmp.com/economy/china-economy/article/3166325/us-china-trade-deal-historic-failure-purchases-more-30-cent
17 https://fivethirtyeight.com/features/how-much-did-covid-19-affect-the-2020-election; https://fivethirtyeight.com/features/even-though-biden-won-republicans-enjoyed-the-largest-electoral-college-edge-in-70-years-will-that-last/
18 https://www.msnbc.com/rachel-maddow-show/middle-east-peace-turns-out-be-harder-trump-thought-msna1009316
19 https://www.reuters.com/article/us-g20-argentina-us-china-idUSKCN1O03SL
20 https://www.speaker.gov/newsroom/8322-2

3. AUKUS: A Survivor of Trump II

1   https://www.sbs.com.au/news/article/i-dont-think-i-know-emmanuel-macron-accuses-scott-morrison-of-lying-about-submarine-contract/1v1g5vhfj

4. North Korea: Spectacle Diplomacy is Back

1   This was a pattern of Trump's. In the talks leading up to the Abraham Accords between Israel and several Gulf nations, Trump unilaterally moved the US embassy in Israel from Tel Aviv to Jerusalem. He did not seek any concession or pledge on Palestine from Israeli Prime Minister Netanyahu, infuriating the Palestinians and further reinforcing their belief that the Abraham Accords held nothing for their aspirations for a state of their own.
2   John Bolton, *The Room Where It Happened*, Simon & Schuster, 2020, p. 33
3   Bolton, p. 109
4   https://www.washingtonpost.com/politics/we-fell-in-love-trump-and-kim-shower-praise-stroke-egos-on-path-to-nuclear-negotiations/2019/02/24/46875188-3777-11e9-854a-7a14d7fec96a_story.html
5   Woodward, *Rage*, p. 181
6   Bolton, p. 434

5. Trump Redux: What Does Australia Need to Do?

1   https://www.smh.com.au/politics/federal/keating-turns-fury-on-labor-and-government-over-aukus-deal-20210921-p58tlc.html
2   https://www.quarterlyessay.com.au/essay/2022/06/sleepwalk-to-war

NOTES

6. Chemistry: 'You Don't Look Like a Prime Minister'
1. https://www.washingtonpost.com/politics/donald-trump-is-holding-a-government-casting-call-hes-seeking-the-look/2016/12/21/703ae8a4-c795-11e6-bf4b-2c064d32a4bf_story.html
2. https://twitter.com/albomp/status/1346929529198055424
3. https://www.theaustralian.com.au/nation/fragile-democracy-is-under-threat-anthony-albanese/news-story/6cf8fbe0d4b1e26e609f0289fd536498
4. https://www.theguardian.com/australia-news/2020/apr/20/malcolm-turnbull-on-donald-trump-you-dont-suck-up-to-bullies

7. Economy: America First in America
1. https://www.nytimes.com/2020/02/05/us/politics/state-of-union-transcript.html
2. https://edition.cnn.com/2020/07/29/politics/trump-economic-approval-rating-analysis/index.html
3. https://abcnews.go.com/Business/trumps-economic-legacy/story?id=74760051
4. https://www.census.gov/newsroom/press-releases/2022/acs-5-year-estimates.html
5. Peter Barker & Susan Glassner, *The Divider*, Doubleday, 2022, p. 79

8. Trade: A World War of Tariffs
1. https://www.piie.com/sites/default/files/documents/trump-trade-war-timeline.pdf
2. https://www.brookings.edu/blog/order-from-chaos/2020/08/07/more-pain-than-gain-how-the-us-china-trade-war-hurt-america/
3. https://www.bea.gov/news/blog/2021-02-05/2020-trade-gap-6787-billion
4. In 2021, steel and aluminium exports were A$1 billion, about 5 per cent of the country's total exports to the United States. Australian beef is Australia's export leader to the United States at A$3 billion in 2021.
5. https://www.nytimes.com/2017/01/23/us/politics/tpp-trump-trade-nafta.html
6. Joe Hockey, *Diplomatic*, HarperCollins, 2022 p. 200
7. Hockey, p. 200
8. https://www.nytimes.com/2021/09/21/opinion/china-biden-australia-tpp.html

9. Climate: Drill, Mine, Burn, Repeat
1. https://www.nytimes.com/2017/06/01/climate/trump-paris-climate-agreement.html
2. https://www.nytimes.com/interactive/2020/climate/trump-environment-rollbacks-list.html
3. https://www.abc.net.au/news/2011-09-05/manne-rudds-downfall-written-in-australian/2869942
4. https://theconversation.com/its-ten-years-since-rudds-great-moral-challenge-and-we-have-failed-it-75534
5. https://www.climatecouncil.org.au/lost-decade-climate-action/
6. https://www.theguardian.com/australia-news/2017/feb/09/scott-morrison-brings-coal-to-question-time-what-fresh-idiocy-is-this

NOTES

7   https://trumpwhitehouse.archives.gov/briefings-statements/remarks-president-trump-prime-minister-morrison-australia-joint-press-conference/

10. Trump 2025: What Can Australia Do?

1. https://www.theaustralian.com.au/nation/nation/malcolm-turnbull-stresses-urgency-of-company-tax-rate-cuts/news-story/a367d37a553fda7c1641811dba63b42a
2. https://australiainstitute.org.au/wp-content/uploads/2020/12/P452-PRINT-Trump-tax-plan-and-the-Australian-response.pdf
3. https://www.smh.com.au/politics/federal/trump-tax-cuts-scott-morrison-warns-business-will-abandon-australia-while-we-are-at-the-beach-20171221-h08r5k.html
4. https://thehill.com/blogs/congress-blog/politics/456708-trumps-meddling-intimidation-played-a-decisive-role-in-feds-rate/
5. In the review of the Reserve Bank announced in July 2022 by Treasurer Jim Chalmers, the appointment mechanism will be assessed as well.
6. https://www.rba.gov.au/monetary-policy/about.html

11. Healthcare and the Coronavirus Pandemic, Lesley Russell

1. https://issuu.com/researchaustralia/docs/research_australia_2021_opinion_poll_on_health_m?e=12222516/93096759
2. https://scanloninstitute.org.au/news/new-research-australians-trust-government-rises-sharply-through-covid-19-pandemic
3. http://tankona.free.fr/trumplancet.pdf
4. https://www.npr.org/2022/05/19/1098543849/pro-trump-counties-continue-to-suffer-far-higher-covid-death-tolls
5. https://www.nbcnews.com/health/health-news/where-despair-deaths-were-higher-voters-chose-trump-n906631
6. https://www.nytimes.com/interactive/2022/12/14/magazine/gun-violence-children-data-statistics.html?smid=nytcore-ios-share&referringSource=articleShare
7. https://www.nytimes.com/2022/08/31/health/life-expectancy-covid-pandemic.html
8. https://www.abc.net.au/news/2022-11-09/qld-health-life-expectancy-australia-dodges-covid19-decline/101625656
9. https://www.theguardian.com/australia-news/datablog/2022/sep/04/covid-pandemic-may-be-causing-more-deaths-than-australias-daily-numbers-suggest
10. https://www.politico.com/news/agenda/2019/11/25/health-care-economics-072145
11. https://edition.cnn.com/2017/02/27/politics/trump-health-care-complicated/index.html
12. https://theconversation.com/labors-medicare-campaign-capitalised-on-coalition-history-of-hostility-towards-medicare-61976#:~:text=Medicare%20as%20a%20safety%20net,continuing%20ambivalence%20twards%20universal%20coverage

NOTES

13 http://www.smh.com.au/federal-politics/political-news/crisis-looms-as-australians-look-to-ditch-private-health-insurance-20160916-grichb.html
14 https://www.hospitalhealth.com.au/content/nursing/article/poll-finds-australian-oppose-medicare-co-payment-plan-848574249
15 https://www.smh.com.au/national/federal-budget-2016-australians-back-higher-tax-if-it-boosts-healthcare-survey-finds-20160428-gohijd.html
16 https://www.commonwealthfund.org/publications/fund-reports/2021/aug/mirror-mirror-2021-reflecting-poorly
17 https://www.aph.gov.au/About_Parliament/Parliamentary_Departments/Parliamentary_Library/pubs/rp/rp1920/LifeExpectancyAustralias Commonwealth
18 https://johnmenadue.com/the-erosion-of-medicare/
19 https://data.worldbank.org/indicator/SH.XPD.OOPC.CH.ZS
20 https://www.rand.org/pubs/research_reports/RR1252.html
21 https://www.healthaffairs.org/doi/pdf/10.1377/hlthaff.2018.05187
22 http://staging.abcardio.org/wp-content/uploads/2016/10/Where-Health-Disparities-Begin.pdf
23 https://www.oecd-ilibrary.org/sites/health_glance-2017-5-en/index.html?itemId=/content/component/health_glance-2017-5-en
24 https://preventioncentre.org.au/news/increasing-spending-on-prevention-is-cost-effective-report/
25 https://www.cnbc.com/2017/07/18/trump-well-just-let-obamacare-fail.html
26 https://www.croakey.org/amid-competing-agendas-and-priorities-some-suggestions-for-ways-forward-for-meangingful-health-reform/
27 https://thewest.com.au/news/australia/i-will-restore-health-rebate-abbott-ng-ya-330604
28 https://insightplus.mja.com.au/2022/19/health-promises-we-must-hold-the-winners-to/
29 https://www.nbcnews.com/news/world/supreme-court-abortion-ruling-will-global-impact-health-organizations-rcna35328
30 https://www.crikey.com.au/2022/06/27/australian-anti-abortionists-celebrate-roe-v-wades-demise/
31 https://www.abc.net.au/triplej/programs/hack/abortion-in-australia/8286896
32 https://www.theguardian.com/australia-news/2022/jun/27/explainer-abortion-laws-australia-is-it-legal-illegal-rights
33 https://www.refinery29.com/en-us/2017/01/135121/donald-trump-abortion-quotes
34 https://www.newsweek.com/trump-attempts-ease-concerns-about-roe-itll-work-out-everybody-1718977
35 https://www.forbes.com/sites/alisondurkee/2022/08/02/vast-majority-of-americans-dont-want-abortion-bans-poll-finds-even-in-states-where-its-already-outlawed/?sh=7383f613795c
36 https://www.smh.com.au/national/abortion-pill-vote-lifts-ban-20060217-gdmzda.html
37 https://www.plannedparenthoodaction.org/communities/planned-parenthood-global/end-global-gag-rule

NOTES

38 https://www.guttmacher.org/gpr/2020/04/unprecedented-expansion-global-gag-rule-trampling-rights-health-and-free-speech
39 https://www.health.gov.au/resources/publications/national-womens-health-strategy-2020-2030
40 https://www.health.gov.au/ministers/the-hon-ged-kearney-mp/media/medical-misogyny-across-health-system-to-go-under-microscope-in-new-national-womens-health-advisory-council
41 https://mdpi-res.com/d_attachment/ijerph/ijerph-19-10400/article_deploy/ijerph-19-10400.pdf?version=1661007089
42 https://www.anao.gov.au/work/performance-audit/australia-covid-19-vaccine-rollout
43 https://www.nytimes.com/2021/09/08/opinion/australia-covid-delta.html
44 https://www.themonthly.com.au/the-politics/rachel-withers/2021/14/2021/1639457497/mistakes-made-and-lives-saved
45 https://mcusercontent.com/8a3d58d1cfb663c4dcefbc00d/files/24613b1d-c960-6a3d-1a71-42012493be39/Halton_Report_Exec_Summary_and_Recs.pdf
46 Australian data at https://ourworldindata.org/coronavirus/country/australia; US data at https://ourworldindata.org/coronavirus/country/united.states
47 https://agedcare.royalcommission.gov.au/news-and-media/coronavirus-covid-19-and-aged-care-royal-commission
48 https://www.health.gov.au/resources/publications/covid-19-outbreaks-in-australian-residential-aged-care-facilities-6-may-2022?language=en
49 https://www.theguardian.com/australia-news/2022/may/19/scale-of-aged-care-covid-deaths-laid-bare-as-staff-prepare-to-strike
50 https://www.smh.com.au/politics/federal/anyone-expecting-an-apology-from-scott-morrison-should-look-to-history-20220817-p5banq.html
51 https://theconversation.com/did-the-morrison-government-really-prevent-40-000-covid-deaths-a-health-economist-checks-claims-against-facts-181052
52 https://www.nytimes.com/2022/05/15/world/australia/covid-deaths.html
53 https://ourworldindata.org/coronavirus/country/united-states
54 https://www1.racgp.org.au/newsgp/clinical/vast-majority-of-australian-population-has-had-cov
55 https://www.actuaries.digital/2022/11/04/covid-19-mortality-working-group-another-month-of-high-excess-mortality-in-july-2022/
56 https://www.health.gov.au/resources/publications/national-covid-19-health-management-plan-for-2023?language=en
57 https://theconversation.com/cutting-covid-isolation-and-mask-mandates-will-mean-more-damage-to-business-and-health-in-the-long-run-189862
58 https://www.whitehouse.gov/wp-content/uploads/2022/03/NAT-COVID-19-PREPAREDNESS-PLAN.pdf
59 https://www.legistorm.com/stormfeed/view_rss/3707802/office/7882/title/select-subcommittee-releases-final-report-culminating-more-than-two-years-of-investigations-related-to-the-nations-response-to-the-coronavirus-crisis.html

NOTES

60 https://www.washingtonpost.com/national-security/2022/12/15/trump-covid-intelligence/
61 https://www.aph.gov.au/Parliamentary_Business/Committees/Senate/COVID-19/COVID19/Report
62 https://www.paulramsayfoundation.org.au/news-resources/fault-lines-an-independent-review-into-australias-response-to-covid-19
63 https://www.gao.gov/products/gao-21-319
64 https://www.minister.industry.gov.au/ministers/taylor/media-releases/mrna-vaccines-be-made-australia
65 https://theconversation.com/view-from-the-hill-scott-morrisons-astrazeneca-hand-grenade-turns-into-cluster-bomb-163680
66 https://www.theguardian.com/us-news/2020/apr/24/trump-disinfectant-bleach-coronavirus-claims-reaction
67 https://www.washingtonpost.com/health/2021/11/12/messonnier-birx-coronavirus-response-interference/
68 https://www.bmj.com/content/378/bmj.o2142
69 https://www.pnas.org/doi/10.1073/pnas.2200536119
70 https://ajph.aphapublications.org/doi/full/10.2105/AJPH.2022.306797
71 https://www.health.gov.au/news/chief-medical-officer-opinion-piece-on-stopping-the-spread-of-covid-19-misinformation
72 https://www.aph.gov.au/Parliamentary_Business/Committees/Senate/Environment_and_Communications/Mediadiversity/Report
73 https://journals.sagepub.com/doi/full/10.1177/0020731421997092
74 https://www.nytimes.com/2022/02/06/opinion/covid-pandemic-policy-trust.html
75 https://www.reuters.com/article/usa-trump-legacy-analysis-int-idUSKBN29P0EX
76 https://www.reuters.com/world/us/most-americans-see-trumps-maga-threat-democracy-reutersipsos-2022-09-07/
77 https://www.theatlantic.com/international/archive/2020/10/donald-trump-foreign-policy-america-first/616872/
78 https://www.brookings.edu/blog/techtank/2017/07/27/how-the-trump-budget-harms-global-health-and-weakens-international-stability/
79 https://www.theguardian.com/global-development-professionals-network/2017/may/31/trumps-aid-budget-is-breathtakingly-cruel-cuts-like-these-will-kill-people
80 https://theconversation.com/trump-budgets-cuts-to-international-aid-put-global-health-security-at-risk-74975
81 https://www.politico.com/news/2021/01/14/trump-billions-cut-covid-vaccine-distributor-459496
82 https://www.bmj.com/content/369/bmj.m1438
83 https://www.washingtonpost.com/world/coronavirus-vaccine-trump/2020/09/01/b44b42be-e965-11ea-bf44-0d31c85838a5_story.html
84 https://www.ncbi.nlm.nih.gov/pmc/articles/PMC5468112/
85 https://www.the-scientist.com/news-opinion/trump-proposes-significant-cuts-to-nih-for-2021-budget-67087

NOTES

86 https://www.voanews.com/a/usa_us-politics_biden-budget-substantially-boosts-foreign-aid-diplomacy-raises-defense-17/6206352.html
87 https://www.washingtonpost.com/climate-environment/2021/09/21/biden-climate-finance/
88 https://apnews.com/article/russia-ukraine-biden-business-europe-foreign-aid-25c8544049165cbabc954e4def27efab
89 https://www.vanityfair.com/news/2021/04/why-the-us-still-cant-donate-covid-19-vaccines-to-countries-in-need
90 https://www.kff.org/coronavirus-covid-19/issue-brief/u-s-international-covid-19-vaccine-donations-tracker/
91 https://www.aph.gov.au/About_Parliament/Parliamentary_Departments/Parliamentary_Library/pubs/rp/BudgetReview202223/ForeignAidBudget
92 https://www.aph.gov.au/About_Parliament/Parliamentary_Departments/Parliamentary_Library/pubs/rp/BudgetReview202021/AustraliasForeignAidBudget
93 https://www.dfat.gov.au/development/topics/development-issues/education-health/health
94 https://devpolicy.org/2020-aid-budget-20201007/
95 https://www.theguardian.com/australia-news/2022/oct/26/foreign-aid-australia-federal-budget-2022
96 https://www.devex.com/news/disrupt-and-compete-how-trump-changed-us-foreign-aid-97955
97 https://floridapolitics.com/archives/460844-land-down-under-lockdown-ron-desantis-blasts-australian-covid-19-rules/
98 https://www.flgov.com/wp-content/uploads/2022/12/Vaccine-Grand-Jury-Petition.pdf
99 https://theconversation.com/trumpism-in-australia-has-been-overstated-our-problems-are-mostly-our-own-154949

12. Trump Political Culture: Earthquakes in America, and the Aftershocks in Australia

1 https://www.washingtonpost.com/politics/trump-raffensperger-call-transcript-georgia-vote/2021/01/03/2768e0cc-4ddd-11eb-83e3-322644d82356_story.html
2 https://www.politico.com/news/2022/06/09/liz-cheney-jan-6-committee-full-statement-00038730
3 https://edition.cnn.com/2022/07/26/politics/cnn-poll-january-6-trump/index.html
4 https://edition.cnn.com/2022/07/20/politics/supreme-court-job-approval-marquette-poll/index.html
5 https://www.politico.com/news/2022/06/09/liz-cheney-jan-6-committee-full-statement-00038730
6 https://www.nytimes.com/2022/06/24/opinion/roe-v-wade-dobbs-decision.html
7 https://www.pbs.org/weta/washingtonweek/video/2022/05/washington-week-full-episode-may-6-2022

NOTES

8 https://www.nytimes.com/2022/06/24/opinion/roe-v-wade-dobbs-decision.html
9 https://www.axios.com/2022/06/19/texas-gop-convention-maga
10 https://www.washingtonpost.com/politics/2022/06/20/how-texas-republican-partys-platform-has-changed-since-2014/

13. Endangered: American Democracy
1 https://www.whitehouse.gov/briefing-room/speeches-remarks/2021/04/29/remarks-by-president-biden-in-address-to-a-joint-session-of-congress/
2 https://www.nytimes.com/2021/05/07/world/americas/blinken-china-russia-in-united-nations.html
3 https://www.whitehouse.gov/briefing-room/press-briefings/2021/06/07/press-briefing-by-press-secretary-jen-psaki-and-national-security-advisor-jake-sullivan-june-7-2021/
4 https://www.smh.com.au/world/north-america/what-s-the-plan-australia-needs-to-prepare-for-the-collapse-of-american-democracy-20220103-p59llh.html
5 https://www.abc.net.au/news/2022-04-24/katherine-deves-transgender-women-culture-wars-democracy/101006068
6 https://www.nytimes.com/2022/04/26/opinion/kevin-mccarthy-putin-ukraine-war.html?referringSource=articleShare
7 https://www.nytimes.com/2022/06/08/opinion/the-jan-6-committee-has-already-blown-it.html
8 https://www.politico.com/news/2022/06/16/j-michael-luttig-opening-statement-jan-6-hearing-00040255
9 https://www.smh.com.au/national/nsw/january-6-inquiry-shines-a-light-on-the-perilous-state-of-us-democracy-20220619-p5auvz.html

14. Culture Wars: Buttons Are Being Pushed
1 https://www.washingtonpost.com/politics/2021/01/24/trumps-false-or-misleading-claims-total-30573-over-four-years/
2 https://www.nytimes.com/2022/02/01/opinion/neil-young-liz-cheney-climate-misinformation.html?referringSource=articleShare
3 https://www.nytimes.com/2022/04/29/opinion/antisemitism-post-trump.html
4 https://www.independent.co.uk/news/world/americas/us-politics/rick-scott-cpac-militant-left-b2024164.html
5 https://www.poynter.org/fact-checking/2022/70-percent-republicans-falsely-believe-stolen-election-trump/
6 https://edition.cnn.com/2022/06/16/politics/read-luttig-statement/index.html

15. The Big Lie: Blunting the Aftershocks in Australia
1 Palmer can take some comfort from joining the Michael Bloomberg club. The billionaire former mayor of New York City sought the Democratic presidential nomination in 2020. Bloomberg spent US$900 million and netted fifty-eight delegates—of the 1991 required to win.

NOTES

2. https://www.theatlantic.com/ideas/archive/2022/05/australia-election-donald-trump/629798/
3. https://www.statista.com/statistics/1245798/australia-percentage-adults-vaccinated-with-covid-19-vaccine-by-state/
4. https://www.abc.net.au/news/2022-05-24/controversial-mp-bernie-finn-expelled-from-victorian-liberals/101093478
5. https://twitter.com/Qldaah/status/1534100836703383552
6. https://www.thesaturdaypaper.com.au/2022/06/11/other-peoples-lies
7. https://www.abc.net.au/news/2022-06-15/aec-rejects-andrew-constance-s-request-for-gilmore-recount/101154090
8. The words in this 'quote' are adapted for purposes of illustration from the transcript of Trump's telephone call to the Georgia secretary of state. Only the numbers have been changed from what Trump said in the call. Public revelation of the actual call and transcript resulted in a grand jury investigation initiated by Georgia's secretary of state to assess whether Trump criminally interfered with the election, vote counting and vote certification processes in Georgia for the November 2020 presidential election.
9. https://www.washingtonpost.com/politics/trump-raffensperger-call-transcript-georgia-vote/2021/01/03/2768e0cc-4ddd-11eb-83e3-322644d82356_story.html
10. https://www.sbs.com.au/news/article/government-drops-push-to-pass-controversial-voter-id-bill-ahead-of-next-election/wif6f7fu1
11. https://www.theguardian.com/australia-news/2018/dec/05/coalition-pushes-for-voter-identification-laws-and-launches-attack-on-getup
12. https://www.sbs.com.au/nitv/article/kill-bill-discriminatory-voter-id-laws-dropped-as-lambie-denies-support/3engi1ivj
13. https://www.aph.gov.au/Parliamentary_Business/Hansard/Hansard_Display?bid=committees/commjnt/ed40663b-3554-4dc7-9817-80a3ad9b0848/&sid=0001
14. E.J. Dionne Jr and Miles Rapoport, *100% Democracy*, The New Press, 2022, p. vii
15. https://www.smh.com.au/national/nsw/sydneysiders-rally-for-abortion-rights-after-roe-v-wade-shock-20220630-p5ay22.html
16. https://www.theguardian.com/australia-news/2022/jun/27/devastating-australian-politicians-respond-to-us-supreme-courts-decision-on-abortion-rights
17. https://twitter.com/mattjcan/status/1540544988987404288
18. https://www.pm.gov.au/media/television-interview-abc-news-breakfast
19. https://worldpopulationreview.com/country-rankings/gun-deaths-by-country
20. https://www.sydney.edu.au/news-opinion/news/2021/04/28/new-gun-ownership-figures-revealed-25-years-on-from-port-arthur.html
21. https://www.abc.net.au/news/2022-05-10/election-2022-morrison-deves-trans-albanese-minimum-wage/101052710
22. https://www.smh.com.au/national/deves-endorsement-shows-pm-is-willing-to-risk-progressive-seats-20220422-p5afb1.html

23 https://www.smh.com.au/national/deves-endorsement-shows-pm-is-willing-to-risk-progressive-seats-20220422-p5afb1.html
24 https://www.theguardian.com/australia-news/2022/apr/19/katherine-deves-claims-key-role-in-controversial-bill-to-ban-trans-women-from-womens-sport
25 https://www.theatlantic.com/ideas/archive/2022/05/australia-election-donald-trump/629798/
26 https://www.theguardian.com/australia-news/2021/nov/12/scott-morrison-says-he-believes-he-has-never-told-a-lie-in-public-life-was-that-a-lie
27 https://www.theguardian.com/australia-news/2021/jun/01/the-morrison-governments-vaccine-rollout-is-not-a-race-nonsense-tells-us-a-lot-about-whats-gone-wrong
28 https://www.abc.net.au/news/2021-07-21/prime-minister-scott-morrison-says-not-a-race/13464362
29 https://www.theaustralian.com.au/breaking-news/scott-morrison-defends-accusing-bill-shorten-of-trying-to-end-the-weekend/news-story/a2e8dd7f361b8bd82942e42cd4a1a87b
30 https://www.smh.com.au/world/europe/i-don-t-think-i-know-french-president-macron-says-scott-morrison-lied-to-him-20211101-p594sx.html
31 https://www.theguardian.com/australia-news/commentisfree/2021/nov/06/writing-a-book-about-scott-morrison-the-fact-he-seemed-boring-wasnt-an-obstacle
32 https://www.theguardian.com/australia-news/2022/jun/15/guardian-essential-poll-albanese-enjoys-post-election-approval-boost-last-seen-with-kevin-rudd

16. Race: Trump's Voice Versus the Voice
1 https://www.theguardian.com/us-news/2016/feb/17/central-park-five-donald-trump-jogger-rape-case-new-york
2 https://www.washingtonpost.com/national-security/trump-race-record/2020/09/23/332b0b68-f10f-11ea-b796-2dd09962649c_story.html
3 https://www.washingtonpost.com/national-security/trump-race-record/2020/09/23/332b0b68-f10f-11ea-b796-2dd09962649c_story.html
4 https://www.adl.org/resources/blog/unpacking-kanye-wests-antisemitic-remarks
5 https://www.newyorker.com/news/q-and-a/a-right-wing-zionist-digests-trumps-anti-semite-dinner-party
6 https://www.politico.com/news/2022/12/04/antisemitic-celebrities-stoke-fears-of-normalizing-hate-00072073
7 https://www.bbc.com/news/articles/cq6lm62vm7zo
8 https://www.timesofisrael.com/trump-told-netanyahu-he-wants-gaza-war-over-by-time-he-enters-office-sources/
9 https://www.haaretz.com/us-news/2024-11-11/ty-article/.premium/why-american-jews-didnt-join-the-trump-wave/00000193-1a95-de99-a9bb-dbb599ea0000
10 https://edition.cnn.com/2022/07/26/politics/trump-dc-speech/index.html
11 https://www.abc.net.au/news/2022-04-24/katherine-deves-transgender-women-culture-wars-democracy/101006068

NOTES

12   The table on p. 167 represents the most recent statistics available from government and official sources in both countries. The intention of this table is to represent disparities between racial groups *within* Australia and the United States respectively, not between the two countries. This is important to note as the data represented presents a fair comparison between populations within a country (using the same methods, representative groupings and data sources and years etc.), but not necessary a fair comparison between the United States and Australia where different methods and years might have been used.
Incarceration rate. The Australian data was retrieved from the Australian Government's Productivity Commission corrective services data. The data is rounded to the nearest full figure and reflects data from the latest reporting period to September 2022. The incarceration rate for 'non-Indigenous' Australians represents *all* Australian adults, including Aboriginal and Torres Strait Islanders, compared with the total Australian adult population. The Indigenous Australian data is the incarceration rate among the country's Indigenous population. The US data is from the US Bureau of Justice Statistics in 2018. Figures represent the rate of prisoners compared with the 100,000 residents within that racial group.
  Sources:
  Australia: https://www.pc.gov.au/ongoing/report-on-government-services/2023/justice/corrective-services
  United States: https://bjs.ojp.gov/content/pub/pdf/p18.pdf page 9.
Median household income. The figures here are measured in local currency (AUD and USD). The Australian data reflects findings from the Australian Institute of Health and Welfare (AIHW) in FY2018–19 for Australians aged over 18 years. Findings were initially measured 'per week' and were multiplied out to match the US data metric of per year. The figures also represent median gross adjusted household income (adjusted for household size and age profile). The US data was retrieved from the US Census Bureau at the latest measurement in calendar year 2021. The figures represent real median household income for Black Americans and white, not Hispanic Americans.
  Sources:
  Australia: https://www.aihw.gov.au/reports/children-youth/income-household-and-individual
  United States: https://www.census.gov/content/dam/Census/library/visualizations/2022/demo/p60-276/figure2.pdf
Life expectancy. The statistics reflected in the table represent the most recent available data from official government sources. The Australian calculation of life expectancy reflects the average years between men and women. According to the most recent statistics by the Australian Institute of Health and Welfare (AIHW), measured last between 2015–17: Indigenous males 71.6 years, Indigenous females 75.6 years. Non-Indigenous males 90.2 years, and non-Indigenous females 83.4 years. In the US data, 'Black Americans' refers to the total life expectancy at birth for the 'non-Hispanic black' population, and 'White Americans', means non-Hispanic whites. These findings were retrieved from the Centers for Disease Control and Prevention.

NOTES

Sources:
Australia: https://www.aihw.gov.au/reports/life-expectancy-death/deaths-in-australia/contents/life-expectancy
United States: https://www.cdc.gov/nchs/data/vsrr/vsrr023.pdf

13 https://www.watoday.com.au/national/western-australia/alleged-murder-of-cassius-turvey-clearly-racially-motivated-says-albanese-20221028-p5btv5.html
14 https://www.aic.gov.au/sites/default/files/2021-12/sr37_deaths_in_custody_in_australia_2020-21_v3.pdf
15 https://www.abc.net.au/news/2022-10-24/murdered-and-missing-indigenous-women-four-corners/101546186
16 https://www.theguardian.com/australia-news/2022/nov/13/queensland-police-service-qps-leaked-audio-recording-tape-brisbane-city-watch-house
17 https://www.abc.net.au/news/2022-11-14/video-shows-dangerous-youth-detention-restraint-on-teenage-boy/101632832
18 https://www.theguardian.com/us-news/2020/jul/08/george-floyd-police-killing-transcript-i-cant-breathe
19 https://obamawhitehouse.archives.gov/the-press-office/2013/07/19/remarks-president-trayvon-martin
20 https://www.washingtonpost.com/national-security/2022/08/04/breonna-taylor-federal-charges-fbi-garland/
21 https://www.youtube.com/watch?v=QFGWoGZwR1Y
22 https://ulurustatement.org/the-statement/
23 https://www.theguardian.com/australia-news/2017/oct/26/indigenous-voice-proposal-not-desirable-says-turnbull
24 https://www.theguardian.com/australia-news/2018/sep/26/scott-morrison-claims-indigenous-voice-to-parliament-would-be-a-third-chamber
25 https://www.abc.net.au/news/2022-05-22/anthony-albanese-acceptance-speech-full-transcript/101088736
26 https://www.theguardian.com/australia-news/commentisfree/2022/aug/15/i--will-be-voting-yes-to-establish-an-indigenous-voice-to-parliament
27 https://edition.pagesuite.com/popovers/dynamic_article_popover.aspx?artguid=9be18c27-c003-4658-a369-a5ff773e0f78
28 https://citynews.com.au/2022/paul-house-offers-a-welcome-of-power-and-inspiration/
29 https://www.pm.gov.au/media/address-garma-festival
30 https://about.abc.net.au/speeches/noel-pearson-boyer-lecture-series-who-we-were-and-who-we-can-be/

17. Media: Will 'The Enemy of the People' Prevail?
1 https://www.huffpost.com/entry/marla-maples-trump-was-th_b_9438540
2 https://www.quarterlyessay.com.au/correspondence/correspondence-bruce-wolpe
3 https://www.quarterlyessay.com.au/correspondence/correspondence-bruce-wolpe
4 Jared Kushner, *Breaking History*, Broadside Books, 2022, pp. 21–22

NOTES

5 https://www.washingtonpost.com/media/2022/01/30/media-trump-war-palin-fox-new-york-times/
6 https://www.bbc.com/news/blogs-trending-42724320
7 https://www.theguardian.com/us-news/2018/aug/03/trump-enemy-of-the-people-meaning-history
8 https://abcnews.go.com/US/wireStory/harris-church-trump-muses-reporters-shot-115447144
9 https://www.theguardian.com/world/2008/dec/04/richard-nixon-recordings
10 https://www.youtube.com/watch?v=TztxwKfud-k
11 https://www.newyorker.com/magazine/2019/03/11/the-making-of-the-fox-news-white-house
12 https://edition.cnn.com/2019/03/04/opinions/trump-fox-news-new-yorker-jane-mayer-hemmer/index.html
13 https://www.newyorker.com/magazine/2019/03/11/the-making-of-the-fox-news-white-house
14 https://thehill.com/homenews/3576601-murdoch-told-jared-kushner-theres-nothing-i-can-do-on-fox-news-arizona-call-book/
15 https://www.wsj.com/articles/the-president-who-stood-still-donald-trump-jan-6-committee-mike-pence-capitol-riot-11658528548
16 https://nypost.com/2022/07/22/trumps-jan-6-silence-renders-him-unworthy-for-2024-reelection/
17 https://www.wsj.com/articles/donald-trump-is-the-gops-biggest-loser-midterm-elections-senate-house-congress-republicans-11668034869?mod=opinion_lead_pos2
18 The *New York Times* reporting of Trump on Twitter is particularly insightful: https://www.nytimes.com/interactive/2019/11/02/us/politics/trump-twitter-presidency.html
19 https://www.nytimes.com/2018/08/29/opinion/trump-bias-google-twitter.html
20 https://www.nytimes.com/2017/06/29/business/media/trump-mika-brzezinski-facelift.html
21 https://edition.cnn.com/2015/08/08/politics/donald-trump-cnn-megyn-kelly-comment/index.html
22 https://www.vox.com/recode/22421396/donald-trump-social-media-ban-facebook-twitter-decrease-drop-impact-youtube
23 https://www.newsweek.com/trump-gets-strongest-show-support-gop-2024-nomination-after-fbi-raid-1733061
24 https://parlinfo.aph.gov.au/parlInfo/download/committees/reportsen/024602/toc_pdf/MediadiversityinAustralia.pdf;fileType=application%2Fpdf
25 On election night, 21 May 2022, Sky News attracted 125,000 viewers. The ABC was the highest rated, with 910,000 viewers, and Seven and Nine networks combined had 1.5 million. https://www.mediaweek.com.au/tv-ratings-may-21-2022-the-abc-and-albo-win-election-night-2022/
26 https://www.canberratimes.com.au/story/7539613/the-grand-irony-of-the-internet/
27 https://www.reuters.com/article/us-usa-trump-qanon-idUSKCN25F2SI

28 https://plus61j.net.au/featured/three-years-after-christchurch-right-wing-extremism-in-australia-still-an-ongoing-threat/
29 https://www.abc.net.au/news/2022-06-17/ita-buttrose-andrew-olle-media-lecture-stronger-press-freedoms/101161494
30 https://www.pm.gov.au/media/abc-90th-anniversary

18. Is Trump an '-ism'?
1 https://clintonwhitehouse4.archives.gov/WH/New/other/sotu.html
2 Ever the cunning, rapacious businessman, alert to every opportunity to monetise the Trump name, Trump issued his picture book before a more official version by the photographers in his White House could be published, with Trump getting the first monies on any official books on his time in office.
3 As a developer, Trump is notorious for stiffing contractors. As a politician, Trump is expert at raising money from his base that he pledges to use in his campaigns, but this money is then diverted to pay legal fees and other non-campaign expenses.
4 https://www.latimes.com/politics/story/2021-06-03/reagan-strategist-stu-spencer-trump-damage-republican-party
5 https://www.presidency.ucsb.edu/documents/resolution-regarding-the-republican-party-platform

19. Trump 2024: We Know What We're Getting This Time
1 https://www.wsj.com/articles/BL-WB-55953
2 https://www.rev.com/blog/transcripts/former-president-trump-announces-2024-presidential-bid-transcript
3 https://www.politifact.com/factchecks/2022/dec/06/donald-trump/trump-said-2020-fraud-calls-for-termination-of-rul/
4 https://www.nytimes.com/2022/09/22/opinion/trump-big-lie-big-joke.html?smid=nytcore-ios-share&referringSource=articleShare
5 https://2015-2022.miniszterelnok.hu/speech-by-prime-minister-viktor-orban-at-the-opening-of-cpac-texas/
6 https://www.businessinsider.com/trump-meets-with-viktor-orban-hungarys-authoritarian-leader-2022-8
7 https://twitter.com/TayFromCA/status/1515072324541693954; https://twitter.com/jdvance1/status/1515075856502177793
8 https://www.washingtonpost.com/national-security/2022/09/22/trump-legal-danger-investigations/
9 https://twitter.com/thehill/status/1516862012180992005?t=SWOwuNI6Qzf7RUSZWy0b6Q&s=03
10 https://www.washingtonpost.com/media/2022/08/21/margaret-sullivan-last-column-trump-2024-media/
11 https://www.theguardian.com/us-news/2022/nov/02/wisconsin-republican-gubernatorial-candidate-tim-michels
12 https://www.axios.com/2022/07/22/trump-2025-radical-plan-second-term
13 https://www.washingtonpost.com/magazine/2022/10/10/country-after-second-trump-term/

NOTES

14 https://www.pbs.org/newshour/show/new-book-the-divider-takes-a-look-at-trump-presidency-and-what-led-to-january-6-attacks
15 Bob Woodward and Robert Costa, *Peril*, Simon & Schuster, 2021, p. 414
16 https://edition.pagesuite.com/popovers/dynamic_article_popover.aspx?artguid=e8972888-d6ff-4942-b083-7f5f07ba347c

20. The Safeguards of Australia's Democracy

1 Dionne & Rapoport, p. xii
2 https://www.opensecrets.org/news/2021/02/2020-cycle-cost-14p4-billion-doubling-16/
3 https://www.ussc.edu.au/analysis/by-the-numbers-per-capita-election-spending-surges-in-both-united-states-and-australia
4 https://www.dailytelegraph.com.au/newslocal/inner-west/prime-minister-julia-gillard-talks-about-the-need-for-compulsory-voting/news-story/8810d8b3aaec1bbd718d310d6c25a4a3
5 https://johnmenadue.com/can-australia-save-americas-democracy/
6 https://time.com/4205867/trump-cruz-illegally-stole-iowa-caucus-win/
7 https://www.politico.com/story/2016/02/trump-cruz-stole-iowa-tweet-deleted-218674
8 https://www.politico.com/news/2020/07/30/trump-suggests-delaying-2020-election-387902
9 https://twitter.com/BeschlossDC/status/1579113415204741120?s=20&t=Pg0Jvuy3po-M3EbNDEyJKA
10 https://www.npr.org/2022/12/22/1139951463/electoral-count-act-reform-passes
11 https://www.aph.gov.au/About_Parliament/House_of_Representatives/Powers_practice_and_procedure/00_-_Infosheets/Infosheet_20_-_The_Australian_system_of_government
12 https://www.pm.gov.au/media/press-conference-parliament-house-canberra-act-1
13 https://www.ministriesinquiry.gov.au/publications/report-inquiry
14 https://www.abc.net.au/news/2022-11-29/morrison-thanks-colleagues-on-eve-of-ministries-censure/101711486
15 https://www.npr.org/sections/itsallpolitics/2012/12/19/167645600/robert-borks-supreme-court-nomination-changed-everything-maybe-forever
16 https://www.c-span.org/video/?45973-1/robert-borks-america
17 For an excellent account of these events, please see *The Betrayal: How Mitch McConnell and the Senate Republicans Abandoned America* by Ira Shapiro, Rowman & Littlefield, 2022.
18 https://www.smh.com.au/national/choosing-high-court-justices-a-matter-of-good-judgment-20220808-p5b867.html

21. Futureproofing Australia's Democracy

1 https://about.abc.net.au/how-the-abc-is-run/what-guides-us/legislative-framework/

2 https://www.parliament.vic.gov.au/images/stories/committees/emc/Social_Media_Inquiry/EMC_Final_Report.pdf
3 https://www.brennancenter.org/issues/reform-money-politics/influence-big-money

22. The Existential Question for Australia
1 https://www.smh.com.au/politics/federal/while-albanese-scores-in-footy-diplomacy-that-other-state-of-origin-china-has-an-end-game-20220715-p5b1wp.html
2 https://www.smh.com.au/politics/federal/japan-joins-us-and-australia-to-counter-china-s-dangerous-and-coercive-actions-20221207-p5c4ag.html?btis=
3 https://www.theaustralian.com.au/inquirer/hold-firm-to-us-but-in-balance-with-our-interests/news-story/2255ec1686584fd6578b4a61f2fdc260
4 https://www.foreignminister.gov.au/minister/penny-wong/speech/speech-carnegie-endowment-international-peace
5 Henry Kissinger, *Years of Upheaval*, Little, Brown, p. 142
6 https://www.fordlibrarymuseum.gov/library/document/0351/1555789.pdf
7 https://www.whitehouse.gov/briefing-room/speeches-remarks/2022/11/03/remarks-by-president-biden-on-standing-up-for-democracy/
8 https://www.mediaite.com/election-2022/jim-clyburn-warns-on-fox-news-digital-america-will-repeat-what-happened-in-germany-in-the-1930s-if-gop-wins/
9 https://www.nytimes.com/2022/09/23/opinion/trump-big-lie-elections.html
10 https://www.washingtonpost.com/opinions/interactive/2022/trump-tapes-bob-woodward-interviews-audiobook/
11 https://www.ussc.edu.au/analysis/us-midterms-2022-the-stakes-for-australia-and-the-alliance

Epilogue: A Letter to Australia from an American Friend, Norman J. Ornstein
1 https://www.bostonglobe.com/2022/08/16/opinion/millions-americans-believe-political-violence-is-justified-heres-how-prevent-it/
2 https://www.theatlantic.com/magazine/archive/2018/11/newt-gingrich-says-youre-welcome/570832/
3 https://www.forbes.com/sites/tommybeer/2020/09/02/majority-of-republicans-believe-the-qanon-conspiracy-theory-is-partly-or-mostly-true-survey-finds/?sh=54acb5825231